LOVE & FAMILY
How the Power of Unconditional Love
Saves and Heals Relationships

JAMES D. JENSEN

Copyright © 2021 James D. Jensen

All rights reserved.

ISBN-13: 979-8-547976-69-8

LOVE AND FAMILY

DEDICATION

This book is dedicated to my loving family who has been my unfailing support throughout this journey of life.

JAMES D. JENSEN

ACKNOWLEDGMENTS

Cover design by: Daniel Alberto Flagel.

LOVE AND FAMILY

CONTENTS

	Foreword	v
	Introduction	vii
1	Children and Charity	1
2	Conditional Love	29
3	Have Patience as They Learn	45
4	Children Learn More from Example Than Word	79
5	We Are Stewards, Not Masters	99
6	Remember Being a Kid	117
7	Service in the Family First	141
8	Seeing Others as God Sees Them	165
9	Teach Correct Principles	179
10	Relationships Are the Key	201
	References	225

JAMES D. JENSEN

FOREWORD

The most important predictor of the health and stability of both individuals and societies is the strength of the family. Yet over the last 60 years we have witnessed the disintegration of the family unit at an alarming rate. When family relationships are damaged or destroyed, individuals are left to cast about in the world seeking a replacement. Often, they resort to gangs, cults, loosely committed companionships, drugs, alcohol, and worse. While many forces in the world degrade the stability of the family, it seems that most of the difficulty families face comes from within the family itself. Many children do not enjoy the benefit of seeing their parents model loving and mature relationships. Before long they become parents themselves and perpetuate a cycle of weak and broken relationships.

The solution to this dilemma and the salvation of our broken world lies in the teachings of Jesus Christ. Specifically, his commandment to love one another as he has loved us. That is: unconditionally.

Love and Family: How the Power of Unconditional Love Saves and Heals Relationships explores the power of the "new" commandment given in John 13:34. It does so from a gospel perspective with an appeal to prophets, apostles, and dozens of family experts who have dedicated their lives to God and strengthening families.

With references to hundreds of well-documented sources, *Love and Family* will define unconditional love and show how it is far superior to all other kinds. You will learn what it means to love unconditionally in your family, have patience with family members as they learn, and how to teach by example. Remembering how we all were children once and realizing we are the stewards of our children, not their masters will help us grow in love and respect for them. *Love and Family* will help you learn how to see others as God sees them through service in the home and family first. You will learn several key principles to help your children govern themselves.

While *Love and Family: How Unconditional Love Saves and Heals Relationships* focuses primarily on parent-child relationships, these family-saving truths can be applied to all relationships. Unconditional love means putting people before principles and being the bridge back home to those who have lost their way.

LOVE AND FAMILY

INTRODUCTION

The message of this book is an unabashed call for increased love and relationship-building in the family as opposed to stern and rigorous discipline regarding raising children. The underlying premise is that family relationships are built on love, and strong and enduring relationships are the most powerful way to influence your children and other family members.

There are many sources for the thinking explored in this book. Many years ago, a seminary principal gathered with his teachers to prepare for another year of the challenging task of teaching religion to teenagers. The principal repeated this simple, well-known proverb about the teenagers enrolled in the course of religious study to the instructors gathered to prepare for another year: "They don't care how much you know until they know how much you care." This principle can be applied to our children and their willingness to be instructed by us. Often, we like to believe that we can coerce our children by the authority of parenthood. But many children don't recognize that authority and, in this work, we will question whether it really exists.

More recently, a philosophy of conflict-resolution found in *The Anatomy of Peace*[1] (Arbinger Institute, 2015), published by The

---

[1] The Anatomy of Peace: Resolving the Heart of Conflict, 2015 by Berrett-Koehler Publishers for The Arbinger Institute.

Arbinger Institute, promotes the idea that we should spend most of our time helping others do what is right rather than focusing on what they are doing wrong. Almost without exception, people know when their behavior is unacceptable to others and pointing it out doesn't really help, and likely makes circumstances worse. This book is an effort to show that building up our children and expressing unconditional love is a more powerful way to influence them than harping on their shortcomings.

There are many competing philosophies, paradigms, psychological theories, styles, and traditions built up around family relationships and how we should interact with, guide, discipline, and raise our children. Some promote permissiveness and treating our children like BFFs. Others prefer "helicopter-parenting" to prevent any sort of harm or opposition from hedging up their way. Some are over-protective and shield from the consequences of choices. Some parenting styles mold children in the image of the parents who live vicariously through their offspring. Some lay down rigid expectations undergirded by a finely tuned system of rewards and punishments. Some put heavy emphasis on praise. Many parent without a plan and their children are molded more by the village than the family. Sometimes children are neglected, or provided for only financially (or not at all) while parents are absorbed in selfish pursuits or personal survival. Some children are raised by other children, whether their own siblings or parents who bore them too early in life. All of these methods and situations have combined to make the prospect of finding your way as a parent quite daunting.

Over and over, we find that parents are only one factor in a child's healthy development. The debate about the "relative importance of an individual's innate qualities as compared to an individual's personal experiences" (nature vs. nurture) rages on.[2] (Wikipedia, 2018) We regularly encounter families with siblings, the one who turns out "great" from a worldly, outward perspective, and another who seems to struggle with even the

---

[2] Nature vs. Nurture, from Wikipedia.

most basic life skills. Presumably, they both received similar treatment from their parents. But as anyone who has raised multiple children knows, the little buggers come pre-packaged with their own personalities, pre-dispositions, and tool kits. Even the best parents have difficulty getting into the heart and mind of difficult children.

Given the wilderness of competing styles, programs, and promises about raising children, what really works? What are the overriding principles we wish we knew starting out, but had no clue about unless we were trained by our own parents? This book attempts to provide some of these answers based on a lifetime of research and experience. There are a few key principles that are true for any situation and provide a framework for constructing healthy and loving long-term relationships with members of your family. These principals foster an environment of trust and confidence for the exchange of important ideas about how to deal with life's challenges and obtain and retain happiness.

The overriding current of thought behind the positions of the author in this book is the Gospel of Jesus Christ as found in the contemporary teachings of the general authorities and general officers of the Church of Jesus Christ of Latter-day Saints. Many of the quotes in this book come from highly educated, devoted people who have spent the better part of their lives being taught and teaching these principles. Is there any organization on earth today that is more driven to build strong families than the Church of Jesus Christ of Latter-day Saints? Is there any other church trying to teach how to build relationships designed to last beyond the grave and into eternity?

There is nothing new or earth-shattering about the concepts to be presented in this work. But take together, hundreds of consistent teachings from dozens of experts over a couple of centuries lend an undeniable force to the conclusions. The idea of love being the law of life is at least as old as Mount Sinai. First it was love God and love your neighbor as much as you love yourself. Then it became love one another as God loves you. We all get an idea of what love is at an early age, but love is not as simple a concept as it might seem on the surface. John, the apostle, writes: "God is love," and shows that we have just as much chance of truly understanding love as we do of understanding God.³ Modern-day ministers, apostles, and prophets of Jesus Christ have been preaching love in the family above all since the earliest days of the restoration of the gospel, but it seems to be lost on many of us. Love for God, between husband and wife, for children and parents, and in the family is the core and center of their teachings on life.

Take for example, Joseph Smith's declaration, "While one portion of the human race is judging and condemning the other without mercy, the Great Parent of the universe looks upon the whole of the human family with a fatherly care and paternal regard, for His love is unfathomable."⁴ (Smith J. , Teachings of Presidents of the Church: Joseph Smith, 2007) Now think about how this relates to raising children. Often, we find that when our children don't meet our expectations for them, we judge them and condemn them without mercy rather than responding to them with love. Many times, we assume our children have the same tool kit we possess and should be able to respond to our expectations with the same enthusiasm with which we would accomplish the task ourselves. We pride ourselves on not asking our children to do anything we wouldn't do ourselves. But if Joseph Smith is calling for us to refrain from judging and condemning others who are perfect strangers or mere acquaintances, how much more then would we be expected to treat those within the circle of our own family with love unfathomable? After all, should we not model our parenting style after the "Great Parent of the universe?" What is His way of parenting? We will pursue answers to these questions in this work.

On the heels of Brother Joseph's merciful declaration, we hear this from Brother Brigham, "How often it is said— 'Such a person has done wrong, and he cannot be a Saint.' We hear some

---

³ "He that loveth not, knoweth not God; for God is love." 1 John 4:8.
⁴ Smith, Joseph, *Teachings of Presidents of the Church: Joseph Smith* (2007), 39.

swear and lie or break the Sabbath. Do not judge such persons, for you do not know the design of the Lord concerning them. Rather, bear with them."[5] (Young, 1954) This advice aligns perfectly with the contemporary teachings on love and law by Dallin Oaks. If applied to a family context, we see that we often consider that a loved one has "done wrong" when they do not meet our expectations for them. These three latter-day prophets are calling for mercy, not condemnation. For patience and forbearance, not judgement. And again, if Brigham Young is asking the early saints to treat members of the congregation with such understanding, how much *more* should we treat the members of our own family in this way?

The quotes from both Joseph and Brigham were taken from an excellent October 2018 General Conference address by Elder Robert C. Gay in the context of loving and accepting family members for who and what they are rather than looking at them through the lens of *our* expectations of what they should be. As President Young said, we "do not know the design of the Lord concerning" those we judge. Can we confidently say that we know the design of the Lord concerning our children? Do we really know who they are or what their purpose and mission in this life is? Who is to say that they are not given to us more to instruct and edify us than the reverse? Yet by virtue of the happenstance that we were born into this world a generation before them, we instinctually rule over them, presuming far greater knowledge and wisdom. To mold and bend them to fit our picture, we instead drive a wedge. When they go astray from the way we think they should go, the wedge prevents us from having any influence in their life and sorrow and regret ensue rather than love and confidence.

If compassion, mercy, forgiveness, and forbearance in the family have been preached for centuries, why do we still find those who fail to hear and listen? Even the most diligent disciples struggle to understand gospel teachings as everything we hear must pass through the filter of our belief system. Unfortunately,

---

[5] Young, Brigham, *Discourses of Brigham Young*, sel. John A. Widtsoe (1954), 278.

it seems difficult to receive pure truth when we encounter it because we can rarely accept it at face value. What we do instead is try to figure out how the new truth fits into our belief system and, when it doesn't, we mold the truth and shape it in the image of our beliefs until it fits. Then we "teach for doctrines the commandments of men" (frankly because the commandments of men are easier to understand and execute on).[6] (Smith J., Joseph Smith - History, 1985) Consequently, all the talk about "the most important work you will ever do" being within the walls of your own home gets lost amidst the rancor to do your duty and serve outside the home.[7] (Lee, 2011)

This work therefore is a collection of gems of wisdom polished and arranged in a way to enhance our understanding of the gospel teachings about love and make it easier to understand what is really being taught by many experts on love and family. We will attempt to take the general teachings and apply them specifically to the circumstances within our home. Our goal is to encourage parents and family members to apply the powerful principles of the Gospel of Jesus Christ to their most important relationships to strengthen and heal them. Failing that, at the very least we have assembled an important body of wisdom with enjoyable and memorable stories and teachings.

To kick off this work, a fear must be confessed. That is the fear that the intended audience of this book, those seeking ways to strengthen relationships in their family, will find nothing useful in its pages. Many of the statements made herein have dawned upon the author like a sunrise over years and, because of their patency, we find difficulty believing that they will be of use to anyone. But experience emboldens us by showing that however "put together" people seem on the outside; we are all at war with the natural man and relentless forces eroding familial bonds which obscure obvious solutions to immediate problems. Ultimately, the fear is overcome by love. A love of and for our

---

[6] Smith, Joseph, *Joseph Smith – History* 1:19.
[7] Lee, Harold B., "Chapter 14: Love at Home," *Teachings of Presidents of the Church: Harold B. Lee* (2011), 128–37.

family. A love of being the parent that God wants us to be and striving above anything else in life to build relationships that will last throughout eternity.

1

CHILDREN AND CHARITY

Let's start with the basics. What could be easier to understand than charity? There have been volumes written on the topic. But we still witness the mental gyrations of authors and teachers as they try to explain it, even after it is defined as "the pure love of Christ."[8] (Saints, 2021) Does it mean our love of Christ or Christ's love of us? The answer is: 'yes.'

In some ways, the word 'charity' has fallen out of favor. Many of the modern translations of the New Testament, not incorrectly, translate the Greek word *agape* as 'love.' Not that the modern translation makes the concept any easier to understand. We all have an idea of what love is, based on our own experience. But for the purposes of this discussion, charity means unconditional love.

Unconditional love means genuinely caring and working for the happiness of another no matter what circumstances we find ourselves in. Unconditional love for another is difficult to obtain. Almost invariably, our love for others, even those closest to us like our spouse or children, is conditional based on our reasonable expectations of our loved one's behavior. It is easy to

---

[8] Topics, *Charity*, The Church of Jesus Christ of Latter-day Saints web site.

love another when they love you. As John said about Christ, "We love him, because he first loved us."[9] But as Jesus asked early in his ministry, "If ye love them which love you, what reward have ye?"[10] Conditional love means that if someone is acting in a way that you approve of, you show them love. But the reward promised by Christ comes from loving those who do not love you, who hurt you, who are your enemies.

We usually assume that those who persecute us or hate us are not the people in our family. But upon closer examination, we conclude that family members are the very people that Jesus was referring to. Yes, of course we could become enemies with our neighbor. Perhaps their dog disrespects our lawn too frequently. Or maybe they steal our apples while we are on vacation. But we maintain that it is much more likely that we will be in a heated disagreement with those closest to us. The powerful emotions between two people in proximity can often lead to hurt feelings. When hurt feelings are not mended and are allowed to fester, they can lead to grudges, harder feelings, vendettas, retaliation, and hatred. Without care, one who we should be closest to is now our enemy, persecutes us, or despitefully uses us. Whereas conflicts between people outside of family bonds have historically been settled by weapons or in a court of law, many family feuds are never resolved so definitively and are allowed to cause pain for generations.

One of the purposes of this work is to take the teachings of the Gospel of Jesus Christ and apply them to the family. We want to strip away misconceptions about who our neighbors are and what is meant by forgiving our brother his trespasses. As Jeffrey Holland has pointed out, "Everybody can forgive sins in the abstract. I've handled Cain and Judas and lot of other people very conveniently. But people who live next me . . . theirs are obviously more serious transgressions and I've got to think a little

---

[9] 1 John 4:19.
[10] Matthew 5:46.

longer about that."[11] (Holland, 1980) What Holland is trying to get at is that having unconditional love for those who are closest to us is not that easy. Their failures and shortcomings have much more of an impact on us than those of our "neighbors" or members of our congregation. Listen to Jesus' call for unconditional love and apply his words to members of your immediate family and they take on a whole new meaning. "Love your enemies, bless them that curse you, do good to them that hate you, and pray for them which despitefully use you, and persecute you."[12]

What if your enemy is your flesh and blood brother or sister? What if the person cursing you is your child? Can you do good to them when they say that they hate you? Can you pray for them when you are feeling used (or abused) by your own parent? Thinking this way brings a whole new meaning to applying the Gospel in your life. We frequently find that we are more courteous to perfect strangers than we are to the members of our own household living under the same roof.

That is why charity, or unconditional love, is so hard to obtain: because it requires that we love our immediate family members even when we don't approve of them or their behavior. It requires that we love them when they disappoint us, disrespect us, or dissemble. It requires that we love them when our love is not returned, when they hate us, or even when they betray or hurt us. Conditional love is not God's love, it is not charity. Conditional love can be snuffed out. Conditional love eventually runs out of gas when our expectations are not met over the long haul.

When you have charity for your spouse or children or parents, no matter what they do, you will not stop loving them. Charity cannot be terminated or destroyed. It will continue to exist if God's love exists. Charity *never* faileth.[13] (Monson, 2010)

---

[11] Jeffrey R. Holland, taken from the transcript of a talk given after he was called to preside at BYU, August 1980. The author is in possession of the transcript.
[12] Matthew 5:44.
[13] Thomas S. Monson, *Charity Never Faileth*, an address given at the General Conference of the Church of Jesus Christ of Latter-day Saints, October 2010.

A Soft Answer Turneth Away Wrath

In family relationships, conflict arises quickly. A main source of this conflict is unmet expectations. We need a tool to defuse the conflict early to avoid arguments and hurt feelings. In this story set forth as a short poem, the father probably has a reasonable expectation that his son will do the work he is asked to do without some special reward. The son is in a gracious mood and, while initially feeling love toward his father, is seeking the attention of the world. He is motivated by the praise of men. The stage is set for a conflict.

> "Father, where shall I work today?"
> And my love flowed warm and free.
> Then He pointed out a tiny spot
> And said, "Tend that for me."
> I answered quickly, "Oh no; not that!
> Why, no one would ever see,
> No matter how well my work was done;
> Not that little place for me."
> And the word He spoke, it was not stern;
> He answered me tenderly:
> "Ah, little one, search that heart of thine.
> Art thou working for them or for me?
> Nazareth was a little place,
> And so was Galilee."[14] (Lyon, 1996)

There are several possible answers to his son that could have run through the father's mind. He could have answered his son authoritatively, "You will work the plot of ground I ask you to work." Or he might have chastised his son for his vanity. But rather than saying, "Verily, ye have your reward," or rebuking him for being worldly, warning him against pride, or expressing disappointment, the father answers with compassion, "tenderly"

---

[14] *Best-Loved Poems of the LDS People*, comp. Jack M. Lyon and others (1996), 152.

not sternly.

While the main point of this story may have been to show that to be like Christ, we don't need to be showy and call attention to ourselves, we find it more instructive to notice how the father answers his son. He can quickly assess that his son's priorities need some work. Any flashes of impatience or disappointment in the father's mind were immediately overcome. The opportunity for a teaching moment appeared. The only question for the father is how the lesson will be presented. Imagine how the son responded to his father's tender care. While he may still have desired a more visible plot, it's now more likely that he took the instruction to heart than if he had received a rebuke or belittlement.

We are reminded of the proverb, "A soft answer turneth away wrath: but grievous words stir up anger."[15] Charity requires that we turn away wrath. Introducing anger into the relationship has a destructive effect. The loving heart hardens a little. Over time, anger between a parent and child erodes the parent's influence as the child begins to learn how to do things on their own, without their angry parent.

William Tyndale, the father of the English Bible, wrote with gospel authority on topics of family relationships. In his counsel to fathers, applying the words of Paul directly to the family as we are doing in this work, he taught, "'Be not overcome of evil;' (Romans 12) that is, let not another man's wickedness make thee wicked also. 'But overcome evil with good;' that is, with softness, kindness, and all patience win him; even as God with kindness won thee."[16] (Tyndale, 1528)

This is especially true of the "wickedness" of children: selfishness, fighting, disrespect, apathy, ingratitude. While we agree our children are born innocent, they can come with a high degree of challenging behaviors (some more than others) that will

---

[15] Proverbs 15:1.
[16] William Tyndale, *Obedience of a Christian Man and How Christian Rulers Ought to Govern,* Set forth 1528, taken from the 1831 edition of *The Works of the English Reformers,* Vol. I, Ed. Thomas Russell, A.M. London, 23.

test our patience and love. Tyndale comes down squarely in the camp of increased love and kindness to overcome these wicked traits in the moment, rather than anger, punishment, and threats. Our responses to our children's shortcomings teach them how to behave later in life when their own expectations of others are unmet.

Almost 500 years ago, Tyndale concluded that ill-behaved parents bring up discouraged and heartless children. By "brawling and chiding," parents teach these same behaviors to their children. But a Christian parent, Tyndale teaches, will be patient and forgiving.[17] (Tyndale, 1528) We do not always need to play the parental authority card with our children. That is, when a child questions an instruction from a us, we shouldn't have to resort to our supposed authority over our children as a reason for our request. If we do, we may observe that we have lost all influence with our child. We have demonstrated that we are unable to change their behavior through love, kindness, and patient teaching, and are now barking orders like a military drill sergeant who never has to deal with questioned authority.

The Heat of the Moment

One of the hallmarks of charity is the ability to overcome, in the moment, the passions raised by those who are placed in our care. To acquire this ability may require the better part of a lifetime, or if you're lucky it's part of your nature. But resolving to show patience, love, and kindness to our loved ones regardless of the situation is what it means to love unconditionally. The following stories illustrate what it looks like when a loving person is placed in a difficult position, and they respond with charity and kindness.

The Insolent Child

Brett Nattress tells a story from his childhood. He adds context by sharing that he was his mother's most difficult child to raise.

---

[17] Ibid.

He recalls finding a goal written by his mother on a sticky note inside her scripture set: "Patience with Brett!" He related an account from his childhood about how his mother would read the scriptures to him and his brother during breakfast. He remembers that neither of them even appeared to be listening, but rather kept reading the back of their cereal boxes. Yet the ritual was repeated daily. At one point, the apparent absurdity of the situation impressed on young Brett's mind must have prompted him to be more honest than usual with his mother. He asked, "Mom, why are you doing this to us? Why are you reading the Book of Mormon every morning? Mom, I am not listening!"[18] (Nattress, 2016)

Getting young boys ready for school each morning can be challenging. Messes are made, outfits are changed, homework is lost and then found. Time runs short and stress mounts. Add to this the requirement to command attention to scripture reading and you have the recipe for a blowout almost any morning. The fact that Brett's mother did not explode at the insolent comment of her challenging son is miraculous and a testament to her ability to "overcome evil with good." Without a doubt angry answers must have run through her mind, but instead, Brett reports, "Her loving response was a defining moment in my life. She said, 'Son, I was at a meeting where President Marion G. Romney taught about the blessings of scripture reading. During this meeting, I received a promise that if I would read the Book of Mormon to my children every day, I would not lose them.' She then looked me straight in the eyes and, with absolute determination, said, 'And I will not lose you!' Her words pierced my heart."[19] (Nattress, 2016)

This is a great example of a parent showing charity toward their child. It's hard to believe it's even true. How could the little brat's bold assertion that his mother was wasting time doing the

---

[18] Brett K. Nattress, *No Greater Joy Than to Know That They Know*, an address given at the General Conference of the Church of Jesus Christ of Latter-day Saints, October 2016.
[19] Ibid.

most important thing to her not be answered with wrath? Did not this smart-mouthed boy deserve to be whacked? How is a family member who is so disrespectful of another's feelings to be treated?

Note that his mother's response was "loving." Also notice that this response was a "defining moment" in Brett's life and his mother's words "pierced [his] heart." This is what it means to overcome evil with good. Her love was stronger than her son's rebelliousness. It sounds as though she completely disarmed him, and her kindness impacted him for a lifetime. This is the kind of influence we want to have in the lives of our family members. Love that is not conditioned on behavior is how this influence is achieved.

The Bishop

In the novel *Les Misérables*, by Victor Hugo, we are introduced to Bishop Bienvenu who lives in poverty in the early nineteenth-century countryside of France. Jean Valjean is released from prison after 17 years and walks for days in search of a new life. When he arrives in the bishop's town, there is not a single person willing to let the convict eat or sleep despite his willingness to pay. Valjean is directed to the home of the bishop who kindly invites him to a supper of soup: water, oil, salt, and bread. Afterwards, the bishop extends his hospitality with an invitation to spend the night in his home where he and his sister live.

While the bishop and his household sleep, Valjean makes off with a basket full of silverware in the middle of the night. Shortly after the bishop's horrified sister discovers the missing silver in the morning, Valjean shows up at the bishop's door escorted by three gendarmes. The bishop was greeted by a brigadier in command of the group with a salute. But before any explanation could be made, the bishop, knowing Valjean had stolen his silverware, assessed the situation and stunned the entire audience with these words, directed at Jean Val Jean, "Ah! Here you are! I am glad to see you. Well, but how is this? I gave you the candlesticks too, which are of silver like the rest, and for which you can certainly get two hundred francs. Why did you not carry them away with your forks and spoons?"[20] (Hugo, 1862)

No one in attendance could believe what they heard, especially Valjean. But the bishop, being the Christlike man he was, showed unconditional love for Valjean who had "despitefully used" him.[21] He overcame evil with goodness and redeemed Valjean's soul with the words, "Jean Valjean, my brother, you no longer belong to evil, but to good. It is your soul that I buy from you; I withdraw it from black thoughts and the spirit of perdition, and I give it to God."[22] (Hugo, 1862) Hugo spends the next 1,300 pages spinning the tale of all the good Valjean returns to the world in exchange for the transformation wrought in his heart through a single act of mercy and love.

Of course, Bishop Bienvenu is a fictional character, but his ability to overcome feelings of disappointment, injustice, or revenge are illustrative of the principle of defeating our enmity in the heat of the moment to respond with charity and forbearance. These stories are related not to suggest that achieving unconditional love is easy, but rather to illustrate the powerful effect acts of kindness and charity can have in the lives of those we love.

If Nattress's mother had responded to his disrespectful remark in anger, imagine the dramatic difference in the outcome from that situation. Rather than having his heart pierced and experiencing a defining moment in his life, the reading session might have ended abruptly in yelling and frustration. On the following day it may have been even more difficult to maintain the sacred ritual. The morning routine could have ended, and evil would have the victory.

---

[20] Victor Hugo, *Les Misérables*, Xist Classics, Kindle Version, Location 2295, originally published 1866.
[21] See Matthew 5:44.
[22] Hugo, *Les Misérables*, location 2315.

Remember Them No More

One of the core elements of charity is forgiveness. Forgiving is important and powerful in a family setting. We find more opportunities to forgive with our loved ones than we do with neighbors, friends, co-workers, or acquaintances. Everything from forgiving the person who drank your last chocolate milk to forgiving the affair of an unfaithful spouse, we cannot have charity without forgiveness. The Lord warns, "Ye ought to forgive one another; for he that forgiveth not his brother his trespasses standeth condemned before the Lord; for there remaineth in him the greater sin."[23]

Holding a grudge against a family member who harmed you is a worse sin than the offense they committed against you. Forgiveness can be very difficult, especially when the pain caused by a family member runs deep. It is beyond the scope of this work to explain how this type of forgiveness of grievous offenses can be achieved. Some wounds from certain physical, emotional, mental, or sexual abuse can be so severe that it will take a miracle to forgive the abuser. But apart from the extreme, there are myriad opportunities throughout our long lives together to overlook and forgive. And forgive is what we are required to do. "I, the Lord, will forgive whom I will forgive, but of you it is required to forgive all men."[24]

Suppose that you had done something to a loved one that would require sincere forgiveness. Is there a way to know when you have been forgiven? Or is there a way to know that you have let go of the pain and hurt caused to you by a loved one? Once again, the Lord offers this clue: "He who has repented of his sins, the same is forgiven, and I, the Lord, remember them no more."[25] When the Lord says that once we have been forgiven, he no longer remembers our sins, that means He will no longer bring those sins up against us. *We* may still remember them, but He

---

[23] Doctrine & Covenants 64:9.
[24] Doctrine & Covenants 64:10.
[25] Doctrine & Covenants 58:42.

won't.

This is the kind of mercy we need to exercise in our families. If we enter into a new disagreement with our spouse and remind them of something they have done to hurt us in the past, can we really say we have forgiven them? This type of forgiveness and forgetting of sins is central to what it means to show unconditional love. Similarly, we do not bring up past failures, missteps, and shortfalls with our children. Everyone knows how deflating and humiliating it is to be reminded of a loss or a miss. We need to spend our time building up our children rather than tearing them down. This means letting our kids start each day with a clean slate, without remembrance of past wrongs.

Express Words of Consolation

People of all ages will have trials to pass through. Part of building up our children and family members is showing compassion when they face hardships. One peculiar thing about trials is they always seem a lot worse to the person going through them than they do from the outside. Many times, it is difficult for those on the outside to understand the severity of your trial. Often, we look at the trial of another and we can easily see a course of behavior that would alleviate or eliminate their suffering. When we do, it can limit our ability to feel compassion. We say to ourselves (or worse, to them) if you would just "fill in the blank" then you would be fine.

There are two problems with this type of thinking. First, when people are suffering, they are rarely open to rational solutions. Especially when they come in the form of words from the outside. When people are sad or faced with difficult situations, they don't always want advice. They usually do want a listening ear. They want compassion and empathy and someone to be with them. Solutions to our problems work better when they come from within us. Sometimes just talking out the problem is all that is needed for the solution to manifest.

Dr. Brene Brown has an excellent video clip produced by RSA

Shorts on YouTube in which she discusses the difference between empathy and sympathy and points out how giving advice when someone is suffering through a trial is rarely helpful. "One of the things we do sometimes in the face of very difficult conversations is we try to make things better. If I share something with you that is very difficult, I'd rather you say, 'Hey, I don't even know what to say right now, I'm just so glad you told me.' Because the truth is, rarely can a response make something better. What makes something better is connection."[26] (Brown, 2013)

A second problem with the approach of solving others' problems is we assume the person we're trying to help has the same tool kit as us. By 'tool kit' we mean the cumulative benefit of our skills, talents, gifts, knowledge, experience, wisdom, and abilities. But a task or problem that looks easy to solve to one person may be completely misunderstood by another. We are all different in our thinking and approach to life. We must deal with and solve our problems with the tools we have. They cannot be loaned or borrowed. We need to refrain from judging another's trial and trying to solution it for them.

The exception to this is when the person suffering a trial specifically asks for our advice. But a better response to a loved one than pontificating solutions would be to first ask them what they think. By doing so, they are encouraged to talk things out which will usually make them feel better and may lead to a more lasting discovery as they uncover the solution on their own.

When our loved ones experience crisis, our answer should be increased love and compassion, not counsel and advice. One extremely sensitive crisis is a trial of faith. For those of us on the outside, the answers seem obvious, but to the person experiencing a loss of faith, the path forward is anything but clear.

Kurt Francom of Leading Saints published a podcast entitled "What Every Leader Needs to Know About Faith Crisis – An Interview with Scott Braithwaite" in which they discussed the dramatic and serious trial of a loss of faith. Doctor Braithwaite

---

[26] Dr. Brene Brown, *Brene Brown on Empathy*, YouTube video published on December 10, 2013.

observes how helpless we are when trying to comfort another going through such a difficult trial.

"I personally believe when it comes to matters of faith and belief in the core of who we are, you are pretty powerless to push anything or to pull any levers. What I think you can offer as a leader in a room with someone who is in the midst of a faith crisis is to be someone who is willing to sit with them and to mourn with those who mourn, to comfort those who stand in need of comfort, because for many of them they have lost their faith. This has been the bedrock of their life. It has evaporated and they don't know what to do. They feel like they are in a freefall. And what they need in that situation is not advice. They need someone who is willing to kind of mourn with them, to sit with them and comfort them and to help them feel loved and supported."[27] (Braithwaite, 2018)

Now to our young children, the trial that brings tears and a great sense of loss is more likely to be on a much smaller scale (to us) than what is being discussed by Dr. Braithwaite. It might be something as small as a broken toy or a misplaced phone, but our response should be the same. Our children do not need to be reminded that we "told you so" or "you didn't take care of it, now it's broken." They already know these things. But the loving path is to get down into the hole of their misery with them and help them feel better. Listen to them. Express words of consolation.

Hugo Montoya teaches the same principle in his General Conference address from October 2015. "Express feelings of compassion to others. If you are a priesthood holder, please use your power on behalf of the children of God, giving blessings to them. Express words of consolation and comfort to people who are suffering or experiencing afflictions."[28] (Montoya, 2015)

Now apply this idea to the responsibilities of being a father. Even though the suffering and afflictions of our children might

---

[27] Scott Braithwaite, PhD., *What Every Leader Needs to Know About Faith Crisis – An Interview with Scott Braithwaite*, a podcast published by LeadingSaints.org, October 14, 2018.

[28] Hugo Montoya, *Tested and Tempted—but Helped*, an address given at the General Conference of the Church of Jesus Christ of Latter-day Saints, October 2015.

not be that great sometimes, we should still be able to look at them and feel compassion for them in their circumstances. We should be able to bless them and help them to come through their trials no matter how great or small.

Feeling What Others Feel

This idea of having compassion and consoling those who are suffering has its roots in a spiritual gift that enables us to see others the way Heavenly Father sees them. When we are blessed to see a struggling soul through God's eyes, we can feel His love and compassion for their suffering.

It may be easier to do this with the young children in our care. But once our loved ones are old enough to exercise their agency to make choices that are not pleasing to us, our ability or willingness to see them in a compassionate light seems to fade. Like we have often heard, we like our children best from the time they learn to talk until the time they learn to talk back.

Cultivating this gift is part of charity. Compassion is being able to understand that our loved ones do not have the same "tool kit" as us to deal with their problems nor do they necessarily want our "solution." Feeling what they feel is empathy. Compassion and empathy drive connection. Connecting with our loved ones strengthens our relationships, which should be a primary objective for us in this life.

Speaking at a Brigham Young University devotional, Sondra Heaston asked: "What if we could really see into each other's hearts? Would we understand each other better? By feeling what others feel, seeing what others see, and hearing what others hear, would we make, and take, the time to serve others, and would we treat them differently? Would we treat them with more patience, more kindness, and more tolerance?"[29] (Heaston, 2015)

A core objective of this work is to help us understand that our neighbors are our own flesh and blood under the same roof. For

---

[29] Sondra Heaston, *Keeping Your Fingers on the PULSE of Service*, an address given at Brigham Young University, June 23, 2015.

example, that the "others" being referred to by Heaston are those closest to us. Our children, spouse, siblings, and parents. What if these "other" people we were making time and taking time to serve are the members of our immediate family? What if we could see into our spouse's heart? Would we understand her better? Would we be able to see what he sees? Would we treat her differently? If we could understand our children's feelings better, we would treat them with more patience, more kindness, and more tolerance.

The Solution is Charity

Just when we are beginning to understand the importance of compassion and empathy in helping others deal with their difficulties, they go and complicate it by making choices that are against our wishes. Our loved ones often make choices or do things that are thoughtless, hurtful, or immoral.

A teenager got involved in drugs in high school. With a desire to be upfront and honest with his mother about the situation, he confessed to what he was doing. What was his mother's response? "How could you do this to me?" The teenager was engaged in behavior he felt in no way affected his mother, and responded, perhaps somewhat naively, "I am not doing this to you. I'm just doing it." Yet his mother took it as a personal attack, a betrayal.

Was this an attempt on the part of the mother to guilt her son into making a better decision? If she could show him how painful his behavior was to her, would this cause him to change? Needless to say, it didn't work.

So, what should we do in cases like these?

Every situation is different. The dynamics at play with every given choice are incalculable. Families are all different. Our backgrounds and experiences and how we deal with difficult situations differ from person to person, family to family, and from culture to culture. We know that what is right or works for one family may not be right for another. But here is one thing that is right in every case: whatever problems your family is facing, whatever you must do to solve them, the beginning and the end of the solution is charity, the pure love of Christ, unconditional love. We can always be sure that the best answer is the loving one, "For 'charity never faileth' – and is never the wrong response."[30] (Craig, 2018)

Henry Eyring shared a wonderful example of unconditional love in his story of a religious grandmother who was given a particularly painful challenge precisely because of her ability to love unconditionally. This story highlights the difficulty of expressing charity for our loved ones when they make choices we don't approve of, but also illustrates how important loving family members are in God's plan.

This woman had been very faithful throughout her life and probably had a reasonable expectation that her posterity would be faithful as well, "Yet one of her grandsons chose a life of crime. He was finally sentenced to prison. She drove along a highway to visit her grandson in prison, had tears in her eyes as she prayed with anguish, 'I've tried to live a good life. Why, why do I have this tragedy of a grandson who seems to have destroyed his life?' The answer came to her mind in these words: 'I gave him to you because I knew you could and would love him no matter what he did.'"[31] (Eyring, 2013)

Can we reach this place to love those closest to us "no matter what" they do?

If you desire to be this type of family member, it may be a good idea, in advance of the situation you fear most, to image how you will deal with it. If your beautiful, pure teenage daughter becomes pregnant by mistake, how will you treat her? Will you condemn and advise, or will you love and listen? Will you have compassion and try to see things through her eyes? Will you be with her in her difficult time or disown her? Will you also love

---

[30] Michelle Craig, *Divine Discontent*, an address given at the General Conference of the Church of Jesus Christ of Latter-day Saints, October 2018.
[31] Henry Eyring, *To My Grandchildren*, an address given at the General Conference of the Church of Jesus Christ of Latter-day Saints, October 2013.

her boyfriend? These are all good practice questions to ponder in advance of the actual experience so that you can be better prepared to love unconditionally when the need arises. For the need *will* arise.

Our charitable role in helping others was taught clearly by Bonnie Cordon in an address about being a shepherding influence on our friends. She noted our responsibility as disciples of Christ to watch out for the needs of others. "Our sheep may be hurting, lost, or even willfully astray; as their shepherd, we can be among the first to see their need. We can listen and love without judgment and offer hope and help with the discerning guidance of the Holy Ghost."[32] (Cordon, 2018)

This guidance was given in the context of how loving friends should watch out for others. How much more then does the Lord expect us, as parents and stewards over our children and other beloved members of our family, to be there for them during their times of trials? Cordon's teaching, applied to our immediate family would sound something like this: "Our child may be hurting, lost, or even willfully astray; as their parent, we can be among the first to see their need. We can listen and love without judgment and offer hope and help with the discerning guidance of the Holy Ghost." The solution to their salvation, both temporally and spiritually, is our charity.

The Spirit of the Lord is Kindness

One thing worse than advising your loved one during a difficult time is saying unkind things. Unfortunately, we find that the people closest to us will make comments and bare their feelings about us at the time when we are most vulnerable. Perhaps it's because we feel so close that we are willing to "be honest" with our loved ones and say things we would never dream of saying to an acquaintance or even a friend. Is there a dark place in each of us that secretly rejoices when we see others struggling or failing?

---

[32] Bonnie Cordon, *Becoming a Shepherd*, an address given at the General Conference of the Church of Jesus Christ of Latter-day Saints, October 2018.

As a child, was it not in the least bit gratifying to see our sibling get into trouble? When our spouse is having a hard time and lashes out in anger, do we console or push buttons? When we are so close to someone, we have an uncanny ability to say the precise things that will amplify their anguish.

This is not the spirit of charity. George Albert Smith taught that "unkind things are not usually said under the inspiration of the Lord. The Spirit of the Lord is a spirit of kindness; it is a spirit of patience; it is a spirit of charity and love and forbearance and long suffering . . . But if we have the spirit of fault finding . . . in a destructive manner, that never comes as a result of the companionship of the Spirit of our Heavenly Father and is always harmful . . . Kindness is the power that God has given us to unlock hard hearts and subdue stubborn souls."[33] (Smith G. A., 2011)

Fault-finding is always harmful. Whether we are finding fault with our loved one's behavior or blaming circumstances on them, it hurts. Most people above a young age know when their behavior is failing to meet expectations. They don't need to be told. Pointing it out is not helping. The power to soften hearts is kindness. Whether we are trying to influence the mind and heart of a child or console a spouse through a failure, soft words, love and kindness trump criticism, fault-finding, and conditional love every time.

Love Before Obedience

Along the same lines as the proverb, "They don't care how much you know until they know how much you care," it may also be said, They don't care to obey until they know how much you care. A beautiful example of the power of patience, forbearance, and long-suffering with a child to influence them was related by Carole Stephens.

This story is so extraordinary in illustrating a divine level of

---

[33] George Smith, *Teachings of Presidents of the Church: George Albert Smith* (2011), 225, 226, 228.

LOVE AND FAMILY

patience and its power, it will do no good but to quote it in full here. Carole took her granddaughter, Chloe, out to give her mother a rest and relates the story:

"I buckled Chloe into her car seat, secured my own seat belt, and drove out of their driveway. However, before we reached the end of the street, Chloe had unbuckled her seat belt and was standing up, looking over my shoulder, and talking to me! I pulled the car over to the side of the road, got out, and buckled her back into her seat. We started again but had gone only a short distance when she was out of her seat again. I repeated the same steps, but this time before I could even get back into the car and fasten my own seat belt, Chloe was already standing up! I found myself sitting in a car, parked on the side of the road, having a power struggle with a three-year-old. And she was winning! I used every idea I could think of to convince her that remaining fastened in her car seat was a good idea. She was not convinced! I finally decided to try the if/then approach. I said, 'Chloe, if you will stay buckled in your car seat, then as soon as we get to Grandma's house, we can play with play dough.' No response. 'Chloe, if you will stay buckled in your seat, then we can make bread when we get to Grandma's house.' No response. I tried again. 'Chloe, if you will stay buckled in your seat, then we can stop at the market for a treat!' After three attempts, I realized this was a futile exercise. She was determined, and no amount of if/then was enough to convince her to remain fastened in her seat. We couldn't spend the day sitting on the edge of the road, but I wanted to be obedient to the law, and it wasn't safe to drive with Chloe standing up. I offered a silent prayer and heard the Spirit whisper, 'Teach her.' I turned to face her and pulled my seat belt away from my body so she could see it. I said, 'Chloe, I am wearing this seat belt because it will protect me. But you aren't wearing your seat belt, and you won't be safe. And I will be so sad if you get hurt.' She looked at me; I could almost see the wheels turning in her little mind as I waited anxiously for her response. Finally, her big blue eyes brightened, and she said, 'Grandma, you want me to wear my seat belt because you love me!' The Spirit filled the car as I expressed my love for this precious little girl. I didn't want to lose that feeling, but I knew I had an opportunity, so I got out and secured her in her car seat. Then I asked, "Chloe, will you please stay in your car seat?" And she did—all the way to the market for a treat!"[34] (Stephens, 2015)

Notice that Chloe did not desire to obey until she understood the love her grandmother had first. Then obedience was simple. Her grandmother showed unlimited patience and love and by doing so was able to influence Chloe's choices. Some people might hear this story and think, 'How ridiculous that this adult can't control a three-year old! If I were there, that bratty little girl would find out that being in an accident wouldn't be the only downside of refusing to wear her seatbelt.' The alternative to Stephens' approach is anger, impatience, and threats. All of these would weaken the connecting relationship between the two. On the other hand, the unconditional love manifest through patience and kindness strengthened their relationship as Chloe came to realize how much her grandmother loved her.

"I Told You So" Is Not Love

Being a know-it-all is not very impressive. No one enjoys being wrong, and it's even worse when it's pointed out. Being right feels good but being right at the expense of another's mistakes should not. We don't need to say, "I told you so," when we learn we were right and our loved one is wrong. Gloating over another's mistake or failure is unbecoming. Obviously, parents are more experienced than their children and can predict with annoying accuracy the outcome of certain behaviors and decisions made by those younger than them. This sets them up with plenty of opportunities to demonstrate their superior knowledge. If we look to the methods of our Eternal Father, we find that He does not. He seems satisfied that we simply learn.

---

[34] Carole Stephens, *If Ye Love Me, Keep My Commandments*, an address given at the General Conference of the Church of Jesus Christ of Latter-day Saints, October 2015.

A friend related a personal experience that illustrates how God teaches us. From this we should be instructed on how to teach our children. Melinda is a spiritual and religious person. She is accustomed to receiving promptings from the Spirit that guide her and protect her. The faithful believe that these spiritual directions come from God and should not be ignored, similar to how parents believe that children should heed their advice and warnings.

Upon arriving at a college sports event and parking her car, Melinda had a feeling she should leave her purse in the car when she went in to watch the game. Normally we like to have our belongings with us at all times in case a purchase needs to be made or some other need pops up. After an inner debate about leaving the purse in the car, she decided to ignore the feeling and consoled herself with a silent promise to keep an extra close watch on the purse and wallet. During the event, the purse and wallet never left her sight. After the game concluded she drove toward home and stopped at the grocery store on the way. To her horror and disbelief, her wallet was missing from the purse. She couldn't understand it. The purse had never left her sight. She prayed about it but did not get the feeling that she should cancel her credit cards. A few days later a friend of hers was at another sporting event when they announced over the loudspeaker that Melinda's wallet was found and if she could come identify herself, then the wallet would be handed over. Her friend called her and asked if she was at the game. She was not. Her friend asked whether she wanted her to pick up the wallet for her. She did. When she got the wallet back, everything was intact.[35]

If we pay careful attention to the feelings that prompt us to make choices and act a certain way, we learn that often when we ignore those feelings, there's a price to pay. But notice how, in this case, Heavenly Father did not "punish" Melinda for her unwillingness to follow the spiritual prompting to leave her purse

---

[35]Melinda Humphrey, related over the pulpit during a sacrament meeting of the Church of Jesus Christ of Latter-day Saints, March 2017.

in the car. We may normally expect to lose our wallet (or even our identity) for failing to follow a clear spiritual direction about what to do with it. We chalk it up to karma. Surprisingly, something much worse didn't happen when it almost would seem to have been justified. Instead, Melinda said, she learned a few important lessons from the experience and God was satisfied with that.

How different that is from how we might parent. We would love to say, "I told you to leave the purse in the car. You should have listened to me. I'm right and you're wrong." Do we enjoy showing how we are the smarter party? But Heavenly Father, being omniscient, does not have the need to demonstrate who is smarter. He only cares for our education and enlightenment. And these should be our main concerns as we guide our children.

Dieter Uchtdorf summarizes with this observation. "Is being right more important than fostering an environment of nurturing, healing, and love? Build bridges; don't destroy them. Even when you are not at fault—perhaps especially when you are not at fault—let love conquer pride . . . Love in the fabric of the plan of salvation, is selfless and seeks the well-being of others."[36] (Uchtdor, 2016) The idea of building bridges to others is a beautiful metaphor. Bridges are a way for a loved one to cross that gulf that can separate us. No matter what we do, life can erode the ground between us and those we love. If that erosion is ignored, over time we find a vast chasm separates us. If we aren't careful, and there are no bridges, a gulf may separate us from those we love for far longer than we wish.

Love Is the Heart of the Gospel

We believe that unconditional love is the answer to many ills in the family. Somehow, we need to learn this ourselves and model it to our children and loved ones. There are many Christian homes throughout the world who have more or less adopted the

---

[36]Dieter Uchtdorf, *In Praise of Those Who Save*, an address given at the General Conference of the Church of Jesus Christ of Latter-day Saints, April 2016.

Gospel as a guiding light for their life. There are likely as many belief systems and understandings of the Gospel as there are Christian homes. But the one thing we should all be able to agree on is that the center of the Gospel of Jesus Christ is love.

Toward the end of his earthly ministry, Christ met with His apostles and poured out sacred teachings that were recorded by the apostle John. In John 15, Christ speaks about love and how He loves us as the Father loves Him. Then He gives His disciples a last commandment, "This is my commandment, That ye love one another, as I have loved you. Greater love hath no man than this, that a man lay down his life for his friends."[37] The commandment is no longer to love your neighbor as yourself. That law has been fulfilled and was a lesser law anyway. The new law is to love as God loves. And note that it is no longer about loving your "neighbor," it is now about loving "one another." Is there any closer brotherhood than that of the twelve apostles? If there is, it is only that of flesh and blood brothers and sisters. And if the apostles are commanded to love each other as God loves them, how much more does He expect us to love our siblings, parents, and children as He loves us? This love He has for us is unconditional. It is charity. It is the pure love of Christ and what we should model for our families. It is the power of this kind of love that will heal all breaches, forgive and forget all sins, overlook all faults and weaknesses. It is patient and kind, not forceful and overbearing.

When Christ gave this new commandment, he no doubt was referencing his upcoming sacrifice when he spoke of laying down one's life for his friends. But if we are going to have the greatest love for the members of our family, must we also lay down our lives for them? Not in a physical sense that we must die for them, but rather we must live for them. This means that the purpose of our lives becomes helping our loved ones achieve happiness. And we do this best through love.

Humans seem to be wired in a counter-intuitive way. When we seek after our own happiness, we come up empty, but when

---

[37] John 15:12-13.

we seek after the happiness of others, and particularly those closest to us, we are fulfilled. Our sadness comes when we focus on ourselves and what we are missing. Our happiness comes when we focus on those we love and what we are giving. So, in the sense that we lay down our own desires for happiness we are laying down our lives. And this is the greatest form of love. The paradox of finding your happiness after you give up striving for it was emphasized by Christ earlier in his ministry when he taught, "For whosoever will save his life, must be willing to lose it for my sake; and whosoever will be willing to lose his life for my sake, the same shall save it."[38]

Thus, the Gospel of Jesus Christ is not a system of commandments and checklists. It is not a program or a service project or even weekly meetings. The Gospel of Jesus Christ is love, and that unconditional. Dieter Uchtdorf related the story of a young girl named Eva who was required to spend some time at her Great-Aunt Rose's house one summer. Aunt Rose was possibly the happiest person Eva had ever known. Over the course of the summer Eva learned that Rose wasn't always so happy.

"There was a time when I was so discouraged, I didn't want to go on," Aunt Rose said. "There were so many things I wished for in my life. Most of them never happened. It was one heartbreak after another. One day I realized that it would never be the way I had hoped for. That was a depressing day. I was ready to give up and be miserable."[39] (Uchtdorf, 2015)

Fortunately, Rose learned that our own happiness comes "when we love our neighbors, we stop thinking so much about our own problems and help others to solve theirs," and that "the one thing that matters most in all the world—the thing Jesus said is the heart of His Gospel . . . is love—the pure love of Christ." Rose taught, "You see, everything else in the Gospel—all the shoulds and the musts and the thou shalts lead to

---

[38] Luke 9:24.
[39] Dieter Uchtdorf, *A Summer with Great-Aunt Rose*, an address given at the General Conference of the Church of Jesus Christ of Latter-day Saints, October 2015.

love."[40] (Uchtdorf, 2015)

Our declaration is that there is nothing more important in the family and in raising children than unconditional love. Love is the heart of the Gospel of Jesus Christ, and this Gospel is the plan of happiness. We understand there are experts out there who bristle at the thought that we show our children love no matter what they do. Proponents of 'tough love' have probably overemphasized the tough at the expense of the love. If not, we may be assured that most families haven't mastered the love part to temper toughness. Being tough is easy. Showing forth "an increase of love toward him whom thou hast reproved" is a lot more difficult.[41] Let us make sure that we have mastered the love part before we attempt to show forth the tough part. For at the end of the day, at the end of our lives, the only thing that will matter are our relationships. Relationships are not built on toughness; they are built on love.

Five Minutes to Express Love

Some reading this may fairly wonder, what about discipline? What about boundaries and rules? They may reasonably argue that without a fair system of rewards and punishments, our children will not excel. While all of these things, and more, have their place in the family between parents and children, the point we are making here is that timing is everything.

Many fathers can relate to this scenario. You are terribly busy. You work a lot and see your children far less than you would like. Kids get busy too. Sometimes it's only a few minutes each morning in a rush on the way to school and work. The failures of your children come to your attention when you are not with them. You need to talk to them about it because you can't just let it slide. The next time you see them is during that 5-minute interval as you cross paths in the morning. You confront them about a missing assignment that is bringing their grade down.

---

[40] Ibid.
[41] Doctrine & Covenants 121:43.

They're tired and rushed and they know the assignment is missing anyway. Tempers flare. Threats are made. It gets their day off on the wrong foot and you're sure the way the conversation unfolded was not what you intended and, in retrospect, was ineffective at best, or harmed your relationship with your child at worst.

As a dad, you may not have a lot of face time with your kids. If you only see your son for five minutes in the morning, that's not the time to ask about missing assignments. We must work to avoid the trap of always using the precious time we have with them to drill them about their accomplishments. That small window is the time to express love.

Take a minute to put yourself in your child's shoes. You don't see your father much. You would probably like to see him more, but every time you do, he starts to drill you about your responsibilities. If you're not on top of *everything*, you know you're going to get a mini lecture, some sage advice, or an expression of disappointment. If this is the pattern, is this an interaction you're going to be looking forward to? More likely it's a conversation you are going to wish to avoid. You will likely begin to figure out ways to avoid your father. The relationship begins to dissolve and there is no plan in place on either side to mend it. On the contrary, if during that brief encounter each morning your interaction is one of love, you will be building up trust with your child. They will look forward to the interaction and be more likely to want to please you.

The question then becomes: When do I talk about these important things with my children? One highly effective means of accomplishing these conversations is by having more respect for your child's time and working with them to set time aside to review the problem. Think of it this way. If you had an important topic of discussion that required facetime with a busy colleague at work, would you try to bring it up when you bumped into her at the coffee machine? Of course not. You would schedule a meeting with her by checking her calendar and finding a time when you both were available for the necessary amount of time to cover the topic. Is your colleague at work more important than your child? Do you respect her more than your own flesh and blood? You shouldn't.

So rather than trying to resolve the missing assignment issue in the five-minute rush before work and school, maybe it would be better to take that time to schedule a meeting to discuss it. This can be done in a light-hearted way that is not threatening. The conversation might go something like this:

"Hey Son, I want to see if I can do anything to help you with your missing assignment."

"There's nothing you can do Dad. I just have to turn it in."

"I'd still like to see if I can help. Do you have some time Saturday morning we can go over it?"

"Uh, yea, that would probably work."

"OK, how about 9 a.m. on Saturday?"

"Can we do it at 10? I probably won't be up by 9."

"How about 9:30? I promised your mom we would go to the store at 10."

"Ugh. OK, but I can't promise I'll be awake."

A little negotiating. A little give and take and you have a time set. Doing this has several benefits. First, it gives you more time to discuss the problem with your child. You can talk to them about it. Understand the reasons for their situation. It gives you time to formulate a plan with them to resolve the issue. It gives you a chance to see if you really can help them. Second, it gives you more one-on-one time with your child. It shows them that you really are interested in what they are doing. It shows them that you really want to help them. All of these things help to build the relationship as opposed to having your child try to avoid or minimize interaction time. And third, scheduling a time with your child gives them a chance to think about the issue and prepare to discuss it with you. Having respect for another person's time is just common courtesy. We should not be of the mindset that just because they are our children, they are subordinate and at our beck and call. Lastly, scheduling a time to discuss gives you a chance to let off some steam and come into the interaction with love and concern rather than anger over your child's lack of attention to their responsibility. If you only have five minutes with your child, use that time to express love.

Conclusion

In this chapter, we defined charity as unconditional love, that is, love that is given that is not contingent on the recipient's conformity to our hopes and expectations of them. When others fail to meet these expectations, it is important that we respond tenderly to express this love. Wise authors have observed for thousands of years the importance of the parents' example and call for us to restrain ourselves in our response to our children. It is important that we anticipate the difficult scenarios we'll face in our relationships and plan our responses ahead of difficult but not unexpected possibilities. This is easier said than done as we find our loved ones often know exactly how to trigger us. Nevertheless, we prove our unconditional love by our willingness to forget offenses and resist the temptation to counsel and advise while developing compassion and empathy for the trials of others. Learning how to feel what others' feel is the essence of empathy. Compassion, empathy, and kindness are the hallmarks of charity.

2

CONDITIONAL LOVE

We've spent a lot of time discussing unconditional love and how important it is to building relationships in the family and how hard it is to achieve. What kind of love do you have for your children if it is not unconditional? What is that love like? The answer is conditional love. And it may not even be love.

Love that is expressed only when certain conditions or expectations are met, or withheld when the conditions are not met, is conditional love. Do we show our love constantly and set expectations for our children when we have their trust and confidence, or do we set expectations for them and show our love and admiration as a conditional reward for their obedience?

Loving based on conditions or expectations of behavior is so engrained in us, that it seems natural. "Loving them who love you" is easy, the Lord said.[42] There is no reward in that. We believe that others show their love and respect for us by meeting our expectations of them. Therefore, when we see them meeting our expectations, we love them. When we don't see them doing that? Not so much.

James Patterson has revealed an understanding of

---
[42] Matthew 5:46.

expectations and love in a marriage and family with deep insight. He has pointed out that, "We all have expectations in life . . . of work and business, of schooling and friends, of marriage and families. We have expectations of spousal relationships, of intimacy and sexuality. We have expectations of how our children should behave; the grades they should receive, and respect they should show. As children, we have expectations of our parents. We have expectations of spiritual things – of family prayer, family home evening, scripture study, missions and even temple service. We even enter into and have 'expectations' of God and of His relationship with us. Our expectations are us – our hopes, our desires, our wants and our needs. They make us what we are and even motivate us in life. Our expectations are created from life's experiences – our upbringings, our parents' teachings and even gospel teachings. There is nothing wrong with expectations. Most of us have good expectations. We're taught to do so and to set high and lofty goals."[43] (Patterson, 2006)

The profound insight Patterson made is that when our loved ones fail to meet our expectations, enmity is placed between us and our loved ones. "Enmity is caused by unmet expectations," he said.[44] And the only power that will overcome enmity is charity, unconditional love.

There are several problems with setting expectations or attaching conditions to our love for our children and spouse:

1) Our expectations can become unrealistic
2) We tend to set the same expectations for all our children when they do not all have the same tool kit
3) When our expectations are unmet, enmity is introduced into the relationship.

---

[43] James Patterson, *Enmity*, from an address given at the Alpine North Stake Conference of the Church of Jesus Christ of Latter-day Saints, January 14, 2006. A copy of the talk was placed into the possession of the author by James Patterson.
[44] Ibid.

Unrealistic Expectations

Patterson outlines some great examples of unrealistic expectations. "If I have the expectation that my home should always be clean with 8 children, it would be an unrealistic expectation. Also, it would be unrealistic to expect my children ranging from 21 to 3 to be at every family prayer or at every family home evening. As well, with some of my children it would be an unrealistic expectation that they would get straight A's. With at least one of my teenagers, it would be unrealistic – at least at this time of their life – to keep their room clean."[45]

Should we not be able to expect all of our children to keep their room clean? It seems like a simple task. Five minutes of work a day and it can be kept very tidy. For many children, depending on their age, this is not much of a problem. For others, it's a big problem. We can ask them to pick up their room. We can explain all of the reasons behind why keeping a clean room is important. We can set up an allowance system or make promises of other benefits. We can count to three or threaten privileges or even bodily harm. Depending on the child, any one of these methods might reach them and motivate them to clean their room. But with another child, any and all of these can be tried and tried to no effect. All of the asking, begging, threats, rewards and help will not get them to meet our expectation. The desire to achieve this must come from within the person. As trial and error has shown, it cannot be forced from the outside with this child. With this child, at least, the expectation that they must keep their room clean is unrealistic. They do not respond to the normal punishment/reward system.

Keeping the room clean is just one of many examples of behavioral expectations we might hold up for a loved one. The point is that some people can easily meet our expectations in one thing or another and others may not be able to meet them. When a loved one fails to meet an expectation, we have arrived at a

---

[45] Ibid.

critical juncture in our relationship and must decide. Do we let go of our expectation and continue to love and support the person? Or do we allow enmity between us? If we refuse to let go of our expectation, then anger, bitterness, and disappointment come between us and the one we love. What appears to be stubbornness in our loved one's refusal to grant our wishes engenders a feeling that the only possible motivation for their actions is that they do not love and respect us. Regardless of their true feelings, our imagination that they do not love us is enough to erode our love for them because we are accustomed to loving them who love us. When we imagine they do not love us, our disappointment becomes sadness and as this state continues, we harden our hearts toward the person we should be loving the most. We have allowed the enmity between us to destroy our love.

Alternatively, we can let go of our expectation. Yes, we run the risk of being judged an incompetent parent or a pushover because we allow our children to get away with whatever they want. But maybe our expectation isn't realistic in this relationship. We cannot see into our loved one's heart to know what it is that is preventing them from fulfilling our desires for them. It is OK to modify or let go of the expectation if it means preserving the relationship. When the relationship is intact, there is a chance of influencing future behavior. When the relationship is broken or hurting, our influence is negligible. Can we still love our child even though they haven't done all that we ask? Of course, we can. Can we also love them if they haven't done anything that we ask? This is much more difficult, but this is love unconditional.

Blanket Expectations

The second problem we have with expectations is that we tend to set the same expectations for all of our children regardless of their abilities or tool kit. Any parent of more than one child will confirm that every child comes with its own set of talents, abilities, baggage, and weaknesses. One sibling may excel at piano, another at football. One may easily master their times tables, and another expresses beautifully in watercolor. So, if our children are all different, how can we expect the same performance from all of them? We cannot. We must be willing to tailor, prune back, or abandon certain expectations for those who are unable to meet them if it means preserving the relationship.

One father learned this quickly with his first-born son. Early on he noticed his son showed a lack of interest in schoolwork, and an unwillingness to buckle down on homework. But in elementary school, that is not necessarily fatal. At the same time, he noticed his son was interested in skateboarding and music. By the time the boy reached junior high it was evident that getting him to excel academically was going to be a problem. Every night was the same routine: Do you have any homework tonight? Nope. Are you sure? Yep. By the time the first term grades came out, the problem was out in the open. No As, One B. The rest Cs and Ds.

Fortunately, this father had access to an online tool that let him review the assignments and grades in each class. This was eye-opening. Almost every assignment that was turned in received an A. The problem was that only about half of the assignments were getting turned in. This was super-frustrating for the father who excelled at being organized and finishing the job. As the year went by, the grades were a constant source of contention between the father and the teen. At first a reward system was tried where $100 a term was offered for straight A's and $5 per A if straight As wasn't achieved. That didn't work. Then came the threats against privileges. The son seemed perfectly fine losing privileges if it meant he didn't have to do homework. The father tried tracking every missing assignment through the online tool, asking questions about them, asking if he could help. Nothing.

By this time, the father-son relationship was very strained. The father thought the son was lazy and possibly an idiot and the son thought the father was an uptight, overbearing jerk who was getting upset over nothing. Finally, when all else failed, the parents made an appointment with a school counselor to see if anything could be done. They met privately with the counselor as their son waited outside. They laid out their concerns and observations and listed all of the things they had tried to do to help their son improve his grades. The counselor listened patiently. When the parents had exhausted their side of the story, the counselor simply observed with a smirk, "This is your first son, isn't it?"

Nothing really came from that counseling session, but as the father contemplated the initial question of the counselor, he realized that the frustrating situation he was in was common. The more he thought about it, the more he realized that he and his son were quite different in many ways. He had explained the importance of education and what a difference getting good grades would make. He had used every means of force and finesse to get his son to live up to the expectations he had for him and what type of grades he should get, and nothing made any difference. Now there was a wall between them that made communication difficult. So, after a lot of thought and re-evaluation, the father concluded that he was not going to ruin his eternal relationship with his first-born son over the grades he made in junior high school.

Dropping the expectation was difficult, but it freed the father from the burden of enforcing it. He realized that, for this child, an expectation of really good grades was not realistic. He was able to accept the child for the person that he was. The relationship began to heal, and they became good friends. Later we found that the son, who drifted through high school, got a great job in sales and did very well. His company paid for him to get his college education. And by the way, his younger sister was a 4.0 student in high school.

It's helpful to the relationships between loved ones if we can learn to evaluate our expectations for each person. Each individual is different, and we can't expect all to live up to the same standards. Our expectations for our loved ones need to be realistic and individualized. Our love "should never be withdrawn when a child, friend, or family member fails to live up to our expectations."[46] (Palmer, 2017)

Expectations and Enmity

What is enmity? Dictionary.com defines it as "a feeling or condition of hostility; hatred; ill will; animosity; antagonism."[47] Webster's defines it as "a mean, deep-seated dislike; a *positive hatred* – showing itself in *attacks* or aggression; repugnance, suggesting a *clash of temperaments*; an intense ill will and vindictiveness that threatens to *kindle hostility*. It is especially applied to *bitter brooding* over a *wrong*."[48]

"What *wrong* could cause enmity so great that it *attacks* and destroys family relations? What *wrong* causes so much *bitter brooding* that a husband is willing to leave his wife and children and sometimes even the Church? What *wrong kindles hostility* so great that a parent is willing to kick a child out of their house? Or what *wrong* would cause "a *clash of temperaments*" so great that a child is willing to leave family and home and live out on the street? Enmity is caused by – **unmet expectations**."[49] (Patterson, 2006)

As the father in the previous story tried to enforce his expectations upon his teenage son, their relationship began to deteriorate. Had he allowed it to continue on the path, could the child have been willing to leave family and home and live out on the street? All because the son would not or could not (who can judge?) meet the expectations of his father. Enmity between the father and son, caused by unmet expectations was destroying their relationship. This is the destructive power of enmity and illustrates the problem with rigidly clinging to the expectations we have for our loved ones. When it comes down to a choice

---

[46] Mark Palmer, *Then Jesus Beholding Him Loved Him*, an address given at the General Conference of the Church of Jesus Christ of Latter-day Saints, April 2017.
[47] https://www.dictionary.com/browse/enmity
[48] Webster's dictionary, emphasis is the author's.
[49] James Patterson, *Enmity*, 1-2. Emphasis in the original.

between holding onto our expectations or our child, it should be an easy decision.

Expectations and Goals

There may be a worry that modifying or abandoning our expectations will lead to lower achievement. We often hear that our children will rise to the level of our expectations. That may be true if our expectations for them are achievable by them. Do not get expectations and goals confused. Goals are expectations we have of ourselves. Expectations are goals we have for others. Of course, goal setting is a great practice used by most successful people. We are not advocating the abandonment of goals. We are pointing out that we can't always expect others to achieve our goals that we set for them.

Children should be taught how to set goals. They should set goals in areas that *they* are interested in, not necessarily in areas that interest *us*. We should help them find their interests and then help them excel in the areas that appeal to them. We should be even more proud of them when they achieve the goals they set for themselves in areas that they are interested in as we would be had we given them our own set of goals and they had achieved those. It may not be easy for the ex-military, hunter, active-duty police officer to support his son's goals in computer nerd, but that is a problem for the parent, not the child. Who knows, but that kid may turn out to be one of the smartest computer programmers around and end up with a great career. He just won't be like his father.

Christ Never Felt Used

There are going to be times when our desires conflict with those of our children. It's OK to express your desire, but then give your desire up to show what being unselfish looks like. For example, one mother and daughter shared clothes. One day they both wanted to wear the same top on the same day. A conflict ensued. They both had plans to wear it and had pictured their outfit already. The mother, being the adult, should be able to give up her desire out of love, but use the moment to teach selflessness. If the mother fights for her desire, refuses to bend, and demands to have her own way, what message is being conveyed to her daughter? What will the daughter learn from that example? But if the mother expresses her desire and the child does not give, the mother can model patience, selflessness, love and kindness. Conflict like this is a perfect opportunity to express charity. When children see their parents' model this type of charity, will they be more or less likely to act generously with others in the future?

But do you have a fear of being taken advantage of by your child when you model charity and unconditional love? This is a valid fear and a good question. Did Christ ever feel taken advantage of? We say, "No. He did not." Christ knew exactly what he was doing and gave up everything and never felt like he was being used because he was showing the way of love, sacrifice, forgiveness and selflessness.

What stops many of us from loving our children and serving them more and honoring them and their agency is a fear of being called weak, of being called a pushover. A fear of letting our children walk all over us. That may be true, we may be accused of that. And in some cases, it may even be true. But was Christ ever accused of being weak? Of course, he was. In many people's minds, meek and weak are synonymous. Was Christ ever accused of being a pushover or someone who was not hard on sin? Of course, he was. What did the Pharisees think of him when he refused to enforce the Law of Moses on the woman taken in adultery? Did people walk all over Christ? Of course, they did. They spat on him and smote him and whipped and tortured him. Could he have prevented that? Of course, he could have. If his kingdom were of this world, he would ask, and his father would send an army of angels to deliver him. Was Christ used? Of course, he was. How many people followed him to get the free bread rather than the bread of life? Did he stop them? No, he loved them even though their intentions were selfish and temporal. Did Christ ever feel like he had been used by others? Of course not. His life was worn out in the service of his brothers and sisters.

Love Initiates Respect

One concern we have in all this is that if our children perceive us as weak or as pushovers, they will not respect us. Parents want to be respected by their children. Some parents demand respect. They do this by virtue of their parenthood. Children are disrespectful by nature. This can lead to a conflict. It seems ironic, but some of the people that tend to demand respect the most are the same people who live in a way and treat other people in a way that causes them to lose respect. There is a big difference between those who demand respect and those who command it.

When a person commands respect, it is because they live in a way that requires us to respect them. They are noble, fair, kind, loving, honest, and full of integrity. When people demand respect, it is usually because they are not receiving the respect they feel they deserve. But respect must be earned. People who don't live in a way to command respect typically end up demanding it from their subordinates. While staff members or children can act respectful toward their boss or parent, they can do so without actually respecting them. Would you rather *earn* the true respect from those whom you love or lead or simply *demand* that they act respectful?

Love is central to earning respect. Love initiates respect. We love to follow and be around and bestow praise and honor on those who we know love us and have our best interest at heart. "Because love is the great commandment, it ought to be at the center of all and everything we do in our own family, in our Church callings, and in our livelihood. Love is the healing balm that repairs rifts in personal and family relationships. It is the bond that unites families, communities, and nations. Love is the power that initiates friendship, tolerance, civility, and respect. It is the source that overcomes divisiveness and hate. Love is the fire that warms our lives with unparalleled joy and divine hope. Love should be our walk and our talk."[50] (Uchtdorf, The Love of God, 2009)

If you want to earn the respect of your children, treat them with charity. We need to show them unconditional love when they disappoint us in our expectations of them. Love them back into the fold. Let our love for them be the main attribute of our relationship toward them.

No Man Hateth His Own Flesh

This attitude of love toward our own children is completely supported by Holy Scripture. It is central to the message of the Gospel of Jesus Christ. We need not fear or heed the advice of the world that is shaming us into harsh discipline, unrealistic expectations of our children, and demanding unearned respect. In one of the core doctrinal chapters in the Book of Mormon, Alma, a high priest urges his people in a heartfelt sermon using these beseeching words:

"I wish from the inmost part of my heart, yea, with great anxiety even unto pain, that ye would hearken unto my words . . . that ye would humble yourselves before the Lord, and call on his holy name, and watch and pray continually . . . thus being led by the Holy Spirit, becoming humble, meek, submissive, patient, full of love and all long-suffering."[51]

If we acquire any of these attributes in our journey to become more like Christ, who would we thus display them to? We often think of ourselves as being humble toward our fellow Saints. Maybe less so at work or in a social setting, and perhaps even least of all at home. Isn't our home the one place where we can let down our guard and be ourselves? No need to put on an air of humility for people who know us so well. But if we think that

---

[50] Dieter Uchtdorf, *The Love of God*, an address given at the General Conference of the Church of Jesus Christ of Latter-day Saints, October 2009.
[51] Alma 13:27-28.

being humble is a Christ-like attitude we should work towards for our church friends, is it not sensible that it should be practiced on those who are closest to us and who we love the most and who love us? If being full of love and all long suffering is how you should be toward all people, how much more then toward your own children, your own flesh and blood?

Is this the flesh Paul referred to in his letter to the Ephesian saints, "For no man ever yet hated his own flesh; but nourisheth and cherisheth it, even as the Lord the church"?[52] Paul says men should nourish and cherish their wives as their own bodies. He says men "shall be joined unto their wife, and they two shall be one flesh."[53] Our spouse becomes our own flesh. Then from that union springs posterity who are also our own flesh and blood. All of these should be treated as dearly as Christ does the church. There is no room for harshness or criticism amongst those closest to us. Rather we should be building each other up with love, encouragement, praise, interest in each other's lives, soft words, forgiveness, patience, and help.

Our children need to feel our love more than anyone else in the world, except perhaps our spouse. They need to know that their home is the one place they are safe to be themselves. They need to feel that they can ask any question and receive a loving response without judgment. All our loved ones need to understand that at home they will be built up and loved, not torn down and belittled.

Some of them, at some point in their life, young or old, will slip off the path we have envisioned for them. They may stray far away. During that critical and dangerous time for them, they will likely feel frightened, broken, and alone. At some point in their wanderings, they may desire to make their way back. When they do, will we be the bridge they can use to cross the awful gulf? Or will we have burned that bridge through our expectations and judgment? Wouldn't it be sad if our own flesh and blood could not return to safety via our outstretched hand, but had to find

---

[52] Ephesians 5:29.
[53] Ephesians 5:31.

another route? Or worse yet, couldn't find another route? "It may break our hearts when their journey takes them away from the Church we love and the truth we have found, but we honor their right to worship Almighty God according to the dictates of their own conscience, just as we claim that privilege for ourselves."[54] (Uchtdorf, Come, Join With Us, 2013) Our charity toward our loved ones must always be beyond doubt in their mind.

Here is wisdom from the mother of a gay man who struggled for years with the conflict between his sexual orientation and his religious feelings. In a gathering with the man's married siblings she said, "The most important lesson your children will learn from how our family treats their [gay] Uncle Tom is that nothing they can ever do will take them outside the circle of our family's love."[55] (Christofferson, 2017) This is the kind of assurance and confidence our children should have about our love for them.

Just Love Him More

As a final witness of our need to show charity to our children, we offer this excerpt from an episode of Perspectives, a Mormon Channel production. In this interview with Gracia Jones, a great-great-granddaughter of the Prophet Joseph Smith, she relates a story about difficulties she was having with one of her sons. Clearly, the son was not meeting her expectations for him. As a mother of eight children, she had little time to customize a solution for the one son that was causing her difficulties. She had, no doubt, tried everything she could think of to get him to change. Finally, she resorted to prayer and her answer came in a dream where she saw the Prophet.

As she relates the story, "I married very young and had eight children. And I had an older child that was extremely difficult. And I was praying a great deal and asking how I could help him

---

[54] Dieter Uchtdorf, *Come, Join With Us*, an address given at the General Conference of the Church of Jesus Christ of Latter-day Saints, October 2013.
[55] See Thomas Christofferson, *That We May Be One: A Gay Mormon's Perspective on Faith and Family* (Salt Lake City: Deseret Book, 2017), 19.

or reach him. And I had a dream. In this dream there were some men standing kind of in a group and they were all in white and one of these people looked at me with the greatest love and the kindest . . . The kindest expression of compassion and tenderness. And I said, "My son is really troublesome. I don't know how to reach him." And he said, "Just love him more and he'll be alright. Just love him more." And then he turned back to his own business, and I woke up. And I knew that the person that I had just interviewed with was the Prophet Joseph Smith, my great-great grandfather. And he was as indescribable as anybody could ever be . . . And his countenance just radiated love."[56] (Jones, 2021)

In this account, the Prophet exhibits the kind of charity toward his great-great-granddaughter that we are calling for toward our own loved ones in our immediate family. He looked on her with "the greatest love and the kindest expression of compassion and tenderness." And because of his attitude of love, his great-great-granddaughter felt connected to him. She felt a trust for him. She confided in him about one of her greatest problems. Is not this the type of relationship we want to engender with our children, with our spouse or parents? One of trust and confidence? A relationship where they seek out our counsel for their problems? One where we have influence over them at important crossroads in their life? This is the type of relationship that charity nurtures. It is not a surprise then that the counsel that this most loving and intelligent of beings gave to Gracia in her time of need was to be more loving. All the things she had tried to reach her son were not working. But the one thing she appeared to be missing was greater love.

Implied in the Prophet's response was the message that she should trust the Lord to take care of her son. "He'll be alright," he said, if you love him more. He may continue wayward and it's all right. If there are lessons to be learned, life will teach them. If the lessons are hard, he'll need a place to come home to where

---

[56] Gracie Jones, *Perspectives – Episode 5*, The Mormon Channel, beginning at minute 22:03.

he knows he will be loved even though he fell. He may reach rock bottom on his journey, but he will return. "He'll be alright" . . . with greater love.

Conclusion

We have shown how different conditional love is from charity and questioned whether conditional love is even love at all. One of the most powerful factors driving us away from unconditional love are the unmet expectations we have of others. We often form unrealistic expectations of people because they are based on the performance of others and not customized to fit the person and situation. A task that is simple for one person may seem insurmountable to another. Consistently unmet expectations introduce enmity into our heart which erodes our ability to feel compassion. It is important that we make our expectations conform to another person's abilities because everyone is different. In some cases, we may be forced to choose whether to hold onto our expectations or our loved one because we can't have both. At the same time, it is important that we not confuse our expectations of others with goals they may have for themselves. Goal setting and achievement are habits for successful people, and we should help others accomplish their own goals and not force ours goals upon them.

Sometimes we fear giving up our unrealistic expectations and believe that our relationship may become a one-way street with all of the giving coming from us. We have made the case that we shouldn't feel used or taken advantage of. We believe it unlikely that Christ ever felt this way about His giving. Instead, we learn that love initiates and is central to gaining the respect of others. Our children need our love more than anyone so they know they can trust us when they have gone astray. Sometimes we feel that no matter what we say or do, we cannot reach them. But the counsel from heaven is that we should just love them more when we feel them slipping away or struggling. It will never work to withdraw our conditional love as a means to causing conformity to our wishes.

3

HAVE PATIENCE AS THEY LEARN

For those of us who have learned all of life's lessons (haha), it can be frustrating sometimes as we watch others make the same mistakes and ignore any sage advice we have to offer. But learning is something everyone does a little differently. We all have different tool kits to learn with and some of us just never learn. People can learn from watching and listening to others who have experience, or they can learn by doing, which is usually the harder way.

Jacob notes this difference as he introduces his sermon in the Book of Mormon. "We labor diligently to engraven these words upon plates, hoping that our beloved brethren and our children will receive them with thankful hearts, and look upon them that they may learn with joy and not with sorrow."[57] Those who receive the plates containing his writings with thankful hearts, and look upon them, may learn with joy. In other words, when we receive the wisdom of those who have gone before us, our learning can be joyful. When we don't, we learn with sorrow, i.e., by experience or what we sometimes call the school of hard knocks.

---

[57] Jacob 4:3.

Many will argue that unless we experience something firsthand, we really don't know it. While that is debatable, must we always learn everything by experience? Should we not be satisfied with knowledge gained by listening to and watching the experience of others? There are many painful things in this life that can be avoided if we follow the instructions of those who have gone before us rather than trying to re-figure out everything on our own. "A page of history is worth a volume of logic," wrote Supreme Court Justice Oliver Wendell Holmes.[58] (New York Trust Co. vs. Eisner, 1921) While this was written with reference to an estate tax, it seems very applicable in the context of life. We can learn so much about "things as they really are, and of things as they really will be" from the writings, teachings, and experience of those who have gone before us.[59] Much of the way things are today can be understood by examining the events, times, people, and places that led up to today. When people interpret today without the context of history, some of the most fundamental truths are hidden and you end up with concepts like a "living Constitution."

Those who read history and the experiences of people from the past tend to have more patience and understanding for the foibles of others today. We learn that the human experience has hardly changed in thousands of years except in the matters of physical conveniences. We have always had love and friendship, motherhood and sibling rivalry, passion and hatred, forgiveness and compassion, selfishness and giving, the birth and death of loved ones, war and fear, triumph and misery. Human nature seems to have hardly changed over the centuries. The experiences that bring us joy and sorrow seem to always boil back to the treatment we receive from those who are closest to us and how we treat them.

So, as we are called upon to raise children, live with a spouse, or please a parent, we must remember that each of us are required to pass through trials of learning. Some of us experience one type

---

[58] Justice Holmes, New York Trust Co. v. Eisner, 256, U.S. 345 (1921)
[59] Jacob 4:13.

of pain and the rest something else. So, unless we have experienced all types of suffering, we are in no position to judge the experience of another, to say how they should have acted in a certain situation or to assume we could have handled it more elegantly. We must have patience as our loved ones learn and hope that they will be patient with us as we do so.

We Learn When We Are Ready

Bradly Foster shares the story of Pablo, a young man from Mexico City who had a father who understood how people learn. When Pablo was a young adult, he grabbed the attention of Foster because of the exemplary way he was living his life. Pablo explained that his father had helped him prepare for life by patiently teaching him when he was ready. Pablo remembered, "When I was nine, my dad took me aside and said, 'Pablo, I was nine once too. Here are some things you may come across. You'll see people cheating in school. You might be around people who swear. You'll probably have days when you don't want to go to church. Now, when these things happen—or anything else that troubles you—I want you to come and talk to me, and I'll help you get through them. And then I'll tell you what comes next.'"[60] (Foster, 2015)

Pablo's father was doing two things here that are extremely important when raising and teaching children. First, he remembered what it was like to be Pablo's age. We wonder how it is that so many children are faced with parents who apparently have forgotten what it was like to be a kid. Now most of us don't remember much from our childhood as we get older, but with a little effort we can recall enough of our mistakes and blunders at any age. And for those of us who do claim to remember what it was like, we often glorify our own childhood by misremembering how it was always colder, hotter, harder, the roads were steeper

---

[60] Bradley Foster, *It's Never Too Early and It's Never Too Late*, an address given at the General Conference of the Church of Jesus Christ of Latter-Day Saints, October 2015.

(both ways), the dogs were meaner, the teachers tougher, etc. How else are we all so familiar with how our father had to walk to school every day in the snow and against the wind, uphill both ways?

In addition to our forgetfulness, we also battle pride. Many of us don't want our kids to know that we are mortal, that we made, and continue to make, mistakes. We fear that if our children know that we are fallible, they will be less likely to listen to our counsel and commands. But wouldn't it be better if our children saw us as real people from an early age? Finding out that your parents make mistakes too should not be like finding out that Santa Claus doesn't live at the North Pole. They were pretending all along to be something they're not. It's OK and healthy to loop our children in on our problems as we are learning. They may surprise us and offer a clarity of view that we don't have.

Most of us will only be in the role of protector, provider, and professor for our children for 25% of their life. The other 75%, we'll want to be their friends and confidants. This can begin by letting them know that you're a real person with struggles and challenges like theirs. And letting them know this can begin by remembering what it was like to be their age.

The second great thing that Pablo's father did was tailor the lesson to the child's ability to learn. "Pablo's father knew our children learn when they are ready to learn, not just when we are ready to teach them."[61] He taught Pablo a little bit at a time, gave him just what he was ready for. He didn't try to teach him everything at once or give him lessons that were out of context for his life. A desire to learn must come from within. Learning cannot be forced on us from the outside. We can preach and teach until we are blue in the face, but if our student is not ready, or is uninterested, all will be in vain.

Teaching is more about timing than anything. Words of instruction have a much greater impact when the soil of the mind is prepared in advance and the season for planting has arrived. Just as the best time to enforce consequences is not in the heat

---

[61] Ibid.

of the moment when an expectation or promise has been violated, but later on when something is needed from us, so it is with teaching that we must wait until all is right to give the lesson. A good coach will not find fault and make correction in a young boy's swing as he is walking dejectedly back to the dugout after striking out. Unless the little athlete has the right mindset and is looking for help at that tough moment, the coaching will be more effective to wait until the next batting practice when the frustrations and hurt feelings are in the past and the batter is in the learning mode.

As parents, we are better off to follow this pattern. While the teaching moment may be right when the lesson first pops into our head, more often it seems that the lesson should be remembered and held until a better time to bring up the discussion. A benefit to this approach is the patience factor. Often when we see someone needs correction, it is because a mistake has been made, and frustration is present in both the teacher and the learner. Teaching in a moment of frustration is rarely effective. When a mistake is made, it is more compassionate and humbler to overlook it in the moment. Divert attention away from the mistake to something more positive. People are almost universally aware when they make mistakes. They don't need someone to point it out and doing so rarely has any positive effect. "We all know where we can do better," teaches Hans Boom. "There is no need to repeatedly remind each other, but there is a need to love and minister to each other and, in doing so, provide a climate of willingness to change."[62] (Boom, 2019)

Wait and see how things go over time. If the mistake is a one-time event, then the learner has probably self-corrected. If a mistake pattern is detected, then perhaps teaching is in order. But it is always better for the learner to come to the realization of what is correct on their own. Few things make more impact on us than discovery. When we learn something on our own, the

---

[62] Hans Boom, from *Knowing, Loving, Growing*, an address given at the General Conference of the Church of Jesus Christ of Latter-day Saints, October 2019.

feeling can be incredible, and the understanding becomes a part of us. Coming to a realization about what is right is one of the most gratifying experiences we can have. Constantly being corrected from the outside is one of the most degrading. So much so, that as a teacher we should be careful about when we step in with a lesson. It may be better to allow a pattern of mistakes to continue to occur until the learner self-corrects as long as no one or no thing is getting hurt.

The obvious exception to this strategy is when the learner seeks our help. But even then, we should give them just enough clues to help them self-discover. There is no need to demonstrate our superior knowledge and come off as a know-it-all. It is more important that a person learn on their own than it is for them to have an answer. Give a man an answer and he will learn for today. Teach a man to think and he will learn for a lifetime. Learning is a life-long process, and we should be good at it. In the meantime, we need to exercise the utmost patience with others as they try to learn.

Giving to Your Children

One life lesson that is particularly important and also difficult to learn is how to work. Much patience is required as people grow into an understanding of what is expected of them. In Ocean City, NJ, in the early 80s, a condominium manager hired a teenager fresh out of high school for the summer to help with maintenance, cleaning, and some janitorial work. One of the tasks assigned to the graduate was maintaining the ocean side pool deck. He was instructed to raise and lower the umbrellas on the tables, spray off the lounge chairs daily to remove residual suntan oil, pick up the trash and dishes, and keep the area presentable. Near the end of the summer, the manager came to the young man in somewhat of a panic. One of the residents complained to him that there was a lot of sand on the floor of the outdoor showers near the pool. When the condo residents came in off the beach, they showered off the sand before going into the pool. By design, the showers were down some stairs to the beach and hidden from view for anyone on the pool deck.

The manager asked the young man, "How long has it been since you hosed out the showers?"

The nervous teenager answered, "I've never done that."

"What?? Why not?" asked the manager.

"Because" came the reply, "Not only was I never told that was part of my job, but I also didn't even know there were showers down there."

The stunned manager held back his anger and politely showed the young man to the showers and instructed him on how to clean them. He knew it was his fault that he didn't put the task in the job description. What was obvious to the condo manager was unseen by the high school graduate. The manager did well by exercising extreme patience while his employee learned what was expected of him.

Helping others learn how to work and what is expected from them either at work or in life should be a primary focus of our teaching of those we are responsible for raising children. But sometimes it seems as if our efforts to teach our children to work become so over-emphasized that we are afraid to *give* our children anything without them having to earn it. Sometimes giving to your children for no reason is fine. Heavenly Father gives to his children whether they earned it or not. "For he maketh his sun to rise on the evil and on the good, and sendeth rain on the just and on the unjust."[63] We should not be made to feel guilty for simply giving to our children because we love them. There will be plenty of opportunities in life to work. Yes, we need to teach the principles of hard work and how to earn our privileges, but those lessons are better received in an environment of love and good will rather than something akin to a forced labor camp.

The importance of hard work is a life lesson that takes years and a certain level of maturity to learn and appreciate. Many adults never learn it. How can we expect a child to have an appreciation in their youth of something we took years to

---

[63] Matthew 5:45.

develop? It's good to remember that basic things that are easy for adults can be hard for children. We need to spend more time *helping* them do what's right than *telling* them to do what's right. Yes, helping them takes longer and it would be easier to just do the work ourselves. Much easier in most cases. But let us also freely give more to our children. Learning how to share and give is a life lesson that even people who know how to work hard struggle to learn, and it's arguably more important.

If a person could only learn one lesson in life and they had to choose between learning how to work or learning how to give, which should they choose? It would seem that knowing how to work would get you "further" in this life but learning how to give brings meaning to life.

Speak With Patience

Being patient with our children as they learn and grow may not be as easy as it sounds. Some of us will have to pass through severe trials to reach the point where we can see others as God sees them and feel his love for them. No parent has more patience for his children than Heavenly Father and one of our main purposes in this life is to learn to love others as he does . . . that is, unconditionally.

Irinna Danielson shared a story about what her friend had to endure as she grew in love and patience for her children. Danielson's friend had struggled in her marriage for a couple years before her husband decided to move out. His choice was devastating for his wife and children. All the hopes and dreams she held for so many years appeared to be lost and broken. Danielson says that for two years, her friend made every effort to live closer to the Spirit to receive guidance about how to deal with her situation and execute on all the family duties that had now devolved to her.

"In these two years that my friend has consciously tried to live closer to the Spirit," Danielson wrote, "I've watched her change. She was always a beautiful spiritual giant to me, but now she is even more so. As more doubt and discouragement has filled her husband's heart, more light and faith has filled hers. You can literally see it. She speaks with more love and patience to her children. She has a deeper appreciation for her family and friends. And where we can be quick to judge and feel anger towards her husband's actions, she feels an increase of love and forgiveness. She said she started to really see him how God sees him and for the first time in her life started to understand what charity really means. Through her heartache, her heart is strengthening. Her faith and trust in God is growing. And I believe it is because she is trying to live closer to the Spirit every day."[64] (Danielson, 2017)

This woman's heartache led to an increase in love and patience for her children. She has begun to learn how to see others as God sees them: without judgement. The changes she has made in her life were a spiritual transformation inside her that is visible from the outside. As she grew closer to God, she began speaking to her children with more patience. God wants us to be patient with our children and loved ones. To love unconditionally demands it. Let us choose to be more patient with our children as they grow before sore trials come upon us and humble us in a way that requires it.

In conversation with a sweet mother of teenage and adult children, she made this statement. "I wish I could go back in time, knowing who my kids are now, and just enjoyed them more when they were young." When pressed for more context around that statement, she noted that her second son, who is very quiet as an adult was much more friendly, outgoing, affectionate and loving when he was younger. "Had I known that his gregarious nature wouldn't last, I would have made an effort to enjoy it more," she said. And of his younger brother, who is now, perhaps, her most loving child she said, "He used to whine and screech a lot as a young boy. If I would have known that behavior wouldn't last, I would have been much more patient with him."

---

[64] Irinna Danielson, *What We Cannot Afford to Live Without*, a blog entry from the website of The Church of Jesus Christ of Latter-day Saints, and since removed and can now be found at webcache.googleusercontent.com.

It's difficult, in the present, to think and believe that the way things and people are now is not how they will always be. We understand the maxim that change is the only constant, but the current moment seems to stretch on into eternity and we often think our situation will never change. But knowing that things will never be the same as they are now should help us to look for the good in this unique moment, embrace with patience the foibles of our loved ones, and forgive ourselves for the messes we've made.

Did That Really Happen?

Further illustrating the reality that we should enjoy the moment while it is with us are comments made by a grandmother in a church meeting. This wonderful woman was near 80 years old when she said, in essence, "I can hardly remember being a young mother. I have grandchildren now that prove to my mind that I must have had young children at some point in the past, but most of that time is gone from me."[65] In addition to the heartbreak that comes with imagining the toddler years may fade from memory, comes the realization that as tough as the moment may seem, it will not last forever.

A similar concept was conveyed by a female survivor of one of the atomic bombs that devastated Japan. In a TV documentary marking 70 years since World War II, this old woman shared this startling insight. Being very close to ground zero as a young girl, but somehow miraculously surviving, she was witness to the devastation and carnage. But now as she looks at the same city which has been restored and is beautiful, she sees young children playing, lovers walking and holding hands, and people going on with life as if the nightmare had never happened. She, herself, can barely remember the horror. She remembers it and describes it, but it was so long ago that the pain and misery no longer seemed real to her, and she is left to ask today, "What

---

[65] Linda Millington, from comments made in a testimony meeting of the Church of Jesus Christ of Latter-day Saints, October 8, 2017.

was that? Did that even really happen?"⁶⁶

What an interesting concept, that the turmoil surrounding raising a bunch of small children can seem like a thing forgotten. Or even the devastation of an entire city being wiped off the map can fade away as if it never happened. No matter how bad things seem at the moment, we can exercise patience with a sure expectation that the misery can be healed. Or, more humorously, as Victor Hugo put it, "In France, there is no wrath, not even of a public character, which six months will not extinguish."⁶⁷ (Hugo, 1862)

Christ Invites

Part of teaching with patience is inviting to learn. As we have seen, people learn when *they* are ready to learn, not when *we* are ready to teach them. We teach those we love with patience and caring for their personal progression, always inviting to learn, never forcing. At times, our invitations will go unaccepted. They may be rejected for years. But we never lose patience and stop extending them.

A group of young men who attended church together had one acquaintance who had come to church a few times and then stopped. The thoughtful boys at church discussed ways to get this young man to join them at church and in their weekly activities. They regularly invited him to join them on one outing or another, but he always turned them down. They asked him to ten different activities, and he declined every time. But they persisted in their invitations. They invited him five more times, with no luck. Then, on the 19th invitation, the boy finally agreed to go with them. They enjoyed their time together. Whether the young man continued to join church activities with his peers is beside the point. The point is that the young men continued to invite him regardless of his lack of response. You can only have a hand of friendship extended to you so many times before you may have

---

⁶⁶ Need source.
⁶⁷ Victor Hugo, *Les Misérables, Jean ValJean*, p. 158.

to finally, begrudgingly, admit that someone really does care about you.

The questioning and doubting mind of youth naturally resists receiving values forced upon them by adults. As teens struggle to see their place in the world, we often find that they are unwilling to accept our beliefs and teachings at face value. Sometimes their questions can seem threatening to us. They seem to be challenging some of our core beliefs. When someone asks, "Why must I give up 10% of my income to the church?" it can be difficult to receive this question as an honest query by someone who genuinely wants to know the reasons rather than a challenge to our, the Church's, or even God's authority. Especially if it is asked with a typical teenage tone of attitude. Our instinct can be to get defensive and, if we're not careful, we jump to the "because it's a commandment" answer rather than digging down for the deeper meaning.

This is why we invite others to discover for themselves. We ask them questions in return to patiently let them find out for themselves. "Come and see," Christ said, in response to his disciples' questions to know more.[68] He did not simply tell them the answer to their question as he could have, he invited them to discover for themselves. Of course, an invitation requires much more patience. It is much easier to just give the answer to a question than it is to look on as a person struggles through a process of self-discovery. It is like how it is often easier to just do the work asked of a child than it is to help them do it right. But when Christ said, 'come and see,' what he was really doing is inviting his disciples to spend more time with him. He knew that if they spent the day with him, they would learn much more than the address of his residence. The same is true with us as we seek to teach our loved ones and each other. There is no substitute for "being with them."[69] (Church of Jesus Christ of Latter-day Saints, 2018)

---

[68] John 1:39.
[69] See *The Aaronic Priesthood Leader Training*, published by the Church of Jesus Christ of Latter-day Saints, 2018.

Jesus Christ, who is the master teacher, never forces anyone to believe his teachings, he always invites. His message, and the invitation to understand it, is extended with love rather than condemnation and threats. And when the message is taught with love, it is much more likely to make it down into the heart of the hearer. "God will invite, persuade. God will reach out tirelessly with love and inspiration and encouragement. But God will never compel—that would undermine His great plan for our eternal growth."[70] (Uchtdorf, Fourth Floor, Last Door, 2016)

The Lord's Way is Patience

Being the patient teacher, making invitations to learn, and waiting until the learner is ready to learn rather than expecting obedience by virtue of parental authority can be hard for some adults. A neighbor noted that when she sees her kids, even as adults, doing things wrong, her instinct is to jump in with fists raised to make a correction. But that is not the Lord's way. His way is patience and long-suffering, working with them and reasoning with them. Lynn Robbins has pointed out, "To discipline in the Lord's way is to lovingly and patiently teach. In the scriptures the Lord often uses the word 'chasten' when speaking of discipline.[71] The word 'chasten' comes from the Latin *castus*, meaning 'chaste or pure,' and chasten means 'to purify.'"[72] (Robbins, 2016)

It's not easy to throw off the shackles of tradition that says adults deserve respect just by virtue of being adults or a couple decades older. Many adults, as persons, are not worthy of much respect, being hardly matured in their thinking and behavior beyond their childhood years. It requires humility and wisdom to patiently wait for your learners to recognize the value of the experience you want to share.

---

[70] Dieter Uchtdorf, *Fourth Floor, Last Door*, an address given at the General Conference of the Church of Jesus Christ of Latter-day Saints, October 2016.
[71] See, for example, Mosiah 23:21; Doctrine & Covenants 95:1.
[72] Lynn Robbins, *The Righteous Judge*, an address given at the General Conference of the Church Jesus Christ of Latter-day Saints, October 2016.

Contention Is Not of Me

Often when our so-called parental authority is challenged, we become indignant, contentious, quick to criticize, and threatening. But can you see a connection between teachings on priesthood authority and parental authority? One of our favorite scriptures in the Doctrine and Covenants is in Section 121: "No power or influence can or ought to be maintained by virtue of the priesthood, only by persuasion, by long-suffering, by gentleness and meekness, and by love unfeigned; by kindness, and pure knowledge, which shall greatly enlarge the soul without hypocrisy, and without guile—reproving betimes with sharpness, when moved upon by the Holy Ghost; and then showing forth afterwards an increase of love."[73]

This divine direction teaches that we cannot exercise power over anyone or even try to influence someone by virtue of the fact that we hold the priesthood. "If fathers would magnify their priesthood in their own family," Dallin Oaks taught, "it would further the mission of the Church as much as anything else they might do. Fathers who hold the Melchizedek Priesthood should exercise their authority 'by persuasion, by long-suffering, by gentleness and meekness, and by love unfeigned'. That high standard for the exercise of all priesthood authority is *most important in the family*."[74] (Oaks, 2020)

What does it mean to "maintain influence by virtue of the priesthood?" Imagine a young married woman without children who desired to be divorced from her husband after only a few years of marriage. Upon meeting privately with a priesthood officer, she is counseled to remain in the marriage. When she objects and desires to understand the reason for the counsel, the man loses patience and offers only that he "holds the priesthood," therefore she should honor this authority and follow

---

[73] Doctrine & Covenants 121:41-43.
[74] Dallin Oaks, *The Melchizedek Priesthood and the Keys*, an address given at the General Conference of the Church of Jesus Christ of Latter-day Saints, April 2020. Italics added.

his instructions. This is an example of trying to influence someone by virtue of the priesthood. There was no persuasion or long-suffering or love unfeigned. There was only a sharp reproving.

Now, would this divine direction still be true if we changed one word? Would it also be true to say, "No power or influence can or ought to be maintained by virtue of our *parenthood*, only by persuasion, by long-suffering . . ."? Do we have enough confidence, wisdom, and love to bear with our children and loved ones while we endeavor to get them to see our point of view? Our parenthood is not sufficient reason to exercise unrighteous dominion over those we love most. When we seek power over the agency of our children by virtue of our parental authority only when things don't go our way, we typically resort to anger and lash out.

But the spiritual guidance from the Doctrine & Covenants, as Robbins tells us, "Teaches us to reprove 'when moved upon by the Holy Ghost,' not when moved upon by anger. The Holy Ghost and anger are incompatible because 'he that hath the spirit of contention is not of me, but is of the devil, who is the father of contention, and he stirreth up the hearts of men to contend with anger.'[75] George Smith taught that 'unkind things are not usually said under the inspiration of the Lord. The Spirit of the Lord is a spirit of kindness; it is a spirit of patience; it is a spirit of charity and love and forbearance and long suffering . . . But if we have the spirit of fault finding . . . in a destructive manner, that never comes as a result of the companionship of the Spirit of our Heavenly Father and is always harmful . . . Kindness is the power that God has given us to unlock hard hearts and subdue stubborn souls.'"[76] (Robbins, 2016)

We hear more often quoted the phrase of this scripture that justifies our parental corrections: "Reprove betimes with sharpness, when moved upon by the Holy Ghost . . ." There are scholarly essays on what, exactly, this means, but more important

---

[75] 3 Nephi 11:29.
[76] Robbins, *The Righteous Judge,* quoting George A. Smith.

is the following phrase: "and then showing forth afterwards an increase of love toward him whom thou hast reproved, lest he esteem thee to be his enemy."[77] (Jackson & Hunt, 2005) And this is the more difficult part of the scripture to implement. How does one show forth an increase in love toward someone who has failed to meet our expectations in such a way as to require reproof? It is natural for someone receiving reproof to feel more like they received a rebuke. Many times, when we are reproved, we feel unliked, if not unloved. Whether this feeling is justified or not is beside the point. When we feel unliked by someone, our desire to please them diminishes. This is why it is so important to offer correction in a loving way rather than in anger. This spirit of contention is not of God.

He Did Not Exercise His Justice

The Lord is very merciful and patient with us as we learn. Even when our learning leads us to go contrary to what we know is right. It is fairly easy to find stories in the scriptures and elsewhere that illustrate the Lord's design in suspending justice.

Juan Uceda related a story from when he was serving a mission in Peru. After an approved visit to the Machu Picchu ruins, some of the young men who were with him wanted to take a dangerous hike to the Inca Bridge. Uceda received a clear instruction from the Spirit to steer his group clear from the mountain pass, but after many pleadings he consented to go, against his better judgement and what he knew was the clear will of God. He said, "I had heard the voice of the Spirit three times before, telling me not to go to the Inca Bridge, but I had not obeyed that voice."[78] (Uceda, 2016) Not unexpectedly, something bad happened. Uceda lost his footing on a very narrow section of the trail and nearly fell 2,000 feet to his death. He hung onto some branches

---

[77] See Jackson and Hunt, *Reprove, Betimes, and Sharpness in the Vocabulary of Joseph Smith*, Religious Educator 6, no. 2 (2005): 97–104.
[78] Juan Uceda, *The Lord Jesus Christ Teaches Us to Pray*, an address given at the General Conference of the Church of Jesus Christ of Latter-day Saints, October 2016.

until his companion was able to pull him to safety.

After relating this story of disobeying the direction of God to him, Uceda made this observation:

"We returned to Machu Picchu very carefully and in silence. On the return trip I remained silent, and the idea came to my mind that He had paid attention to my voice but that I had not paid any attention to His. There was a deep pain in my heart for disobeying His voice and at the same time a deep sense of gratitude for His mercy. *He did not exercise His justice upon me*, but in His great mercy, He had saved my life."[79] (Uceda, 2016)

Sometimes it seems as though not exercising our authority to mete out the consequences and punishments that our children "deserve" is one of the most difficult parts about parenting. We are stuck in this dilemma: If you are too kind and loving and patient with her while she learns, you will "spoil" her and she will turn out to be a brat. Yet if you are too harsh and really do require him to "pay the uttermost farthing,"[80] then he will "esteem thee to be his enemy."[81] While it is a fine line to balance, we should be in favor of erring on the side of love and mercy. For that is how Heavenly Father lets us learn in this life. As Eric Huntsman rightly declared, "We should never fear that we are compromising when we make the choice to love."[82] (Huntsman, 2018)

Another great example of a teacher siding with mercy and patience was heard when Dale Renlund related a story from his youth about setting off a firecracker in church: "One Sunday, my friend Steffan, the only other deacon in the branch, greeted me at church with some excitement. We went to the chapel's adjacent overflow area, and he pulled from his pocket a large firecracker and some matches. In an act of youthful bravado, I took the firecracker and lit the long gray fuse. I intended to snuff out the fuse before it blew up. But when I burned my fingers trying to do so, I dropped the firecracker. Steffan and I watched in horror

---

[79] Ibid., emphasis added.
[80] Matthew 5:26.
[81] Doctrine & Covenants 121:43.
[82] Eric Huntsman, *Hard Sayings and Safe Spaces: Making Room for Struggle as Well as Faith*, a devotional address given BYU August 7, 2018.

as the fuse continued to burn. The firecracker exploded, and sulfurous fumes filled the overflow area and the chapel. We hurriedly gathered up the scattered remnants of the firecracker and opened the windows to try to get the smell out, naively hoping that no one would notice. Fortunately, no one was hurt, and no damage was done."[83] (Renlund, 2016)

Needless to say, many adults were very aware that something had happened when they arrived at the chapel for church. Like Juan Uceda, Renlund also knew that what he had done displeased God. After church, Renlund was called down to meet with the branch president, the man in charge of the church meetings. Through tears, Renlund told him about the firecracker, and it was evident how sorry he felt. Was it the job of the branch president to fabricate some kind of consequence for this youthful indiscretion? Apparently, the wise man didn't think so. Instead, he opened a copy of his scriptures and had the young man read, "Behold, he who has repented of his sins, the same is forgiven, and I, the Lord, remember them no more. By this ye may know if a man repenteth of his sins—behold, he will confess them and forsake them."[84] By sharing this scripture, he showed the youth that he had already been forgiven of his mistake . . . within hours. The fear, sorrow, and regret the boy felt was punishment enough. There was no need to make him feel worse by adding to that list.

This story also shows that the Lord would prefer to exercise patience than justice. Juan Uceda should have known better as a missionary. He was old enough to know right from wrong and received spiritual communications to help keep him safe. By the time he was rescued from the cliff's edge, his heart had already smitten him. What more did the Lord need to do? Life sets up its own consequences that make things hard enough. What we need as children is to be taught ways to avoid the sadness in life. Not have man-made punishments heaped upon us for every tough learning experience.

---

[83] Dale Renlund, *Repentance: A Joyful Choice*, an address given at the General Conference of the Church of Jesus Christ of Latter-day Saints, October 2016.
[84] Doctrine & Covenants 58:42-43.

But the reader may notice that both Renlund and Uceda were religious and good young men. Is that why the Lord had mercy on them? How does he treat those who don't "measure up"? Does the Lord mete out harsher judgement for those who do not love him? What should we do with our rebellious children? Let's look at some examples from the scriptures to answer that.

Why Did He Not Judge Us?

In the Book of Mormon, we hear the story of Alma the Younger. His father was the high priest of the church in his civilization. Without doubt, Alma was raised in a manner similar to Renlund and Uceda. He was taught right from wrong. When he began to rebel, he was likely smitten by his conscience in a similar manner. Yet, he went on to find his own experiences and chose a path to "learn with sorrow."[85] As we have discussed, this is OK. Some people just have to experience things for themselves to learn anything. We should not judge them. If there is an ultimate truth, then we will all arrive at it one way or another because it is true.

In one of the most arresting sections of the Book of Mormon, Alma relates his experience and how he came to himself. As a young man, while his father presided in the church, he and some of his friends (who also happened to be the sons of the king), decided to leave the church of God. These young men were the children of the prestigious in society. It could be they were thinking that being taught their religion from their youth somehow infringed upon their agency and prevented them from making up their own mind. And as it is with many who apostatize, they could leave the church, but they couldn't leave it alone. When we are blinded by darkness, we feel that we do God a favor by trying to disabuse his faithful followers of their delusions. As Alma describes it, "we went forth even in wrath, with mighty threatenings to destroy his church."[86]

This Alma was remarkably effective in his efforts. He was a

---

[85] Jacob 4:3.
[86] Alma 26:18.

man of many words and flattered the people and led them away from the beliefs of their youth. So successful was he in his campaigns that he later recalled the punishment he expected in this way: "I had murdered many of [God's] children, or rather led them away unto destruction; yea, and in fine so great had been my iniquities, that the very thought of coming into the presence of my God did rack my soul with inexpressible horror."[87] If anyone has felt they deserved to be punished for their actions, it was Alma. Fortunately, men are not called to judge their own souls, or the souls of their brothers.

As he and his friends went on in their rebellions against God, an angel appeared to them. One might suppose the angel would be wielding the sword of justice in defense of truth and virtue; that he might slay Alma and his friends in a miraculous display of protection for the church. But rather, the angel said that God had heard the prayers of Alma's father and "for this purpose have I come to convince thee of the power and authority of God."[88] He didn't come to threaten him or cause him to fear. He came to "convince" him. This is persuasion, long-suffering, gentleness and meekness, and love unfeigned.[89]

Alma didn't understand the mind of God or how he deals with his children, even his rebellious ones. He asked, "Why did he not consign us to an awful destruction, yea, why did he not let the sword of his justice fall upon us, and doom us to eternal despair … Behold, he did not exercise his justice upon us, but in his great mercy hath brought us over that everlasting gulf of death and misery, even to the salvation of our souls."[90] This is the bridge back across the gulf we have referred to. God is always the bridge back to Himself, just as we need to be the bridge back to our loved ones who stray. God can see the good in us that we can't even see in ourselves. This is why we must learn to see others in the way God does. While God knows each of his children

---

[87] Alma 36:14.
[88] Alma 27:14.
[89] See Doctrine & Covenants 121:41.
[90] Alma 26:19-20.

perfectly and can see things in us that cause our behaviors that we can't see in ourselves, we must trust that those good things are there. And we must also trust that those good things are in others even though they are obscured to our view by their behavior.

The Evil Spirit

Another example of how the Lord views his relationship toward his children is related by Luke. In this story, the Lord has made up his mind to go to Jerusalem because it was his time to be received up. His planned course of travel to Jerusalem would take him through a village of the Samaritans. The Jews and Samaritans were not on friendly terms at the time, and Jesus sent some messengers ahead of him to find a place for him to stay on his trip.

When the Samaritans learned that Jesus intended to merely pass through on his way, they refused to receive him in their town. Perhaps they were offended that Jesus was not going to preach or perform miracles for them. Who knows? But when his apostles James and John saw how inhospitable they were to their beloved Lord, they were angry. Apparently, they did not understand the motivations of the Samaritans any more than we do. In their wrath, they asked Jesus if he would like them to call down from heaven fire to consume the villagers for their affront to the Lord of Heaven.

In a response that must have surprised the apostles and illustrates how far many of us are from understanding God's relationship with his children, the Lord "rebuked them, and said, 'Ye know not what manner of spirit ye are of. For the Son of man is not come to destroy men's lives, but to save them.'"[91]

When the Lord said that his disciples did not know what spirit they were of in their quest for what they felt would be a justified punishment, it seems implied that the spirit he had in mind was the spirit of the devil. It is the adversary who is gratified with

---

[91] Luke 9:55.

severe punishments for sins and mistakes. When we take satisfaction in seeing justice served upon others, it may be the evil spirit guiding us. Punishment humiliates and degrades; it does not help correct. As we have seen, we are almost all perfectly aware when we are falling short.

This is not to say that there should not be laws in society. And we understand that laws without penalties are not laws.[92] The point is for us to not take satisfaction in seeing others punished. Instead, we should feel sorrow for those souls who have not been able to understand or abide the law. We cannot see inside their souls or know the sort of experiences, from their perspective, they have had or the tool kits they were given. But we can trust that God knows them and can see it. We can be sure that he will be perfectly just in his dealing with them. In the case of our children and loved ones, we seek to patiently wait for when they are ready to learn and teach with patience and kindness.

Some may hear these examples and call to mind the devastations suffered by the Israelites in the Old Testament. They may recall the plague that wiped out 24,000 souls of the idolaters,[93] or the time when the earth "opened her mouth" and swallowed Dathan and Abiram at the same time that 250 men died by fire.[94] To say nothing of the time "the LORD sent fiery serpents among the people, and they bit the people; and much people of Israel died."[95] We hear of these stories and are inclined to think of God as being full of wrath and justice. It seems natural to impute the bad things that happen to people to their sins. But we don't know the mind of God and may be premature in assigning other people's misfortunates to the same God who sends his rain on the just and unjust or allows missionaries in his service to be indiscriminately injured in a terrorist bombing at an airport.[96] (Andersen, 2018) It is our lot to withhold our

---

[92] See Alma 42:17.
[93] See Numbers 25.
[94] Numbers 26:9-10.
[95] Numbers 21:6.
[96] See Anderson, Neil L., *Wounded*, an address given at the General Conference of the Church of Jesus Christ of Latter-day Saints, October 2018.

judgement, feel compassion for those who suffer, bear with and love those who are confounded and rejoice in their successes.

A Parent-Teacher Conference

A young, adopted girl was struggling in elementary school. The previous year, her teacher told her parents that not only was she the most disruptive child in the class, but she was also the most disruptive child the teacher had ever had. The next year when it was time for parent-teacher conferences, she was very worried and stressed after learning that her parents had every intention of meeting with her teacher. It was almost as if she had something to hide. She dreaded the evening of the meeting and watched in anguish as her parents left.

The news the parents received at the conference was only marginally better than the news they had received from her previous teacher. But the parents recognized that this child was struggling. They had tried everything they could think of to help her. They paid for lessons, activities, counseling, sports, and eventually, even medicine. Nothing really seemed to work. While their frustration was high and the report from the teacher added to the burden, their attitude was that they just wanted to help their little girl rather than punish her for wayward behavior.

When they returned from the meeting, their daughter was, somewhat irrationally, petrified that some huge punishment was forthcoming. Instead, her parents talked calmly with her about their meeting with her teacher. They discussed quietly the school's concerns and how they were just trying to help her in her life. They agreed on hopes and dreams for better days ahead and encouraged her to always do her best.

The parents reported that they could see the fear and worry drain from their daughter's countenance as she realized that she wasn't going to be punished, however much she may have thought she deserved it. She expressed her gratitude to them for not being mad and the experience strengthened their relationship. Being mad at someone doesn't really help them get better. Loving them unconditionally, being patient with them as they learn, and helping them do what's right does.

Contrast this story with a hypothetical alternative outcome. The parents getting mad, yelling when they got home. Threatening, punishing. The young girl feels stupid, berated, angry at the teacher for ratting her out. She is resentful at her parents for the way she is treated. Love is extinguished. Hatred is fostered. The parents' opinion of the girl is diminished, as is the daughter's desire to please them. Everything that occurs tends toward a negative outcome, nothing improves the chances of solving the problem.

In reality, the problem isn't the young girl's rebellious attitude, it is a much deeper issue. The acting out is a surface symptom of a core need being unmet. We assume she is doing the best she can with the tool kit she has. Who can imagine what effect spending the first year of your life in an orphanage can have on your ability to cope with even some of the simple things in life? We cannot see into her heart and do not know her history or inner ability. And this blind spot is not caused by the fact that she spent that first year on the other side of the planet. We all have missing pieces that others can't see. Most of us don't even know which pieces are missing from ourselves, let alone have the ability to see what's missing in others. This is why we are patient and do not judge when others are failing to meet our expectations.

Hearts Will Not Change Where Love Is Not Present

If we are seeking to influence those we love, patience is the key. Patience with their unwillingness to learn. Patience with their inability to learn. Patience with the timing of the lessons. Patience with their performance. We must keep our emotions in check and have passion for their learning, but not at the expense of our relationship with them.

This point was powerfully made by Mark Palmer who observed, "No true teaching or learning will ever occur when done in frustration or anger, and hearts will not change where love is not present. Whether we act in our roles as parents, teachers, or leaders, true teaching will happen only in an atmosphere of trust rather than condemnation. Our homes should always be safe havens for our children—not hostile environments."[97] (Palmer, 2017)

Shut Up Kid, and Listen to the Grown-Ups

There is a video on YouTube, taken from the Southland TV series, that shows an example of the kind of "tough love" mentality some like to watch because, "Shut up, kid. Things were way tougher when I was your age." The child in this clip has two adults ganging up on him. He's not feeling the love.[98] (Southland, 2014)

The clip begins with two police officers knocking on the front door of a woman's home. The woman answers and we see the following dialogue take place.

First police officer: "We're here to investigate a child abuse complaint."

Mother: "I didn't call the police."

12-year-old son, Daniel, comes up behind the mother and in a bit of a belligerent tone says: "I did. She hit me with the belt."

First police officer: "Is that true ma'am?"

Mother: "I found out from Daniel's teacher he's been cutting class. But when I asked him about it, he lied. So I hit him."

Second police officer motions to Daniel to come outside in front of the house: "Come here, kid."

Daniel follows the officer out to the sidewalk in front of the house.

Second police officer: "How long ago did this happen?"
Daniel: "A few hours ago."
Second police officer: "How many times did she hit you?"
Daniel: "Three. Whopped me right on the butt."

---

[97] Mark Palmer, *Then Jesus Beholding Him, Loved Him*, an address given at the General Conference of the Church of Jesus Christ of Latter-day Saints, April 2017.
[98] Southland: "The Winds" Clip, published March 20, 2014.

Second police officer: "Did she hit you anywhere else?"
Daniel: "No."
Second police officer: "Did she hit you with her fist or another object?"
Daniel: "No. Just the belt."
Second police officer: "Has this happened before?"
Daniel: "No."
Second police officer: "Let me take that belt and put it into evidence."
Mother overheard in the background: . . . "acting out a little and I felt like I had to . . . Am I going to jail?"
Second police officer turned back to Daniel, and in a tone of disbelief asked: "You called the police on your mother because she disciplined you for ditching school?"
Daniel: "That's child abuse. I've got rights."
Second police officer: "Who told you that?"
Daniel: "My friends."
Second police officer turning back to the mother and holding out the belt: "Hit him again."
Second police officer turning back to Daniel in a very angry tone: "You know what? You got some bad advice from your buddies on the playground, pal. You don't ever call the police on your mom. Had that been my mom, you'd be calling me from the floor. If I got to be back here again because you have been ditching class, I'm going to peel this big belt off and I'm going to hit you myself! You got it? Get inside."
Daniel looks very afraid and runs into the house.
This is a popular video clip with almost 400,000 views (2019). But what is really shocking (as is usually the case on YouTube) is what you find in the comments. Almost without variation, those commenting on the video are encouraging the type of interaction that takes place between Daniel and the second police officer. Here is a sample of the comments pulled from directly under the video without editing:
Jake: "Hitting a kid with a belt on the butt is not child abuse. Its discipline."

jimmykicker7775: "Hit 'em again! Hahahaha!!! Sounds like that cop was raised in an Irish household."

r71oats6: "If parents don't discipline their children the courts and DOC will. Have a nice day."

Sean Griffin: "Physical abuse and discipline are two different things and people are sensible enough to know which is which. This privileged generation thinks so little of authority and believe when they do wrong, it is okay. In the long run, they and others will suffer for it."

Moro Moco: "You people are so soft thinking hitting a child is abusive so what! There's so many kids who aren't discipline in this dang generation. It's not called child abuse it's called Discipline!"

kevin texter: "Hit him again 😊 God I love it"

Mike Wang: "This clip should be made into a PSA."

Benjamin Masters: "Im 17 years old and i was disaplined this way, i didnt like it but it taught me, now i am glad my parents disaplined me, now i am a good student working hard everyday on everything cuz my parents taught me how to work, its not abuse its teaching the child, cuz now i see all the kids who rnt disaplined and there introuble all the time, now i am glad im not one of them [sic]"

A.A. Coming At Yah!: "People here are ridiculous. I'm thinking the main reason there are kids out there smoking and drinking or disrespecting parents is because they don't get disciplined! How are they going to learn?! Have you watched Super Nanny?! Those kids are literally yelling and hitting their parents. And they don't do a thing. Do you think parents like hurting them? Of course they don't! They love them! They actually love them so much they discipline their kids because they don't want them to grow up as a bad person. I was raised right, and I'm thankful that I was whooped! And my parents after would apologize and tell me the reason they disciplined me. They don't do it for no reason. It's not child abuse, it's discipline."

Michael D. Durham: "Man, I'll bet that boy won't be pulling a stunt on like this again."

ItalyMan rome: "that cop is right"

One interesting theme to note in the video and the comments is the tendency for people who were harshly disciplined to think that they were somehow better for it. The police officer sounds proud that his mother would have hit him harder than Daniel's mother hit him. Those in the comments who were disciplined with physical force agree that they are glad they were disciplined that way and think that those who don't discipline their children that way are a problem for society.

A.A. Coming at Yah! believes "the main reason there are kids out there smoking and drinking or disrespecting parents is because they don't get disciplined." What we are saying is that the main reason kids are exhibiting these behaviors is because they don't get loved. Hardly anyone, kids or adults, enjoy harsh discipline. Why are children disrespecting parents? In many cases it's because parents have not done much to deserve a lot of respect. But shouldn't children respect their elders? Yes. People should respect each other. Even if a person is a slob, they should be treated with respect. Parents teach their children this by showing respect for them and their feelings.

In reality, children are adults in immature bodies, but they have instincts about what kinds of behavior merit respect. If they don't see this modeled in their parents' behavior, they naturally don't respect them. Should parents have to earn the respect of their children? Yes. And they do this through the natural course of love, kindness, forgiveness, teaching, forbearing and patience. The same attributes that earn respect in an adult social or work setting.

When parents discipline harshly, they teach their children this behavior. The children grow up and discipline their offspring the same way. A cycle ensues. What we are trying to do with this work is to break the cycle for families. We do not have to treat our children harshly with anger, but rather we can show them love and respect. Unfortunately, the world is filled with people like "A.A. Coming at Yah!" and "kevin texter" who will challenge this premise, belittle those who don't agree with them, and continue to call for discipline bordering on violence to be applied to our children.

The following story illustrates how this cycle was broken in one family. The father gave up corporal punishment after noticing something peculiar with his first-born son. The son was about 5 or 6 years old, old enough to know better than the mischief he was causing. The father had warned several times against a certain behavior. The warning went unheeded. Upon learning that he had been ignored, the father decided, in anger, to emphasize his wishes with a spanking. He reports that he hit his child so hard on the bottom that he actually hurt his own hand. After several swats he noticed that his son was just sucking it up and taking it. After a couple more he saw that it made no difference to his son that he was being spanked even though the father knew that it was painful. By the time the spanking had ended, the father could clearly see that the child had no intention of changing his behavior because he had been spanked. The father realized at that moment that physical punishment of this kind had no positive effect on this child's behavior, surmised that it had no positive effect on anyone's behavior, and resolved at that moment to never again use that type of discipline. He reports never returning to that behavior or regretting that decision.

Take a moment to ponder the effects of harsh discipline, whether it is spanking, berating, or severe punishment of any kind. How could it affect behavior?

First, we have been taught to believe that harsh discipline is typically used to instill fear in the person being disciplined. We reason that because we cannot persuade a child to reform his behavior, we will make him fear the punishment. The hope is that the fear of punishment will prevent the undesirable actions. But this hope is not founded in research. Search the term "does the threat of prison deter crime" on the internet. Note how easy it is to find search results showing research and studies indicating that the fear of harsh punishment does little to deter crime. If reasonable adults are not deterred from committing serious crimes by the threat of doing time in prison, how much less can we suppose that the threat of a far lighter punishment (a spanking, for example) will influence the behavior of a less rational child?

Second, rarely does a person believe that their behavior merits some kind of harsh discipline. When children are disciplined severely, they can feel that the punishment is not justified. When Jean Valjean, in *les Misérables*, was sentenced to 5 years in prison for stealing a loaf of bread to feed his sister's hungry children, the result of his punishment was that he grew to hate "society" and believe that it was flawed. We can rightly expect our children to believe that we are flawed because of our inability to persuade them to correct behavior and our willingness to lash out when our expectations are not met.

Finally, when a person is punished harshly and, as they almost invariably believe, unjustly, their desire seems more likely to remove themselves from the presence of the discipliner than to reform their behavior. Our argument is that this type of harsh discipline tends to break families apart. And when a person has left our presence, our influence over them is all but gone. Persuasion with love and patience tend to unite families and draw them closer where our influence over each other can grow and expand. There is no need to be one who disciplines gravely if we can learn to be one who persuades positively with love.

Our philosophy is that life has its own consequences. We teach our children correct principles and let them govern themselves (within the bounds of physical safety) and we do not come between them and the natural consequences of their choices and behaviors. We need to clearly lay out the consequences of their behaviors so they can make informed decisions about how to behave. Sometimes those consequences can be implemented by society, teachers, police officers, attendance policies, bosses or parents, but we have to be clear. And then when the consequences are in force, we have to stand back and let them fall. If we intervene and lighten the burden, any rational person would expect that type of rescue in the future and their behavior will continue to generate undesirable consequences.

Enforcing Consequences the Right Way

One common mistake made by parents is not waiting for the most natural time to allow the consequences of choices affect behavior. It usually seems like the best time to inflict the consequences is at the moment of the undesirable behavior is discovered. But this is actually a very ineffective time for implementing consequences. When poor behavior is discovered or witnessed, there is disappointment and anger to deal with. At that time, it is best to work to avoid harsh feelings and words. The best time to enforce consequences as discussed is when the child needs or wants something.

Many children believe they can get along fine without their parents. They have no idea how much they depend on them. They don't realize how often they ask for things they need and want. At the precise moment when a child has a desire that only their parent can fulfill, a parent can fairly inflict the most devastating enforcement of a planned consequence. To implement consequences in this fashion requires discipline on the parents' part. The power of the moment a child asks for something can easily be dissipated in the passion of the moment the unwanted behavior is discovered. When a parent flies off the handle in anger or disappointment, we tend to threaten all types of consequences, many not fitting the behavior, many not planned in advance, and many that we neither want to, nor are able to, enforce later when things have cooled down.

Instead, when you are presented with unwanted behavior, rather than threaten with consequences in anger, wait until the time a child asks for something to enforce the consequence. It works like this. The parent desires the child to pick up their room. They agree that Saturday morning will be the time the room is picked up. As part of the agreement, it is understood that the child will not be able to borrow the car if the room is not picked up. Since the teen does not need the car Saturday morning, and since they seem almost completely incapable of foreseeing a time when they might need to borrow it in the future, Saturday morning comes and goes, the room is not picked up. Sound familiar?

So instead of blowing up on the child right before lunch making all kinds of unenforceable threats, the parent patiently waits. Not too much longer, probably on the same evening, perhaps it's the next day, the child who has forgotten to pick up the room, suddenly remembers they need to borrow the car. Without a thought about their promise to pick up the room, they come up in high spirits and ask to borrow the car. At that moment, the parent remembers the thing they were asked to do. The conversation goes like this:

"Dad, can I borrow the car for my date tonight."

The father, in a calm, unemotional way replies, "Sure you can, son . . . just as soon as you're finished picking up your room like you agreed to."

Can you imagine the pain this response inflicts? There will be weeping and wailing and gnashing of teeth because of a half dozen different reasons. But none of that rationale has an effect on the dispassionate enforcer of consequences. The father stands his ground in a smug, concerned way. The teen has no choice. He wants something. He wants it bad, and the only way to get it, he now sees, is that he does what he agreed to do. It is amazing how fast the room can be picked up at that point.

This is a remarkably effective and correct way of enforcing consequences. It does require patience and remembering, but any little agreement made between parent and child can easily be enforced this way because children always need something from their parents. And when they ask for it, then is the time to remember any and all past unfulfilled agreements, pick one, and agree to help them when they have fulfilled their promise to help you.

Teach with Tenderness

The bottom line in these teachings is that love, tenderness and the spirit of kindness is the best way to teach. We stand firmly against the need for harsh discipline as a method of teaching. Patient teaching is not only the Lord's way, but also our duty as well. We have been given the tools and knowledge to reach those who are struggling to learn. No matter how futile things may appear with someone we love, we must be their bridge back and strengthen that crossing with our example and love.

We agree with J. Reuben Clark: "It is my hope and my belief that the Lord never permits the light of faith wholly to be extinguished in any human heart, however faint the light may glow. The Lord has provided that there shall still be there a spark which, with teaching, with the spirit of righteousness, with love, with tenderness, with example, with living the Gospel, shall brighten and glow again, however darkened the mind may have been. And if we shall fail so to reach those among us of our own whose faith has dwindled low, we shall fail in one of the main things which the Lord expects at our hands."[99] (Clark, 1936)

Conclusion

We all learn differently and come equipped with different tool kits for learning. We can learn a lot from studying the experiences of those that have gone before us. One of the most important learnings from history is that we are not qualified to judge the experiences of others because we don't live in their shoes. Two important ways to improve your teaching quality of your children is to remember what it was like when they were young and remember that they learn at their own level and in in their own time, when they are ready. Teaching is about timing. And a good time to teach is some time after the frustrating period following a mistake. Waiting to teach requires patience. Sometimes the patience shows us teaching is unnecessary because the lesson has already been learned.

Teaching our children to work is extremely important, but it

---

[99] J. Reuben Clark, an address given at the General Conference of the Church of Jesus Christ of Latter-day Saints, in *Conference Report*, Oct. 1936, 114.

should not override our desire to give freely to them. Being generous and giving is just as important of a life lesson. One important way we give to our children is by being patient with them. It seems that if we could see how things will be different in the future, we would be more patient in the present. The necessary patience might come more quickly if we can realize that the hardship we are currently experiencing will be a faded memory in the future.

Make inviting to learn a habit. This is the way Christ teaches. Of course, our invitations may be rejected, but that's where the patience comes in. Patience, not contention, is the Lord's way. We are counseled to persuade with love, with long-suffering (patience), and gentleness. Kindness is the power God has given us. We related examples where people who made mistakes and felt deserving of some punishment, were impressed for life when they were shown mercy instead, the story of Alma being so dramatic as to land a place in scripture. We contrasted alternative outcomes for an adopted orphan who was failing in school to highlight how awful an angry response can be. True teaching can only occur in an atmosphere of trust.

There is a raging debate between tough lovers and patient teachers. It's easy to find examples of people who feel that lack of discipline with children is the root of all evil in society. Our argument is that it is the lack of love. There is little evidence to support harsh penalties as an effective deterrent to bad behavior. But there is plenty to show it engenders a desire to remove oneself from the presence of the discipliner. It seems more effective to let life be in charge of discipline. Timing is everything when it comes to teaching, especially when it comes to enforcing consequences. Our example and our tenderness will be the support to those who need to correct their path.

4

CHILDREN LEARN MORE FROM EXAMPLE THAN WORDS

It is here we must take a moment to consider the role that our own behavior as parents influences the behavior of our children. Which father and mother has not taught, or at least tried to teach, the Golden Rule: Do unto others as you would have them do unto you? Of course, the Golden Rule was taken from the Sermon on the Mount. Interestingly, and logically, it is found in Matthew right after the verses telling us not to judge others: "Therefore all things whatsoever ye would that men should do to you, do ye even so to them: for this is the law and the prophets."[100] When Jesus says, "this is the law and the prophets," he means that this Golden Rule is the summation of all of the scriptures in the Old Testament. The Law being the Pentateuch, or the first five books of Moses, and "the prophets" including writings from Joshua to Malachi.

In other words, this injunction to treat others the way we would wish to be treated is core doctrine for all Judeo-Christian civilization. Yet often when we hear this principle taught, it is an adult teaching a child that this is the way that they should treat

---

[100] Matthew 7:12.

their friends and acquaintances, or even strangers. We're not so sure that these same adults necessarily apply this teaching to themselves in regard to how they treat the children they have stewardship for.

Perfect Stranger Rule

Think about how you, as an adult, like to have others treat you. In no certain order, we commonly expect to be treated with respect, consideration, and kindness. We like to be listened to and have our opinions valued. We enjoy having others take interest in our lives and expect to be extended common courtesies. If we arrive at the end of the line at the same time as someone else, we may act happy (emphasis on "act") to let them go ahead. When someone signals a lane change, we let them over. (Well, maybe there are limits to our courtesy.) This is how we have grown accustomed to treating others and interacting socially with perfect strangers. But if we are called upon to treat others outside our family with kindness, respect, attention, and courtesy, how much more then are we expected to treat in this manner those who reside under the same roof with us?

Many of us still treat members of our own family with less courtesy than we do those we hardly know. If this sounds familiar, you may want to consider implementing the "Perfect Stranger Rule" along with the "Golden Rule" in your household. The Perfect Stranger Rule says, "You have to treat members of your immediate family with at least as much courtesy and respect as you would extend to a perfect stranger."

For example, if you were in an airport waiting to board a plane and trying to read a book to pass the time and a person seated nearby was talking so loudly on their phone that you can't concentrate, you would most likely just say to yourself, 'This situation won't last long, so I won't ask them to speak more softly.' We all seem to be more tolerant of others when they are not known to us. Whereas, if you were in your own living room trying to read and an immediate family member were talking loudly on their phone, you would think nothing of asking them to be quieter.

Of course, asking a person to be more aware of how loud they are is perfectly fine in either situation. It's how you ask that becomes the problem. With the stranger we are patient and tolerant. With the family member, we often feel so familiar with them, that common courtesy goes out the window in our interactions and we jump straight past patience and forbearance and straight to the annoyed question, 'Will you keep it down or go in the other room? I'm trying to read here.'

In moments of frustration and impatience we would do well to ask ourselves, how would I approach this interaction with my family member if they were a stranger in a public place. For some odd reason, we typically show more courtesy in our interaction with strangers than we do those we love most. In the case of the airport situation, had the situation appeared that it might extend for more than a few minutes, you might have found it necessary to ask the stranger to be quieter. We would expect the interaction to go something like this: You reach over and softly tap the person talking on the phone to get their attention and when they pause, in a polite tone, you say, 'Excuse me, sir, would you possibly be able to talk a little more quietly? I'm trying to concentrate on my reading.' Likely, the stranger would offer an apology and immediately talk more quietly or move to another area so as not to disturb you. It is surely odd how we more frequently follow the Golden Rule with others who are not well known to us than we are with those we love most.

Wayward Parents

There are plenty of examples of parents who hardly follow either rule. This is nothing new in our generation. Five hundred years ago, William Tyndale observed the effect of unloving parents on their children: "Where the fathers and mothers are wayward, hasty and churlish, ever brawling and chiding, there are the children anon discouraged and heartless, and apt for nothing;

neither can they do any thing aright."[101] (Tyndale, The Obediance of a Christian Man, 2000)

Wayward means unpredictable, stubborn, or defiant. Churlish means impolite in a mean way. Chiding is scolding or rebuking. None of these behaviors are unfamiliar to us in a family setting. We see them in children and parents. The difference is that parents should know better. And when they are seen to act this way, their children, who have instincts for how people should interact and naturally expect love to be the dominant force, become discouraged, lose confidence in their abilities (apt for nothing) and often dejectedly think that they can do nothing right. These are horrible traits to foster in a child and could take years to overcome, if it's even possible in a lifetime.

It seems to be common sense that children learn by example. When we are treated disrespectfully by someone on a regular basis, we begin to treat them that way back. It is interesting to note that respect is gained by be respectful. In much the same way that the merciful obtain mercy, or in the way that we are measured with the same measuring stick we use to judge others, respect comes to us by showing respect for others. While it is evident that people come into this life predisposed to act in a certain way, we can also be sure that acceptable behavior is learned. We say this after observing that the common lot for very young children is to be selfish, noisy, stubborn, messy, undisciplined, and destructive. The primary institution for transmitting values and behavioral standards is the family. Behaviors that children learn in the home largely influence the behaviors they exhibit outside the home and foster in their own families when they create them. To break free from this observed-adopted behavior cycle is difficult.

---

[101] William Tyndale, *The Office of a Father and How He Should Rule*, from The Obedience of a Christian Man, Penguin Books, 2000, first published in Antwerp, 1528.

Being Tender-Hearted

In his letter to the Christians at Ephesus, Paul offered good advice on how the faithful should act toward each other in social situations. We often take these words to be guidance concerning our behavior towards friends and acquaintances; perhaps those we associate with at church. But take these words and apply them to your most important relationships, to your spouse or children: "Let all bitterness, and wrath, and anger, and clamor, and evil speaking, be put away from you, with all malice: and be ye kind one to another, tenderhearted, forgiving one another, even as God for Christ's sake hath forgiven you."[102]

Why does this counsel fit better within a family rather than between friends? Perhaps it has to do with being forced into such close living quarters with others; perhaps it has to do with familiarity breeding contempt or letting our guard down with those we are not trying to impress. But where is the place you are most likely to encounter anger during the day? Is it in the home with the child who leaves his cereal bowl on the counter above the dishwasher again no matter how many times you've explained how to load it? Or the one whose bedroom is miraculously trashed less than 12 hours after you spent the afternoon helping them straighten it up? Or the sister who keeps borrowing your phone charger and never returning it. There may be nothing as efficient at provoking wrath and malice as the myriad idiosyncrasies and character flaws we face every day and are forced to abide for years in the people who are closest to us.

This is why we need to apply Paul's teachings inside the walls of our homes. And as the adults in the room, we need to lead by example. In the face of these annoyances, we are called upon to be kind to one another. Kindness and common courtesy are in order within familial relations, not frustration, impatience, and bursts of bitterness. Be tender-hearted, meaning have a soft heart. That is to say, do not harden your hearts against one another. When one has a soft heart toward a person he loves, he has

---

[102] Ephesians 4:31-32.

empathy for them, meaning he understands and shares their feelings. We are quick to forgive because we believe that the other person is doing the best they can with the tool kit they have been afforded.

Inside the family, perhaps the best way to accomplish this and demonstrate it to others is when we "put away" clamor from ourselves. Clamor is shouting. A tender heart is manifest in a soft voice, not in voice-raising. We don't need volume, as if the louder we speak the more weight our words will carry. Remember the wisdom of the Proverbs, "a soft answer turned away wrath?"[103] Whether we are turning away from or putting away wrath, we do so with quietness. Do we want our children to learn the example of yelling to get what they want? If not, then we must not do so to get what we want.

Being in Their World

At the same time, it is not uncommon to feel as if our children are training us to yell at them. We are like Pavlov's dog because initially we only get what we want when we yell.[104] (Wikipedia, 2021) The scenario typically unfolds like this: We make a simple request of our child, for example, turn off the television and come eat dinner. The first time the request is made, it is done calmly, in kindness, with a soft voice. "OK," comes the robotic response. Five minutes later everyone is gathered to eat except the child in front of the TV. The second request is made more urgently. "OK, I'm coming!" sounds the rather annoyed response. Within minutes, the meal is cooling off awaiting a blessing, the TV is still going downstairs, and still no Robby. Finally, the burst of anger and the threat: "Turn off the TV right now or it will be off all weekend for you!!" Within seconds, the TV is off, and the child is pulling up a chair at the table.

The "classical conditioning" we have undergone is that a soft request equals no results; a yelled request equals fulfilled

---

[103] Proverbs 15:1.
[104] See Wikipedia, Ivan Pavlov.

desires.[105] (Wikipedia, 2021) We may inquire of our children, "Do you enjoy being yelled at? You are training me to yell at you. When I ask you nicely, I get no response until I begin yelling." How do we turn away wrath in situations like this? How do we reach a child with a simple request when they seem to be in their own world?

One answer is to leave our world and go find the person in their world. This requires more time and patience, and we often feel as if we shouldn't be required to go so far out of our way, that our children should be "obedient" to our every desire. To find the person in their world means to be with them rather than yelling to them from our world. We take the few minutes to walk into the room with them. We find out what they are doing. We really find out in the sense that we engage with them about their activity. At first, we may be ignored or wished away, but if we persist, we can meet the other person where they are and extend a meaningful invitation. We learn what they are thinking and feeling. Another person's interest in me is a powerful motivation for me to do things that please them.

How can we acknowledge to them that their activity is important? While it may seem unimportant to us, it clearly is to them. Can we find a way to patiently disconnect them from their world and lovingly draw them into ours? When we make every effort to meet them where they are, and when our invitation is extended with a feeling of love, the likelihood of reaching them and drawing them into our world is much greater.

When we meet others in their world, they intuitively know of our love for them. A great story and real-life example of meeting a child in their own world was related by Michelle Craig who had received an email about this from a mother who heard one of her speeches. The story related in the email went like this:

"After coming home last night from a couple of long days of helping at our elementary school, a flat tire, doctor's visit, radiology appointment, and emergency room visit for one of my sick children, I was greeted with a kitchen full of dishes and life

---

[105] See Wikipedia, Classic Conditioning.

mess all over my house. I was exhausted, . . . and honestly, I just wanted to shower and climb into bed. . .

"While I was trying to tidy the kitchen, my seven-year-old approached me and asked if I would walk down to our basement to help him find a particular toy. My first thought . . . was, 'I just want to get the kitchen cleaned and kids to bed without interruption.' He again asked if I would help him. . .

"I then remembered the following from your talk in conference: *'When prompted, we can leave dishes in the sink or an inbox full of challenges demanding attention in order to read to a child, visit with a friend, babysit a neighbor's children, or serve in the temple [my insert: or help your child find a toy] . . . [We can] see people not as interruptions but as the purpose of [our] life."*

"I looked at my son, who was looking up at me, and I looked at my sink full of dishes and countertops littered with clutter, and I said out loud, "Dishes, you have to wait." As he and I proceeded to walk down our stairs to the basement, my son, Andrew, said, "Mom, you love me more than dishes, huh?" To which I responded an unequivocal "Yes!" . . .

"Then, this morning, while helping him finish his homework for school, I said, 'Andrew, I love you.' He responded with, 'Yup, you love me more than dishes.'"[106] (Craig M. D., 2018)

While the response of the seven-year-old is cute and inspires a smile, consider the corollary. If he thought that his mom leaving the dishes meant that she loved him more than the dishes, what would he have thought if she had chosen not to leave the dishes to help him? The time we spend in the world of those we love shows our love for them in a way that can even be recognized by a young child.

Influencing Generations

When we find our loved ones in their world, meet them there, learn about them, and invite them into ours, not only do we build

---

[106] Michelle Craig, *This is My Day of Opportunity*, a devotional address given at Brigham Young University, December 11, 2018.

our relationship with them and find more things in common, but we also teach them about respecting others and show them how good it feels to have someone take interest in the things that interest you. When they see their parents treat them this way, they are more likely to treat others and their children this way. "The way you treat your wife or children, or parents or siblings may influence generations to come," teaches Dieter Uchtdorf. "What legacy do you want to leave your posterity? One of harshness, vengeance, anger, fear, or isolation? Or one of love, humility, forgiveness, compassion, spiritual growth, and unity?"[107] (Uchtdorf D. F., 2016)

Learning What Love Really Is

Some may fairly question, "I put all the effort into planning, shopping, and preparing this meal. Why should I have to call more than once to get him to come eat it? Doesn't that just show how ungrateful he is for my sacrifice?" This is a tempting line of inquiry. But what we are calling for in this work is a transformation in the way we think and view our roles and responsibilities in this life. We are all saddled with myriad mundane tasks that consume large amounts of our time on this earth. Daily we make our beds and clean our teeth, prepare food and clean up the mess, wash clothes and sweep floors, pay bills and commute to work, feed the animals and take care of the yard. The list goes on. Who wouldn't rather be free of all these menial tasks? Have you ever wondered why we were created to dwell in a world that requires so much daily maintenance? Couldn't we just as easily have been created in a condition where the struggle for survival didn't consume us?

Instead of viewing these tasks as sacrifices, can we see them for what they really are or what they can be: opportunities to demonstrate our love. "True Christlike service is selfless and focuses on others. One woman who took care of her invalid

---

[107] Dieter Uchtdorf, *In Praise of Those Who Save*, an address given at the General Conference of the Church of Jesus Christ of Latter-day Saints, April 2016.

husband explained, "Don't think of your task as a burden; think of it as an opportunity to learn what love really is."[108] (Esplin, 2016)

Wouldn't it be great if we could look upon all our burdensome tasks around the home as opportunities to show our family members how much we love them by performing them. Sometimes we are tempted to feel like we are being used because others are not doing their "fair share." But in the end, will it matter whether we all did equal amounts of tasks? No. It will only matter if we loved. Some may ask, "But what will happen to our children if we don't teach them to take care of things and to work? Won't we spoil them?" We *are* teaching them to work. They see us doing it. We are teaching by example. We are saying "Do as I do," not "Do as I say." In other words, we are saying, "Come, follow me."

Transitioning to this mode of thinking is not easy. We must first overcome the natural man, who is lazy and selfish. We seem to be programmed to compare what we have, and what we have to do, to everyone we see. If we are constantly vigilant to make sure that everyone shares equally in the work, we have little chance of performing service. That is to say, we will hardly be able to do anything for others that is not our duty to perform. We will always be expected to do that which is our share. This is not to say that duty is not important and that we should ignore it. Duty suffices where love is not present.

A Higher Motivation

A higher motivation for work than duty is love. We plan for, shop for, and prepare the meal, not because it is our duty as a parent to take care of our children, but because we love them. We clean up the dinner messes night after night without complaint, because it is a small act of service, we can perform that grants our loved ones that one bit of leisure after dinner. In fact, all our

---

[108]Cheryl Esplin, *He Asks Us to Be His Hands*, an address given at the General Conference of the Church of Jesus Christ of Latter-day Saints, April 2016.

effort and sacrifice for those we love can be sanctified if we do it for the love of the Lord. We do not need to do all our maintenance tasks because it is our duty, or our job, or our role, or because we are expected to. When we do the type of thankless work required to bring order, cleanliness, and happiness to our home for which we never receive any recognition, we can do those tasks in the name of the Lord. We need not even do these daily maintenance tasks because of our love for those we are sacrificing for. We can do them for our love of the Lord. This is an even higher motivation than doing it out of our love for others. We do these tasks for him, in his name. Is not this the meaning of one of the first commandments that Adam received from God through the angel after he was cast out of the Garden of Eden?

Even though Adam and Eve were shut out of the presence of God, so that they could not see him, they still heard the voice of the Lord "from the way toward the Garden of Eden," and "he gave unto them commandments, that they should worship the Lord their God, and should offer the firstlings of their flocks, for an offering unto the Lord."[109] After many days, God sent an angel to Adam and Eve to test their knowledge and obedience. For a long time, Adam had been offering the firstlings of his flocks as sacrifices. He didn't know why. It's almost as if it was a burdensome, routine task that he was doing. Something he did regularly. He didn't know what was being accomplished by doing it. The ritual obviously hadn't done him much good yet because he couldn't cite a single benefit as a reason for doing it. To Adam, this routine was almost akin to doing dirty laundry (but a lot more expensive). The only reason he did it was because he was obedient. When the angel greeted Adam and Eve, he asked, "Why dost thou offer sacrifices unto the Lord?" And Adam answered, "I know not."

Let that sink in. For "many days," Adam performed this arduous ritual for no other reason than he felt it was his duty. One wonders how long he could have sustained it had the angel

---

[109] Moses 5:4-5, The Pearl of Great Price.

not intervened. Our guess is that "many days," in terms of Adam's longevity, was an awfully long time. It would have had to been. Firstlings don't appear daily unless your herd is unimaginably large.

At least when you pick up after you kids or do their laundry for many days, you know you do it out of self-respect and you have the benefit of a cleaner home. But to sacrifice valuable assets day after day without knowing the reason? Remember, the firstling is the firstborn of the females in a herd of sheep. The sheep being sacrificed would have grown up and provided wool for clothing, reproduced and created more valuable assets, and eventually provided food when it was slaughtered. But to sacrifice it was to kill it and burn it on an altar. It was to destroy a productive asset. We hardly have a parallel in today's society other than maybe to make a regular withdrawal from an investment account and light the cash on fire. Anyone without knowledge of the custom observing him would have likely thought him insane.

"This thing (meaning the sacrifice) is a similitude of the sacrifice of the Only Begotten of the Father," explained the angel. Then he gave two additional commandments for Adam and Eve to follow. "Wherefore," he said, meaning, "as a result of which," in other words, as a result of the sacrifice of the Only Begotten of the Father, thou shalt:

1. Do everything that you do in the name of the Son, and,
2. Repent and call upon God forevermore (in the name of the Son, of course, it having already been established in the first command that *everything* he does must be done in the name of the Son.)

It is this interesting first commandment, given to mankind early on in our sojourn here on Earth, that applies to our discussion here. Adam and Eve, and by extension, their posterity, must from now on do everything that they do in the name of the Son. This may be the most widely unfollowed commandment ever given to mankind. Think about it. Do everything that you do in the Lord's name. Everything. When you wake up in the morning and get ready for your day, do it in the name of the Lord. When you take the train into work, do it in the name of the Lord. When you clear your lunch dishes off the table at Zupas, do it in the name of the Lord. When you fill your tank with gas, do it in the name of the Lord. Are we beginning to get the picture? Who does this? Anyone we know? Why would the angel of the Lord give this commandment without any known explanation? What kind of effect would this mindset have on our daily interaction with our routines and other people?

Many of us have as our personal motto, Do your best! We try to be the best we can be and do our best in everything we do regardless of whether we will be seen or recognized for our efforts. In more religious vernacular, we repent daily. But fighting off the tendencies of the natural man to cut corners is a constant battle and often our own personal drive to be better is not strong enough to overcome. It is at times like these when we can call upon a higher motivation. We can fulfill our responsibilities in the name of the Son. That is to say, we can do the things that are required of us because of our love for the Lord. This is another way that we can remember him and fulfill our promise to do so. When the angel commanded Adam and Eve to do everything in the name of the Son, he was really calling upon them to remember him. And by remembering to do everything in his name we can fulfill our witness to "always remember him."[110] This is another tie between the sacrifice of the Old Testament, the baptism of the New Testament, and the sacrament ordinance in the latter days.

This should not seem foreign to Christians who are called on to "pray always,"[111] and "to stand as witnesses of God at all times and in all things, and in all places."[112] In the latter days, we have been commanded that our "vows shall be offered up in

---

[110] Doctrine and Covenants, Section 20:79.
[111] Luke 21:36.
[112] Book of Mormon, Mosiah 18:9.

righteousness on all days and at all times."[113] One way this is done is by doing things in the name of the Lord. For example, when you are finished wiping off the counter, and on your way to the sink to rinse out the cloth, you notice a few crumbs that were missed, instead of just leaving the crumbs there, or thinking someone else should do something around the house, or wiping them off in frustration or impatience, we think about the Lord and how much he has done for us. You then wipe up those last few crumbs "for Him." We do a better job than we would have naturally done because we are doing it for Him, because we love Him, and because we know He loves us. With practice, we can begin to perform more of our tasks in this manner and with this mindset and be in a constant remembrance of him. This seems to be what the angel had in mind when commanding Adam and Eve to do everything in the name of the Son.

With this mindset, we begin to understand those grandmothers we recall from our childhood who seemed to live in the kitchen. They were up early cooking breakfast, and we kids woke up to the smell of bacon. We mechanically and, in retrospect, somewhat ungratefully, slammed down our poached eggs with toast and bacon before running out to play. Not a thought was given to Grandma, who was left behind to clean up the entire mess, until we heard the call for lunch.

Little did we notice, but there was not a trace of breakfast dishes in sight when we rushed in to enjoy some homemade chicken noodle soup and cornbread before rushing back out to finish the summer day. If we did return momentarily for a bathroom break or a drink to cool off, there was Grandma in the kitchen, wiping up crumbs or putting things away in the fridge. Her apron never came off from dawn till dusk and neither did her smile. There was always something mixing or baking. Looking back, we now realize that she was not slaving away in the kitchen over ungrateful grandchildren, but she lived to love and serve, and was happy to spend her life in the service of her posterity.

---

[113] Doctrine and Covenants, Section 59:11.

Is this not what love really is? Will it matter in the end that Grandma served us for years and we did nothing for her in return? Of course not, because she expected no reward. But it is up to us to learn from her example and influence future generations to pay it forward. Our influence on our loved ones can know no bounds.

They Watch and Learn

One young adult woman related the story about a requirement in her family to study the scriptures regularly. Growing up she was not naturally drawn to the scriptures. Most children aren't. Her mother would repeatedly ask her for a report on how her study was going. Being behind where she thought her mother expected her to be, she bristled at the thought of being checked up on. She confessed in church that, "My mother's constant checking up on me made me feel rebellious and made me not want to read the scriptures."[114]

But her mother took the higher road and studied on her own. Her children noticed. Later in life when the young lady moved away from home, she realized that life is not as black and white and simple as it seemed at home. Whereas happiness was a familiar feeling as a child, the competition and confusion of the world brought stress and doubting. Despite being taught the "plan of happiness" as a youth, the pursuit of happiness begins anew as a young adult. On visits home from college, she couldn't help but notice that her mother seemed to be truly happy, not like so many others she had been around outside the home. It was then it dawned on her that her mother's happiness came from doing the things she was teaching her children to do. She realized how important a regular escape to the edifying influence of the scriptures is to achieving happiness. She did not doubt that her mother knew it and from then on felt a desire to follow counsel and study on her own.

---

[114]Bailey Hendrickson, in a testimony given during Sunday School, Highland, UT, June 26, 2016.

This story illustrates the powerful effect that modeling the behavior you want to see in your children has. Unfortunately, our poor behavior is picked up on just as readily as our best behavior. Always keep in mind that you are demonstrating how to be and other can make the connection between your actions and your enjoyment of life.

Serve Your Children?

Many may remember the following commandment as the one which seemed the hardest to keep. "Ye will not suffer your children that they go hungry, or naked; neither will ye suffer that they transgress the laws of God, and fight and quarrel one with another, and serve the devil, who is the master of sin, or who is the evil spirit which hath been spoken of by our fathers, he being an enemy to all righteousness. But ye will teach them to walk in the ways of truth and soberness; ye will teach them to love one another, and to serve one another."[115] Teach your children to love one another and serve one another? How can you teach them to serve one another without serving them? What will that service look like, they may wonder. Childish ideas of serving someone invoke images of a butler or maid standing with a neatly folded napkin draped over their forearm patiently waiting for their master's next command. But this isn't it at all. One central theme of this work is describing what this service looks like for those who haven't seen it.

Will we expect it to suffice if we simply *tell* our children to serve each other? It won't. If we want our children to love and serve one another, we must love and serve our children first. We love Christ, the apostle John reminded us, "because he first loved us."[116] They will learn from us, and they will treat each other the way they are taught to be treated. They will yell requests at each other if they are taught by having requests yelled at them. They may not want to help each other do their chores, but if we love

---

[115] Mosiah 4:14-15.
[116] 1 John 4:19.

them, speak softly to them, help them do what is right rather than telling them to do what is right, they will be much more inclined to do so with each other.

This principle was pondered after witnessing the behavior of a mother staying out of town at a condo with her teenage daughter for a volleyball tournament. The mother was good at teaching her daughter how to work, we were informed. The mother sat around and commanded her daughter, telling her to clean up the lunch mess, get her a drink from the fridge, run upstairs and grab her phone for her from the other room. This appeared to be a good practice because the daughter was obediently doing everything that her mother asked her to do. The situation was good, we heard, because the mother was teaching her daughter how to work.

Yet we wonder what the actual lesson being taught was. Was it how to work or how to be lazy? What lesson would you conclude from someone who sat around and barked orders at you? From the daughter's perspective, we may have thought, "Why don't you get up and get your own phone?" Or "Why don't you clean up your own mess after lunch?" Or we may have thought, "I can't wait until I'm a parent so I can force my kids to get me whatever I need." We are impressed with the young woman's willingness to serve and not rebel at the "do as I say, not as I do" teaching style of her mother. Her actions demonstrate one thing for sure: her love for her mother. When we serve each other out of love, the arduousness of the tasks melts away.

You might say that a parent has the right to do this because they are the parent. But we wonder what gives a parent the right to treat another like their personal servant. While some may try to teach others how to work by sitting around and making demands of them, we are saying that a better way to teach them how to work and serve is by serving them. We need to show them by example. We teach our children how to work best by working hard and by consecrating the results of our work to them. Most people prefer a role model or leader when they know that the leader will not ask them to do anything that they wouldn't do themselves. We like leaders who get down in the trenches with us, who lead us into battle rather than sending us in. This is the principle Christ taught saying, "Greater love hath no man than this, that a man lay down his life for his friends."[117] Our willingness to sacrifice any portion of our life for someone shows our love for them.

Conclusion

We believe that children learn more from example than they do from words. We should teach our children how to treat others by the way we treat them. In a household, we should be showing each other at least the same courtesy that we would extend to perfect strangers.

The folly foisted upon children by "wayward parents" has been a problem in society for centuries. We may have been born into such a home and the duty is upon us, if we are able, to soften our hearts toward our children. A tender-hearted parent showing love by example can influence generations of posterity for good. We see how we can transform our thinking into viewing our mundane, repetitive tasks in a holier way, as acts of service for those we really love. It's not easy, but we can serve our children and, at the same time, teach them to serve and to work. There is nothing wrong with this type of service which Christ himself demonstrated as the greatest form of love.

The Golden Rule is the summation of the most basic doctrine underpinning Judeo-Christian civilization. Therefore, we need to apply it to our familial interactions, not just our encounters with acquaintances. We may want to see if we are more courteous to strangers than we are to members of our household and adjust accordingly. Wise authors have pointed out for centuries how the bad example set by parents influences their children for a long time. We follow Paul's advice to be tender-hearted as we try to set a better example for our children regarding personal

---

[117] John 15:13.

interactions.

The importance of getting into the world of our children cannot be overstated. This small act can influence them and their posterity for generations. It is a challenge to view the menial tasks that consume our time as opportunities to show our love, but when we do, others take note of our example. With practice we can learn to do these things out of love and in the name of the Lord. This effort will not go unnoticed by our loved ones. When we serve each other out of love, the tasks we perform become easier. At the same time, our example shows them how to be.

5

WE ARE STEWARDS, NOT MASTERS

It seems to be an uncommon perspective for parents to view their children as regular people with their own rights, feelings, interests, and wishes. We have lots of other ways of viewing them. Some people view their children as small versions of themselves and try to relive their childhood through them vicariously, planning and guiding them through the type of life they wish they had. Others view them as little servants without rights who are there to do everything for them. In many cultures, children are put to work at a very young age and the fruit of their labor is taken to help sustain the family.

The Christian perspective is that we are all children of our Heavenly Father making us brothers and sisters of our children. From this perspective, we are truly responsible for our children's care for maybe 25% of our life. The other 75% of our lives we hope to have a good relationship with them and learn from them as much as teach them. In the end, we are temporary stewards of our children's souls until they reach adulthood. A steward is someone employed to manage domestic concerns. That's really what it boils down to for the first years of our children's lives until they are on their own: we manage their domestic concerns. We are stewards of our children, not their masters.

Honor and Obey

As parents, we are often particularly fond of the 5th commandment: "Honor thy father and thy mother: that thy days may be long upon the land which the Lord thy God giveth thee."[118] When we are failing to gain the respect of our children, we can call on the authority of God and His word in the Bible to shame our children or play to their sense of duty or guilt. As a last attempt, since nothing we have done has merited our children's honor, we can appeal to God and perhaps our children will listen to Him. But this commandment to honor and obey parents is given to the children. It is not given to the parents to use as leverage to keep their children in line. The children need to learn this commandment and internalize it but are often delayed by tyrannical parents demanding honor.

It is a tough pill to swallow to change our mindset to believe that we have to earn respect and honor from our children. We feel entitled to respect and reverence, much like Bill Cosby's father as described in his comedic monologue, "My father established our relationship when I was seven years old. He looked at me and said, 'Ya know, I brought you in this world, I'll take you out. And it don't make no difference to me cause I'll make another one that look just like you.'"[119] (Cosby, 2012) We're bigger, stronger, and for a short time, smarter, and because of this we often think we deserve respect. In reality, our relationship may be more like that of David and Goliath or Jack and the Giant. Respect does not necessarily follow size and precedence.

A Steady Ministry

A big part of our stewardship with our children and loved ones is to act as minister to them. We are regularly faced with trial and sadness caused by the agency of those we love. The gift of agency

---

[118] Exodus 20:12.
[119] Bill Cosby, *Fathers*, YouTube video.

is the greatest of God's gifts to his children, but unfortunately it is often used unwisely to follow a course that brings grief either for the agent, the steward, or both. A minister in this situation applies the Balm of Gilead, he doesn't use his position of authority or respect to impress guilt or shame. "With the gift of the Holy Spirit to guide, we can perform a steady ministry to lessen the pain of poor choices and bind up the wounds insofar as we are permitted."[120] (Christofferson D. T., Finding Your Life, 2016) This is love and our duty as stewards: lessening the pain and binding up the wounds of those who make poor choices. Love is not "teaching them a lesson" or saying they deserve their pain or inflicting more pain by ridicule or indifference.

Showing Gratitude to Our Children

Part of being a good steward or shepherd to our children is treating them like whole people and showing gratitude to them. Obviously, our young children have much more to be grateful to us for than we do to them. Children rely on their parents for so many things. Because of this, we can feel they should be constantly indebted to us. It may not be easy to see the things they do for us to remove our burdens and it is much easier to see what they do to add to them. This means that we should be on the constant lookout for things where we can show our gratitude if we want to show them how to be grateful.

We should be on the lookout for every way possible to show gratitude to our children in even the smallest things. The best part of this is that regular expressions of gratitude to your children teaches them how to be grateful. It helps them feel what it is like for someone to be proud of them, instilling in their souls a desire for the blessings of service. For there is never a service given for which the recipient does not feel grateful. And the feeling of the gratitude expressed for your service is enough to strengthen your desire to continue to serve. So, when your children feel the feeling of your gratitude, it motivates them to continue to do things for

---

[120] Todd Christofferson, "Finding Your Life", *Ensign*, March 2016.

which you will be grateful.

What kinds of things that your children do can you show gratitude for? One father gave his daughter a ride to school every day. It wasn't that far, so it would seem like something that his daughter should be expressing gratitude for to him. But one day his son had a meeting at the high school and had to be there before the bus could get him there. Because of this, if his daughter wanted a ride that day, she would have to get up early and would arrive at the junior high 15 minutes early. The day before, he let her know the conditions for getting a ride and reminded her before she went to bed. The next morning when her alarm went off, he reminded her about needing to be ready early if she wanted a ride. She didn't complain, got up, got busy and got herself ready on time so they could all leave early. When he dropped her off at school, he thanked her for getting ready early. It was a very small thing, but he thanked her anyway.

While it may not seem like much, picture what could have happened. His daughter could have chosen to sleep a little longer and get up at the last possible moment. Then when it was time to leave, she would not be quite ready. She would need another 3 minutes or so. The father would have been placed in a position of making his son later for his important meeting at high school or having his daughter freak out that he couldn't wait a measly 3 minutes. Undoubtedly, a fight between siblings would break out. There would be screaming and yelling, hard feelings, and a wedge would be placed between brother and sister. If the father had chosen to help his son keep the important appointment time, he would have been considered rude and impatient by his daughter. Had he chosen to wait the extra 3-5 minutes, he would have sent a signal to his son that being late for important meetings is OK or that he cares more about his daughter than his son. It would be a no-win situation for him. (Thought of this way, perhaps that small effort by his daughter was much more impactful than it appeared on the surface, as are most small acts of thoughtfulness.)

Fortunately, his daughter did not place him in that situation, and everyone was happy. Kudos to the father for not expecting the little sacrifice of waking early and waiting 15 minutes at the school. He hoped that his little show of gratitude would make her feel better and have a desire to do more good. This is all part of spending 90% of your time helping your children do what's right.

Parents or Friends

There are two mainstream schools of thought about how to parent. One is restrictive parenting. The other is permissive parenting. Restrictive parents place all kinds of rules and expectations upon their children without regard for their agency. They adhere to the roles of parent-child and regularly remind their children who is who in the relationship. The children's personal space is regularly invaded, and they are regularly judged according to their willingness and ability to meet parental expectations. These types of parents are viewed by many as proactive, good parents who take responsibility for their children's actions and outcomes. While this type of parenting can trigger the rebellious spirit in a child, when one of these children gets off track, the blame is typically placed on the child.

Permissive parents, on the other hand, tend to allow their children more space to make mistakes and are not seen as demanding. While some delinquent parents fall into this category, it is possible to be a responsible parent and still be viewed as permissive. These parents are viewed more as "friends" to their children than parents and whenever one of their children is going astray, it is generally agreed that it is because "nothing is expected of them." That child has plenty of friends, it is said, what they need is a parent.

It seems that prevailing contemporary wisdom says that children need to have parents first and then friends later. To be a good parent, adults should actively "parent" their child, teach them and restrict them rather than being a friend and letting them confide in them and trust them. While the wisdom in this is evident, our question is, after spending a generation being a parent to your child and telling them what to do all the time and how they're doing well and how they're not doing well and correcting them constantly, at what point, exactly, does one stop being a parent and become a friend to your child? When does one become someone who your child can trust; who they can come to with their feelings and problems without the fear of being judged? Or when do you stop trying to tell them what they're doing wrong or trying to solve their problems for them? When do you become someone who counsels with your children rather than dictating solutions to them?

Bruce McConkie explained how he counsels with his children as a wise friend. "I bring my children in," he said, "and we counsel on a problem. I don't tell them what ought to be; I say, "What do you think? What's your evaluation? What do you want to do in this situation? What's the best thing to do?" And they tell me what they think."[121] (McConkie, 1973) After they had talked it out, Bruce would share his views if any.

Some may ask, but how old were his children when he was counseling with them in this manner. And the answer is, at the time, he was referring to his adult children. But when are your children too young to counsel with? When are they too young to have views on how they should direct their course? When are they too young to be asked what they think? When are we humble enough to just listen and not thrust our solution upon them? Unfortunately, our children reach the age when they have thoughts about how they should act at a far younger age than we reach the wisdom and humility to let them reason things out in their mind and ask us if it be right.

Responding to Confessions

An experienced father was working in his garage one evening after dinner when his 13-year-old daughter came in and surprised him with some alarming information about her best friend.

---

[121] McConkie, Bruce R., *Agency or Inspiration – Which?*, an address given at Brigham Young University, February 27, 1973.

"Taylor is being a butt," she said.

"Oh?" asked her father, "What's she doing?"

"She's mad at me because she's in trouble for sending nudies to a boy."

As the father processed this sensitive confession, a number of possible responses rushed through his mind. The first was the panic response: "OK, you are never hanging out with Taylor again." The second was the lecture response: a monologue on the long-term consequences of sending nude photos of yourself over the internet. Third was the conditional love response: to tell his tell his daughter that she should choose better friends. But finally, he resolved to take the calm approach and see if he could get his daughter to open up and talk about the situation more. Without hardly looking up from his task or showing any signs of urgency, he calmly asked, "So why is Taylor mad at you then?"

He inquired first into his daughter's feelings about how her friend was treating her. This helped his daughter put her guard down and open up about her friend, their relationship, and the complexities of social life in junior high. They had a good conversation in which he was able to get a good, honest assessment about his daughter's attitude toward sending nude pictures. He was able to tell her a story about another girl her age that did the same thing and the types of difficulties she faced. And he was even able to get his daughter to think about the permanent nature of internet images and what perverts do with pictures of children without clothes. The conversation was peaceful and edifying for both father and daughter and would have only been possible following the calm response to the frightening announcement.

When people are faced with problems, rarely do they come to us looking for advice or solutions. Usually, it is just to have someone to talk to. Many times, we are confided in by others simply because a listening ear is sought after. The same is true for our children. Jumping to conclusions and solutions is the worst thing we can do. Nothing will prevent a youth from confiding in us more than them learning they are going to be:

a) judged for what they tell us,
b) get in trouble for what they tell us, or
c) have an unwanted solution forced upon them.

Who wants to appear before or confide in a know-it-all who consistently solves our problem with their superior solution, judges us as stupid for not following it, and says, "I told you so," when our solution doesn't produce results as good as the imagined results of their solution?

Contrast for a minute the mature conversation this daughter had with her father to what might have happened had the father followed one of his instinctual impressions when he heard the dilemma.

The Panic Response

The father's first instinct was a reaction based on fear. He recognized the danger to his daughter posed by sharing nude selfies and, because of his love for her, he wanted to remove her from the situation to protect her from harm. He recognized his daughter's friend had made a terrible decision that was probably preceded by several poor decisions. By cutting his daughter off from her best friend who made a bad mistake, he assumed he would be reducing her exposure to ideas and activities that could lead to a very regrettable situation for her. The Panic Response is one where a parent takes out of the equation any possibility of compromise or discussion and dictates the solution with very little patience, or input from the child.

There are a few problems with this response. First, it assumes that his daughter's friend is the problem and not his daughter. While most of us as parents find it difficult to believe that our child would be the leader in taking risks, in a relationship with two BFFs, your daughter has a 50% chance of being out in front. When people are friends, they find that they have values, experiences, and interests in common. Second, it assumes that it is even possible to cut off the friendship. The Panic Response seems to forget that the child spends a good portion of her school day, countless text messages, Snap Chats, or video calls, and probably a weekend activity at the mall with the friend she is barred from associating with. When two people are friends, an edict from a parent can rarely end that. What it does instead is give the child a reason to lie and deceive as she seeks to find ways to continue the relationship without parental permission. Telling me you never want me to see someone who I like ever again doesn't change my feelings toward them or my memories of the fun we've had together. And finally, when a child, especially one in their teen years is forced to choose between a relationship with their friend or one with their parent, the friend is likely to win out. This is perhaps the most undesired outcome of the Panic Response.

The Lecture Response

Hopefully, we can all remember as kids how awful it was to endure a lecture from parents, adults, or other authority figures. They always acted like they knew everything, when in reality, as a teen, we knew that they knew nothing, and we knew everything. Lectures rarely have the intended effect, probably because kids have a "parents channel" and a mental remote they can use to switch channels at the first sign of undesired communications. Who knows? But one message that is commonly received from a lecture is that you are showing me how much you know, but not how much you care. Lectures, by definition, are a form of one-way communication. What is really needed in tough relationship situations is more love and peace, not a parent droning on and a child tuning out.

The ultimate example of a parent's calm response to a child's shocking confession comes in a story by the authors of *The Anatomy of Peace: Resolving the Heart of Conflict*, by the Arbinger Institute. In this story, the main character of the book, Lou, a successful businessman, is struggling to deal with his older son's unwillingness to comply with any of his father's life expectations for him. During this experience, a memory of his teenage years is triggered that helps Lou come to terms with a better way to be in his relationship with this son.

Lou's father was a poor apple farmer in upstate New York in the mid-20th century. As a kid, Lou's family had only owned one vehicle, an old, flatbed farm truck that barely ran. When Lou was sixteen, his father bought a new car, which was a huge deal for his family. Of course, Lou wanted to take it to run some errands the day after his father brought it home. Surprisingly, Lou's father was OK with him taking the new car. When Lou was getting ready to leave, he started the car in the driveway and then had to run back in the house to grab his wallet. Unfortunately, he forgot to put the new car in park, and it slow-rolled down the driveway and dumped off a 20-foot bluff into the Hudson River.

Try to imagine the fear and trepidation that must have gripped Lou as he located his father in the house to inform him about the accident. When he found him reading the newspaper in his favorite chair, he awkwardly stumbled around for the words and finally blurted out that the new car was in the river and apologized in tears. His father's response is at the heart of the book *The Anatomy of Peace*, and cannot be related better than by the authors.

"[Lou] remembered trembling while waiting for his father to respond. His father didn't turn to him but still sat holding the newspaper wide before him. He then slowly reached his left hand to the top corner of the right-hand page and turned it to continue reading. And then he said it, the sentence Lou would never forget. He said, "Well, I guess you'll have to take the truck then."

"Lou realized in this moment that his father's heart was at peace toward Lou, a peace so powerful that it couldn't be interrupted even by a provocation so great as the sudden loss of a hard-earned car. Perhaps in his wisdom he knew Lou was now the last person who would ever put another car into the river. Perhaps in that instant he divined that a lecture would serve no purpose, and to start one would only hurt an already hurting son."[122] (Arbinger Institute, 2015)

It is essential that we realize that when our loved ones or friends are confiding in us or confessing to us, they are probably already hurting. It is better to give them space to work things out and be there for them and try to feel their pain rather than offer the advice and opinions and predictions that they will likely tune out. People need to figure things out on their own. We can't learn for them, and we need to be there for them if we love them.

The Conditional Love Response

Another unhelpful, if not hurtful, response is to tell your kids that they have made a bad choice in friends. Yes, choice of friends is particularly important for youth, but by encouraging them to abandon their friends, are we not training them to do the very thing we are trying to overcome in our own life? Isn't abandoning your friend in their time of trouble really just conditional love? Are you not teaching your child that it's OK to be there for someone when they are meeting your expectations, but if they don't, you need to move on?

This is an hard saying. We all want to protect our children from the evils of the world and if they get hooked up with the wrong "crowd," they can be hurt themselves. If it is hard to see your own flesh and blood child as the offspring of our Heavenly Father who needs to be loved, cherished, and treated with respect no matter how rough the going gets, how much harder is it, then, to see their friends, souls from another family, class, culture, or lifestyle as children of God? But if loving all mankind unconditionally is the goal of the Gospel, we must view our children's friends as our children, once removed.

A better response than telling them to get new friends is to ask your child how they can be a *better* friend to their friend in their time of need. Teach them to love the person, not shun them because they have a problem. Help your child ponder and

---

[122] The Arbinger Institute, *The Anatomy of Peace: Resolving the Heart of Conflict*, Berrett-Koehler Publishers, Oakland, CA, 2006, 61, Kindle version.

discover ways they can be a help to their friend during their time of trial.

If encouraging a loving relationship between your child and their friend who seems to be on a collision course with hard times seems like a risk to your child, you can talk to your child about what it means to be a leader in a friendship. A good leader is always looking out for the best interest of others. Talk to your child about being a leader in their friendships instead of a follower. Tell them to build up their friend rather than tear them down. Someone has to be a leader in a relationship, and it might as well be your child. Try to remember that your child's friend has a mother who cares and is wondering how to reach her child. Let your son or daughter know that their good example and friendship may be an answer to their friend's parents' prayers.

A loving, patient, and calm response to a confession from a loved one will encourage them to open up. It will teach them they can rely on you as a friend in a time of need. It will increase your influence over them rather than diminish it. And it will show them the way to be with their own loved ones, perpetuating the cycle of love.

A Child's True Identity

It is helpful during stressful times when loved ones seem to be going off the rails to remember who they really are. They were the children of Heavenly Parents before they were your children. It takes some of the burden off you as an individual to recognize that every soul has its agency. And while you can lovingly guide, encourage, suggest and invite, who they become is their own choice and they will ultimately be accountable to God only. Seeing them as God's children first helps in a couple ways. It requires that you treat them with the respect due a prince or princess, that is, the child of the King of Kings. It helps you teach them that God is in the details of their life in the same way that He is in yours. And seeing your children as a child of God will help you feel more love for them during their times of transition.

"I like this variation of a quote attributed to Goethe," said Lynn Robbins. "'The way you see [a child] is the way you treat them, and the way you treat them is [who] they [will] become.' To remember a child's true identity is a gift of foresight that divinely inspires the vision of a righteous judge."[123] (Robbins, 2016)

We are stewards of our children at least as much as we are their parents. Our primary role is to feed, clothe, shelter, teach, and transmit our faith. We give them a fighting chance in this world and hopefully our faith and witness of their true nature will be powerful enough to counterbalance the negative self-image they will receive from the world.

Helping Things Go Right

Another core philosophy found in *The Anatomy of Peace* is the principle of helping things go right rather than just pointing out the things that go wrong. Yusuf, the wise counselor in the story, observes, "So for many problems in life, solutions will have to go deeper than strategies of discipline or correction. I won't invite my child to change if my interactions with him are primarily in order to get him to change."[124] (Arbinger Institute, 2015) This is the same principle we discussed elsewhere in this work where we said that if we only get to see our child for five minutes before school, that's not the time to be working on strategies for getting better grades. If every time I speak with my child or loved one, it is on the topic of how they need to change, it won't be long before they tire of speaking to me. This is not inviting them to change, it is turning them away. Instead, we should be using every moment we have to build our relationship. A strong relationship and loving example are where our invitations should be coming from.

"I become an agent of change," Yusuf continued, "only to the

---

[123] Lynn Robbins, from *The Righteous Judge*, an address given at the General Conference of the Church of Jesus Christ of Latter-day Saints, October 2016.
[124] The Arbinger Institute, *The Anatomy of Peace: Resolving the Heart of Conflict*, Berrett-Koehler Publishers, Oakland, CA, 2006, 18, Kindle version.

degree that I begin to live to help things go right rather than simply to correct things that are going wrong. Rather than simply correcting, for example, I need to reenergize my teaching, my helping, my listening, my learning. I need to put time and effort into building relationships."[125]

Pointing out others' flaws and shortcomings is not helpful. This is an incredibly important point. Most of us are deeply aware of our issues. We know when we have done things we shouldn't have done or have said things we shouldn't have said. Instead, we should be focused on creating an environment of love to learn in.

"There is no need to constantly tell our spouse or children how they can improve; they know that already. It is in creating this environment of love that they will be empowered to make the necessary changes in their lives and become better people . . . . We all know where we can do better. There is no need to repeatedly remind each other, but there is a need to love and minister to each other and, in doing so, provide a climate of willingness to change."[126] (Boom, 2019)

Instead, if we can teach behavior by example, if our example is worthy of emulation, then those who admire it will seek change within themselves because they will desire to possess the quality that they love in you. Finding ways to take time to help those we love with whatever they need help doing (whether it is leading them in the direction you desire or not) is showing them that we care about them and their interests. Listening to them, and, yes, learning from them, rather than always advising them or attempting to solve their problems for them will ingratiate you to them. If someone is not where *you* think they should be or doing what *you* think they should be doing, it's OK. Everyone is different and seeks happiness in their own way and in their own time. Insofar as we can help things in their lives go right, we should endeavor to do so. This requires time and patience and

---

[125] Ibid. p18.
[126] Hans Boom, from *Knowing, Loving, Growing*, an address given at the General Conference of the Church of Jesus Christ of Latter-day Saints October 2019.

being there for them.

Looking Inward for Solutions

It is also helpful to consider that time spent focused on the inadequacies of others is time that could be better spent focused on your own spiritual improvement. Spirituality is teaching, helping, listening and learning. These are the skills we need in ourselves if we have any hope of being a benefit to others. Good insight into this tradeoff is beautifully illustrated in a marriage self-help book by authors Henry Cloud and John Townsend. "When we neglect setting boundaries with ourselves and focus instead on setting boundaries with those we think sorely need limits, we have limited our own spiritual growth. As in any growth process, spiritual growth proceeds to the level that we invest in it. When we only invest in changing someone else, they get the benefit of our efforts, but the important work we have to do has been neglected . . . If your spouse is . . . angry, irresponsible, inattentive, and self-centered, you will not grow if you continue to react to his sins. This is not seeking first God's kingdom and righteousness (Matt. 6:33); it is seeking satisfaction from another person (codependency).

"We must become more deeply concerned about our own issues than our spouse's. We cannot overstate the importance of this idea . . . Boundaries with yourself are a much bigger issue than boundaries in your marriage. In the end, while we are only partly responsible for growing our marriages, we are completely responsible to God for developing our very souls. You are responsible for half of your marriage and all of your soul. Boundaries on yourself are between you and God."[127] (Townsend, 2002)

This principle of placing focus on self-improvement is essential to building relationships that work and last. Self-improvement is a worldly phrase for repentance. Repentance and

---

[127] Cloud and Townsend, *Boundaries in Marriage*, published August 12th, 2002, by Zondervan (first published January 1st, 1999), 65-66.

forgiveness are at the core of the gospel of Jesus Christ. But the gospel is not so much about our desire for others to repent so we can forgive them as it is about our deep need to repent so that we can be forgiven. Unfortunately, the problems in relationships most often appear to be something wrong with the other person. If my daughter would just stop wearing such short shirts when she knows that bugs me, we think, or if my son would just start doing his homework like I told him to, or if my husband would just stop spending so much time fishing and live his life the way *I* think he should, then we would get along just fine, and everyone would be happy.

Rarely do we look inwardly to see if the problem is in us. Rarely do we ask, "Lord, is it I?"[128] As Dieter Uchtdorf relates it, "It was our beloved Savior's final night in mortality, the evening before He would offer Himself a ransom for all mankind. As He broke bread with His disciples, He said something that must have filled their hearts with great alarm and deep sadness. "One of you shall betray me," He told them. The disciples didn't question the truth of what He said. Nor did they look around, point to someone else, and ask, "Is it him?" Instead, "they were exceeding sorrowful, and began every one of them to say unto him, Lord, is it I?"

"I wonder what each of us would do if we were asked that question by the Savior. Would we look at those around us and say in our hearts, "He's probably talking about Brother Johnson. I've always wondered about him," or "I'm glad Brother Brown is here. He really needs to hear this message?" Or would we, like those disciples of old, look inward and ask that penetrating question: "Is it I?" In these simple words, "Lord, is it I?" lies the beginning of wisdom and the pathway to personal conversion and lasting change."[129] (Uchtdorf D. F., Lord, Is It I?, 2014)

Christ's disciples appear to have understood what he meant when he instructed, "Thou hypocrite, first cast out the beam out

---

[128] Matthew 26:22.
[129] Dieter Uchtdorf, from *Lord, Is it I?*, an address given at the General Conference of the Church of Jesus Christ of Latter-day Saints, October 2014

of thine own eye; and then shalt thou see clearly to cast out the mote out of thy brother's eye." At the Last Supper, they each presumed that the problem they were facing originated within themselves.

This is a theme reiterated by the prophets and apostles of the Church of Jesus Christ of Latter-day Saints. Henry Eyring related the story of a conversation he had with a wiser Church leader. He confided to his friend, "That because of choices some in our extended family had made, I doubted that we could be together in the world to come." His leader replied, "You are worrying about the wrong problem. You just live worthy of the celestial kingdom, and the family arrangements will be more wonderful than you can imagine."[130] (Eyring H. B., 2019)

Six months later we hear similar advice from Dallin Oaks. "After the death of his beloved wife and the mother of his children, a father remarried. Some grown children strongly objected to the remarriage and sought the counsel of a close relative who was a respected Church leader. After hearing the reasons for their objections, which focused on conditions and relationships in the spirit world or in the kingdoms of glory that follow the Final Judgment, this leader said: "You are worried about the wrong things. You should be worried about whether you will get to those places. Concentrate on that. If you get there, all of it will be more wonderful than you can imagine."[131] (Oaks, Trust in the Lord, 2019)

It is easy to see from this counsel that the more important path is to focus on our own behavior and how we can improve than on that of others. Our own is the behavior we have control over, and we know we are far from perfect. Therefore, let us focus on love and supporting those we love rather than finding fault and criticism.

---

[130] Henry Eyring, from *A Home Where the Spirit of the Lord Dwells,* an address given at the General Conference of the Church of Jesus Christ of Latter-Day Saints, April 2019.
[131] Dallin Oaks, from *Trust in the Lord,* an address given at the General Conference of the Church of Jesus Christ of Latter-day Saints, October 2019.

Conclusion

Just because we were born 25 years before our children doesn't mean that we instantly merit their honor, no matter who we have become. Most people have to earn respect from others, and we should strive to earn it from our children. We have a stewardship for our children for a short time and hopefully we manage that small thing in a way that we will enjoy loving relationships with them throughout the larger portion of our life when they have more stewardship for themselves. One way of earning their respect is by showing our genuine gratitude for the good things they do right. Yes, we need to be the parents, but more importantly we need to be their friends and confidants.

We know our children will get off track because we are off track. We hope they will confide in us when they are in trouble (or before) and our response to their confessions will determine the extent to which they will be willing to trust us with other private information about their lives. Of the many ways we can build trust through our response to our children, listening without judgement makes great headway. We need to remember their true identity and help them do what's right. And remember, a focus on how we can improve is the right problem to receive our attention. We really can only improve ourselves. We are promised that if we do well ourselves, then Heavenly Father will take care of everything else.

6

REMEMBER BEING A KID

You Were a Kid Too

One of the hardest things for a young person to wrap their heads around is the fact that their parents were ever their age and therefore can somewhat understand what they are going through. It may be just as hard for a child to view an adult as a young person as it is for an adult to view a child as a mature spirit in a small body. And as we have seen, this inability can lead to a parent demanding underserved respect and treating children more like ignorant servants than children of God capable of great things. There may be a number or reasons for this.

The concept of passing time is difficult for any of us to grasp. Our pictured future never precisely materializes the way we expected and our memories of the past fade. One year of time is 20% of a kindergartener's conscious life, but only a small fraction of her grandmother's life. Growing up in the 70s, the thought of listening to "oldies" music from the 1940's would be unfathomable to a teen of that era. But as she ages, she thinks nothing of listening to 80s music in the 2010s.

The point of this is that we should make a valiant effort to remember what it was like being a kid for the sake of our own children. Not misremembering it, as in how we had to walk to school uphill, both ways, in 10 feet of snow. But remembering it in a way that we recall the excitement and risk-taking, the newness, the terrors and fears, the mistakes and triumphs. These thoughts should always be close to our minds when dealing with youth.

When we remember what it was like for us, we have more compassion, patience, understanding, and humility towards the younger generations. It helps us to avoid the temptation to tear down their confidence by quickly pointing out the "obvious" solution to every dilemma they face. Having years of experience in this life is definitely an advantage when it comes to solving life's problems but telling someone about our Maui experience doesn't get them one inch closer to putting their toes in the warm, foamy water.

"Let the fathers and mothers mark how they themselves were disposed at all ages; and by experience of their own infirmities help their children, and keep them from occasions."[132] (Tyndale, The Obediance of a Christian Man, 2000) Note that Tyndale here reminds parents that they will be able to help their children, not by their greater knowledge or wisdom, but by the experience of their infirmities. In other words, our memory of our weaknesses and mistakes, related to our children, will help them avoid occasions that they will benefit least from. This reinforces the notion that it is our humility and presenting ourselves to our children as the fallible creatures that we are that will make them feel better and more like they will be able to trust us.

We've Made That Mistake

A young man early in his career was learning a new tool that allowed him to query and make changes directly to a database. It was a powerful tool and also capable of wreaking much havoc on a customer's data if it was used improperly. At one point, he made

---

[132] Martin Tyndale, *The Obedience of a Christian Man*, Office of a Father and How He Should Rule.

a mistake that caused all of the receivable accounts for one customer to unreconcile. This meant that if the customer looked at their accounts receivable at that moment, it would appear as if none of their customers had made a payment on their account for months.

This was a bad mistake which, at the very least, would cause a lot of work for the customer of the man's employer. The young man was horrified once he realized what had happened. He searched on his own for a way to restore what he had done but could not quickly find a remedy. Knowing that the clock was ticking, and it would be a short time until the customer noticed the problem and called his employer, he had no choice but to go quickly to his boss and confess the error. He imagined all kinds of worst-case scenarios for how his boss would respond. But much to his surprise, when he informed his boss about the situation, his boss said, "We can fix that."

The young man was shocked. "Really?" he asked.

"Sure," said his boss, "it's not like *I've* never done something like that before."

Now his boss could have made an example of the situation. He could have pretended that he'd never made a similar mistake, but through his superior wisdom, he could fix up the mess. Instead, he chose to defuse the situation and confess his own fallibility and by so doing, made the day for his young mentee. The lesson had already been learned. The pain and agony of realizing what a foolish action had been taken had already been suffered. Now the wise boss was building the confidence in his employee and putting them somewhat on equal footing and earning a great deal of trust and respect.

This type of response to mistakes, remembering how things were for you early on, is a powerful way to strengthen a relationship. If we can mark how we ourselves were disposed at all ages, we will be reminded that we made some classic blunders as well. Stop pretending like you didn't do those kinds of things when you were a kid. The problem is you can't remember how you behaved. Either that or those times are recalled through rose-colored memories.

Kids Roll Their Eyes

As an adult, we do have greater experience than children. This is an unavoidable fact. Children, on the other hand, don't seem to grasp this fact well. This may be because, as a human, we usually seem to believe that the extent of our experience is equal to the greatest amount of experience anyone can have. This attitude starts at a young age and seems to be carried with us throughout our life. Because of this, people at all ages (but particularly in their teen years it seems) believe that they know it all.

It's not clear at what point in life we begin to realize that our accumulated experience isn't worth the space on the head of a pin. The author of Proverbs believed, "the fear of the Lord is the beginning of wisdom."[133] It's true that, as we begin to grasp our place in the universe, we see our wisdom and experience doesn't amount to much. But until that time, we tend to be know-it-alls and have little patience for those who are still learning.

The attitude of knowing everything develops at an early age. And our children show' their impatience with our ignorance in a myriad of ways, some of them quite childish and annoying. Having not mastered the social graces, they routinely say and do things that, if we're not careful, can trigger a vengeful response from us as their parents. But as a parent, the best response is to take a deep breath and remember that this too will pass. If we mark how we ourselves were disposed at that age, when we see a child's display of disgust with our answers, it will remind us of ourselves, and we are much more likely to respond pleasantly and with a chuckle. It's also good to remember that things that bother you and seem disrespectful in the heat of the moment, become cute and expected later in life.

In that story about the young girl who was made to stay at her great-Aunt Rose's house for the summer for reasons she did not understand, Dieter Uchtdorf observed that Eva was dead set

---

[133] Proverbs 9:10.

against her parents' decision. "But no amount of arguing or eye-rolling could change the decision."[134] (Uchtdorf D., A Summer with Great-Aunt Rose, 2015) Hearing that now brings a chuckle. No doubt it tipped her parents over at the time. Kids roll their eyes and sigh, it's what they do.

Don't Criticize Your Kids Interests

Unfortunately, when we are the subjects of our children's disrespect, it tends to anger us. A natural reaction to being angered by someone is to do or say something that angers them in return. Even though it's not a fair fight, adults will often criticize children, putting them down to make themselves feel better. This is easy to do. Children do and say many things that look ridiculous to parents when seen through eyes without understanding. As the adult in the room, we should be the ones building up our children, not tearing them down.

But often our children will take interest in things that we don't understand . . . such as Kim Kardashian or Anime. Because we don't understand them and haven't taken the time to learn with them in their space, we can become critical of their interests. This is a particularly harsh form of criticism because you are at once belittling them or making them feel stupid and putting down the thing they like. This is not good for relationship-building. It's a conversation killer. It puts up a barrier between you and them. It is one less thing you have in common.

During the Christmas season, a family met together one night to discuss with the teenagers social media and its potential downsides. In the discussion, the topic of Snapchat and the particular dangers and temptations that go with an app that lets a recipient glimpse a picture for a moment before being "deleted forever." The teenage daughter really liked Snapchat and used it all the time.

---

[134] Dieter Uchtdorf, from *A Summer with Great-Aunt Rose*, an address given at the General Conference of the Church of Jesus Christ of Latter-day Saints, November 2015.

At one point, the father, whose analytical mind could never understand the draw of the app, lost his cool and blurted out, "Snapchat is the dumbest app ever made." Coming from someone who designs apps for a living, he spoke from a position of some authority, which probably added to the sting. Right after the words came out, he felt the Spirit smite him because it hurt his daughter's feelings. A person who she looked up to and whose approval she seeks just dissed one of her favorite things.

How does it feel when someone you admire and respect (like your parents, even though you don't admit that you do) disparages something you really like? It hurts your feelings. You harden your heart toward them and care a little less about their opinions and what they say. You *must* care less what they say because what they say hurts your feelings if you care. Don't criticize the things your kids like even if you think they're stupid. Remember what it's like to be they're age. If it really is immature, they'll grow out of it. Promise.

One new couple were in the maternity ward of the hospital while the young mother was giving birth to her first son. Some of us cannot even imagine what the prospect of giving birth for the first time must be like to a young woman in her early twenties. Here they are faced with one of the hardest things they will ever do and, having had no training and little preparation, they must wonder if they can even do it. All kinds of fears must be faced.

During this birth, the baby paused for a couple hours when its head was just beginning to crown the cervix. Staying in this position caused a small deformation of his soft head as it pushed through to the air. Because it was pushing against the cervix, a little lump the shape of the hole protruded on the back of his head when he was out. He was a beautiful baby . . . but he had a big lump near the top of his head. The timid couple were horrified. Images of the Hunchback of Notre Dame or a circus sideshow spectacle taunted their fears. When they pointed out the misshapen head to the doctor a little later, the doctor assured them, "It will be fine and grow into shape. You don't see very many adults walking around with lumps on their head, do you?"

The same is true for kids and their misshapen habits and interests. They "grow into shape." It's part of being a kid, so don't worry so much about it.

Be Excited with Them

You will have plenty of opportunities to strengthen your relationship with the youth you're in charge of. At certain ages, they can hardly contain their excitement about things. One wise Cubmaster observed, "I love Pack meetings with these boys. No matter what I plan, no matter how lame and immature, they are totally into it and go for it with all their might." Get in there and be excited about the things they're excited about. If your teenage daughter can't wait for One Direction or Little Mix to come in concert, hang on the edge of your seat with her. Even if you think their music sucks.

Remember what it was like to be their age. Think about the bands you're probably embarrassed you liked. It's OK that you don't have the same taste in music now. Look for the good in her music. Have her play some songs for you. Make a connection. You don't have to prove your superior taste in music since you've had longer to refine your palette.

Watch for the things that make them excited. Figure out how you can spend time with them doing what they love. Of course, Road Runner and Bugs Bunny are different than Sponge Bob and Invader Zim, but your kids are going to find that their own kids roll their eyes at Sponge Bob soon enough. You need to show them how to not let their favorite things become a wedge, even if it's annoying.

The Teenage Disease

After years watching teens go through the near crash landing of youth only to later pull the plane nose up and come in for a safe touchdown, we are tempted to see the teen years as a congenital disease to which we should respond with compassion rather than a condition that requires constant correction. What would it be like to have any of the following symptoms, let alone all or most of them at once?

Teens Don't Think Logically.

Logic is the ability to arrive at a conclusion about a proposition based on the analysis of other propositions or premises. For example, safety belts in vehicles have been proven to prevent injury and death in accidents. Parents always check and admonish children to wear a seatbelt. Laws have been passed to make seatbelt wearing mandatory. Yet for some reason, many teens will get into a vehicle and choose not to put on a seat belt almost every time. Can you imagine how hard life would be if you couldn't make the connection between obvious, simple facts and an appropriate course of action when you're an adult?

Center of the Universe Syndrome

Not having a clue about how the world works, a teen, for example, could be petrified at the prospect of having their parent speak with their coach. They have no idea what adult relations are like and assume it must be like what occurs between them and their peers even though it is almost nothing like it.

"Please don't talk to my coach! It will be so awkward!"

"Son, adults talk to each other. We do it all the time. It will be fine."

What would it be like to have a constant concern about how you fit in? We usually stop worrying about this later in life, but for years our focus is on what group of people will accept us. The reality is that teens spend way more time worried about what others think of them than those people they are worried about spend thinking about them. It's what we call the Center of the Universe Syndrome. That is, we assume that since we are the center of our own universe that we are also the center of other people's universe as well. (This is a common malady that also afflicts people in business.) It's a fallacy. Other people do not spend anywhere near the amount of time thinking about us as we spend thinking about ourselves.

First, they are too busy worrying about their own universe to think much about ours. Not fully understanding social mores and rules, teens sometimes make a faux pas and then spend hours and days obsessing about it over and over, worrying non-stop about how they were perceived by their peers. Additionally, they assume others think about their mistake just as much as they do and are constantly evaluating, judging, and conspiring to knock them down a few notches in the pecking order.

In reality, any member of the audience of your awkward act most likely had one fleeting thought like "cringe," "dork," "rude," or "funny," and then never gave it another thought. What they observed was just one frame of a 24-hour movie they watched that day that contained many more important scenes that were much more relevant to themselves. "Note how other people's embarrassments mean little to you when you are an observer. That's how much your embarrassments mean to them. Nothing."[135] (Adams, 2019)

Every person carries with them a microcosm of the universe. Every person has people they love and hate. People they are trying to build relationships with and others that are fading from their life. They have health and sickness, prosperity and poverty, and thousands of daily, insignificant decisions to make and consequences to consider. They have mountains of problems pressing in on them just like you do. And unless you are one of the main actors in the play of their life, they probably rarely give you a second thought.

Most other people in this world are like props to us. We have the neighbor props, the teacher props, and the co-worker props. We have the cashier props at the grocery store and the props that give us the high sign on the freeway. In some sad cases we even have a father prop or a sister prop. In many ways they are like

---

[135] Scott Adams, *Loserthink: How Untrained Brains Are Ruining America*, Chapter 3, The Ego Problem, Audible Edition, 2019.

two-dimensional characters to us, cardboard cutouts that exist solely to aid our imagination in believing that our world is real. We rarely pause to consider the universe they carry with them or even that they have a universe that is just as deep and varied as our own. It's overwhelming to see people in a crowded mall and consider all the relationships, crises, aspirations, hurt, likes and dislikes each one carries with them and many if not all of which are completely different from our own. We could not even begin to try to get to know all these people and become attuned to their universe and really understand what they are going through. Because of this we tend to project onto them a portion of our own universe and assume that they think and worry about the same things as we do. And since the main thing that occupies our attention is ourselves, we are worried that we are the main thing that occupies the attention of others.

Some of us never get over this. We never come to realize that we are just a prop in the world of almost everyone we know. Rarely will they ever give us more than a second thought. If teens could understand this, their fears could cease about almost everything they worry about. It seems many of us never really grow out of this, but we do begin to understand socially acceptable boundaries and stay within the customary guardrails that keep us from driving off the cliffs of the devastatingly embarrassing behaviors we suffered as a teen. But can you imagine what it would be like if you were constantly burdened with this kind of worry? Terrifying.

Anticipating Consequences

Teens fail to anticipate the consequences of their choices. It is a biological and physiological fact that our brains are not fully developed by the time we reach our teen years. "Brain studies show the frontal lobe – which is responsible for decision-making, impulse control, sensation-seeking, emotional responses and consequential thinking – does not finish developing until our early-to-mid 20s."¹³⁶ (McCue, 2020) This is probably why we have our offspring live at home for so much longer than any other species on earth. Decision-making and controlling impulses are two coveted skills in the professional, adult world. You'll for sure want to have a handle on sensation-seeking and your emotional responses before you venture too far away from home. Consequential thinking is the product of a mature frontal lobe which occurs in your early to mid-20s. In other words, the ability to fully comprehend the consequences for your behavior doesn't really take root until you are a young adult and that's assuming your brain growth wasn't stunted by some type of trauma.

It's a witch's brew of hormones and stimuli that marinate the maturing teenage brain. If "teenageism" is not a disease, it is at best a disadvantage. We cannot view teenagers as adults with respect to our expectations of them even though their bodies may suggest otherwise. Physically, they may be at their peak, as we often note the alarmingly young age at which some young women develop or at which Olympic gold medalists achieve their awards. But mentally and emotionally, they should be viewed with patience and compassion as they muddle their way through some treacherous years. It takes great patience, but they'll get through.

Living Carefully

One important theme you can stress with those in your care is that it is important to live carefully, not carelessly. Who doesn't want to live a carefree life? But that's just not realistic. Living carefully mean living deliberately. It means slowing down and thinking through your actions and their consequences. With so much going on in the world and so many distractions, it is easy to lose focus. When you stop paying close attention, life has a way of loading on the inconveniences.

A young man, barely out of high school, decided to leave the comforts of home and go to work in a big city in China for a

---

[136] James McCue, *A Parent's Guide to Why Teens Make Bad Decisions*, "The Conversation" website, accessed January 19, 2020.

semester. He was both encouraged and warned by his supportive parents. They built up his confidence in his ability to do hard things and at the same time warned of the difficulties of living in a foreign country. It won't be like it is at home. There will be a lot more crime and people who don't care.

During his first week in Suzhou, just outside Shanghai, he left his debit card in an ATM machine. This was not a great surprise as he had never really needed to use an ATM machine back home and was not used to handling and caring for a debit card. With the double fear that he had no way of buying food and that someone could be draining his bank account, he texted his parents in somewhat of a panic.

"My first thought," his father reported, "was, 'That didn't take long.' My second thought was, "Good. We've all made mistakes like this and survived." His father remembered that he had warned his son about pickpockets and the need to watch his stuff carefully. Rather than taking the opportunity to say, "See? I told you," the young man's father went to work on helping him solve the problem.

These types of experiences are a real drag when you're going through them. You feel stupid. You want to get a replay. You think about all the things you shoulda, coulda, woulda done differently, but none of those changes the reality. We all have them, youth and adults alike. It doesn't take many of these experiences to get your attention. We quickly learn to be much more careful in the way we do things. And at the end of it, we are much better off. In the meantime, parents can recognize that these things happen and can be helpful and supportive and take the opportunity to build confidence rather than erode it. Careful living is a good lifestyle habit.

Letting Them Fail . . . Safely

As our youth are learning to live carefully, we will find opportunities where we can help them . . . by letting them fail. Failure is a great teacher. But the proper mindset is that we only fail when we give up. There is nothing wrong with multiple attempts. Failures are a learning experience. We find out about things that *don't* work and if we try something different, we will eventually succeed.

A long-time associate of Thomas Edison, named Walter S. Mallory, visited Edison in his laboratory where he and his researchers had been working on the development of a nickel-iron battery for more than five months.[137] (Quote Investigator, 2020) In a biography published in 1910 called "Edison: His Life and Inventions," Mallory relates the anecdote as follows:

"I found him at a bench about three feet wide and twelve to fifteen feet long, on which there were hundreds of little test cells that had been made up by his corps of chemists and experimenters. He was seated at this bench testing, figuring, and planning. I then learned that he had thus made over nine thousand experiments in trying to devise this new type of storage battery but had not produced a single thing that promised to solve the question. In view of this immense amount of thought and labor, my sympathy got the better of my judgment, and I said: 'Isn't it a shame that with the tremendous amount of work you have done you haven't been able to get any results?' Edison turned on me like a flash, and with a smile replied: 'Results! Why, man, I have gotten a lot of results! I know several thousand things that won't work.'"[138] (Dyer, 1910)

Leaders and mentors of youth need to allow for the accelerated learning that can come to youth through their attempts and failures. When kids want to do things on their own, we should always let them as long as no one gets hurt. A perfect example of letting kids learn occurred on a Handcart Trek sponsored by the Church of Jesus Christ of Latter-day Saints.

On a handcart trek, hundreds of teenage members and friends of the Church dress up like pioneers and pull handcarts fashioned

---

[137] Quote Investigator, "I Have Gotten a Lot of Results! I Know Several Thousand Things That Won't Work," retrieved January 20, 2020.
[138] 1910, Edison: His Life and Inventions by Frank Lewis Dyer and Thomas Commerford Martin, Volume 2 of 2, Chapter 24: Edison's Method in Inventing, Quote Page 615 and 616, Harper & Brothers, New York.

after those used to cross the Great Plains in the latter part of the 19th century. They load their food and supplies on the handcarts and spend several days pulling them through the desert or mountains in a re-enactment of the plains crossing. The large group of youth are divided into "families" of 8-10 teens with two energetic adults acting as the "Ma and Pa." This is a great opportunity for the youth to face some challenges in a carefully controlled environment.

On one such trek, a 16-year-old in one of the families rose up to take on some leadership responsibilities. After a couple days of watching "Pa" tie down the provisions on the handcart, he felt confident that he could do it. At first the "Pa" was hesitant, knowing about the roughness of the trail and how secure everything needed to be. But then he thought, "What's the worst thing that could happen? A few things could tumble off into the dirt and sagebrush." He also thought about the boost to this young man's confidence if he was able to properly secure the load, so he let him try.

As the young man made several loops around the cart with the long rope, the "Pa" could see it wouldn't work. He debated whether to step in and correct it, but since the teenager seemed confident and wasn't asking for help, he decided to let it go and see what happens.

Less than an hour into the trail up Rocky Ridge in Wyoming, the cart ran over some man-sized boulders. The constant jarring motion had wiggled things around, and the rope was now loose. Tipping the cart over the big boulders was all it could take. The family's two five-gallon water coolers dumped out on the hot dusty trail. That water supply was supposed to last them the rest of the day. Leaders from other handcart families came running over to help get everything back together. The "Pa" that had let the young man take the lead stood by as other adults jumped in and re-secured (or should we say "rescued?") the load. No one asked who it was that tied down the load and the "Pa" didn't volunteer that information. The "Pa" let the other adults assume it was him that didn't know how to tie a good knot and suffered a little embarrassment. Within minutes, other families contributed some of their water rations, the load was tied down tight, and the young leader stood on the side looking somewhat dejected about his failure. In truth, the fact that it was the young man's "failure" was only known to him and the "Pa." No one else in the family had taken enough interest in securing the load that morning to even know (or care) who tied it down.

Was that the right thing for the "Pa" to do, to let the young man fail like that? He knew the way the load was secured wouldn't survive the terrain. Did that experience build up the young man or bruise him? It depends on the young man. This one was a noticeably confident and up and coming leader and based on his comments at the end of the trek, we think it was good to let him fail. He said he appreciated the opportunity to make the attempt. It didn't turn out the way he hoped, but he definitely learned from it, he said. Nothing bad came out of that and it was a chance for him to grow and learn.

Letting those we love fail safely is important for their growth. It requires that they be taught that failing is not the end and it doesn't mean they are a failure. It's good to let them see our failures and we can show them how we learned and overcame. Life is full of setbacks, and it's only when we quit trying that we truly fail.

Why Don't They Like Church?

Many faithful parents have spent hours in church agonizing and wondering why their children don't seem at all interested in church. How could something that is so important and meaningful to us seem so useless and trivial to them. We worry and fear. Haven't I set a good example? If they don't have the guidance of the church in their lives, what types of immoralities and sadness will they have to suffer through? What if they end up going away from the church as an adult?

It may be good to be reminded that a Christian church service doesn't really speak to people who don't feel a need to be reconciled to God. For those who feel that their life is fine the way it is, the Gospel doesn't do much for them. And perhaps our children fit this profile. Being young, believing, and innocent, not having strayed much from the right path, they may think that all the talk of repentance and faith is for others who need it. For those without grievous sin that has wrenched their heart from God, they don't feel like a stranger to God.

For those who feel sadness in their life or feel like they left God, or they miss Him, or they've done things that they know aren't right with God, then is the time that the Gospel and the church is meaningful to them, and it will help them become reconciled to God. When there is a breach in your life that needs to be mended, then the Balm of Gilead is desired. When we feel estranged from Him, we desire to be brought back into His presence. But for those who have barely left it, the need may just not be there yet.

This is not to say that we shouldn't worry if our children show no interest in church. But we should understand that we are giving them tools they will need later in life. Church for young people is a theoretical discipline. They hear weekly about what they should do "if they ever" fall into transgression or experience deep sorrow. But at their age, it must seem that it's too far in the future to worry about. Continue teaching as if they were engaged. If there's anything we should know about children it would be that they are always listening, even when they act like they're not. The proof of that is how they all seem to pick up on conversations you don't want them to hear.

10 Years of Perspective

It's amazing how much perspective a decade can bring. One family relates the horrifying story of their oldest son being arrested. As a young teen, he made a trip to the local grocery store with some friends. Without thinking too much about it, he grabbed a tube of lip balm from the shelf and slipped it into his pocket. After the store detective followed him around the store, he headed for the exit. When the detective determined there was no intention to pay for the $0.59 Chapstick, he stopped the young man and took him to the store office. From there, parents and police were called.

With him being the oldest, his parents had never experienced anything like this before. This was a new level of embarrassment and humiliation. Where did he get the idea that this behavior was OK? Have we not taught him right from wrong? Oh, woe is us. While one parent had never dreamed of stealing, the other was reminded of their past and some of the crazy things they did at that age. (We will leave it to the reader to decide whether it was the mother of father.) The store decided to make an example of their son and he ended up in court and performing public service. For his parents, it was the low point in their life of parenting thus far.

No more than 10 years later, the extended family got together and was reminiscing about the hardships of parenting and the topic of the arrest came up. By this time, the event was more of a battle scar for the parents than a poignant memory. Everyone in the family had a good laugh about it. No feelings were hurt, the son by this time was a contributing member of society, and all was forgotten.

Unfortunately, in the heat of the moment, it's hard to maintain the 10-year perspective. But if we could, life would be much easier. We would know in the moment that everything is going to work out and be OK and we might be a bit less harsh in our words and discipline.

Living Vicariously

The other aspect to this story is what the parents went through. We all experience anxiety over our kids when they appear to be underperforming. We intervene in their lives and do everything we can to convince them if they would apply themselves more fully, then they could be more like us. It's natural to long for the praise of teachers and others outside the home about our kids.

It's almost as if we somehow take credit for their performance or feel honored vicariously. When they go amiss from our expectations, we take it as defiance.

We need to ask ourselves a question and be 100% honest with ourselves when we answer: How much of our anxiety over the performance of our children is us worrying about other people's perception of us as a failed parent? Do we feel just as anxious when we see the children of other parents underperforming? Of course not. And in a sense, it is sort of a relief to us. We fear that others will think we didn't teach our children or spend enough time with them. We are worried that they will think we don't teach them the value of good performance. We are concerned they will think that we don't care about our children.

These types of thoughts and feelings are natural, but they are really more about us than they are about our children's performance. Children come pre-packaged with talents and interests. And while we can influence them in some ways, much of their performance and deliverables have nothing to do with us.

One young father was a police officer and an ex-Marine. He was athletic and a hunter. He surfed, skateboarded, and lifted weights. On a bow hunt, he took down an elk, dragged it home, cleaned it, made chili, and had the head mounted over his fireplace. A true outdoorsman, he was the definition of a man's man. Naturally, he was asked to be a Scoutmaster when his oldest son was nearing his teenage years.

Not too far into his Scouting career it became quickly and painfully obvious that his oldest son was not going to follow in his footsteps. He was not athletic, did not particularly care for camping, and took little interest in hunting or other manly activities. This was the source of much frustration and bewilderment for his father. It didn't take long for the boy's parents to realize that their son was a sort of genius. Amazing at math and science, he loved to read, and required little direction when it came to getting straight A's. Before long he was well on his way to a great career in computer science.

This example of the stark contrast between father and son is interesting. No matter how much this father envisioned all of the outdoor adventures he would be taking with his firstborn son, in the end, he had little influence on the direction of his son's life in those areas. This illustrates the principle that our children are their own people and while we can teach them correct principles, they will ultimately end up governing themselves and we need not suffer the anxiety of the underperformance in the areas that we think they should perform in. The reverse of this principle is also true. That is, many times we have truly little influence over their successes, so we can stop taking credit for them and instead place the praise where it belongs: on our children.

Church Fireworks

Earlier we related the story of the young man the set off the firecracker in the church. He was not disciplined at all by the church leader. Perhaps that wise leader could remember what it was like to be a boy full of adventure and mischief.

Why did the leader forgo punishing the young man? Did he not get the boy's parents involved? After all, it was an extremely dangerous thing he did. Someone could have gotten hurt. Something could have caught on fire. He knew right from wrong. He chose the wrong anyway. Isn't the church leader teaching him there are no consequences for his actions?

The answer is that life meets out consequences in its own due time. This young man had suffered because of his fear of getting caught, his embarrassment of doing something stupid. He already judged himself unworthy of partaking of the sacrament. His leader found no need to further the consequences. He merely needed to show the young man the path to repentance, the path to joy. As parents, we rarely need to mete out consequences for our children's actions. We want to highlight some of the potential consequences so that when they occur the child can make the connection between his actions and the consequences.

Over a lifetime, we have rarely seen parent-defined consequences have a positive effect. Fear of punishment never deterred us in our youth from making wrong choices. If anything, the fear added to the exhilaration of disobedience. It's much more important that we lovingly point out the connections and let "life" or "karma" or "opposition" have its full sway, and then be there with the balm of comfort when the consequences become difficult.

At the same time, it is not wise for a parent to stand between their child and the consequences. Whether we teach them that the bad thing is not their fault, or we do their dealings with other adults for them, removing the consequences is as hurtful as inventing consequences for them. Let us remember what it was like to be their age and be there to help them through.

Safe Places

The idea of a "safe place" is not new, though in the first couple decades of the 21st century they have been created and ridiculed by opposing groups of people. A safe place is somewhere a person can go to avoid uncomfortable interactions with others. On a college campus, this might be a place where students with a progressive mind-set might be free from having to interact with and be confronted by ideas that don't agree with theirs.

In a home, it might just be a child's bedroom, the living room, or a tree house. We all like to draw a line around a space that we call our own. We arrange everything in it to our liking and impute meaning and memories to the things we choose to keep around us. In our safe space, we are in charge and at peace. We don't tolerate others coming in changing the way we have things set, whether it's the lighting or the TV volume. These places seem to be important to our well-being and we look forward to retreating to them. One father reported that his safe place was the family room. It was his go to place for unwinding after work and while everyone was welcome to join him there, he noticed that his children didn't share his desire to be together with him. Most of us feel comfortable inviting others into our safe place. And inasmuch as they are extensions of ourselves, we welcome the visit and feel like we have the home field advantage.

Our children create safe places of their own and they increase in importance as they grow older until they finally move out and work to make a home of their own. These places are out of the way of traffic and commands. Parents and siblings make infrequent intrusions. Messy or tidy, our children seem to have them organized the way they want them.

Perhaps these places are created for the same reason the safe places on college campuses are created: to protect their occupants from uncomfortable interactions with others. Children learn soon enough that hanging out in their parents view leads to undesired consequences. Statements like, "How long are you going to just sit there and watch TV? Get outside and play;" or "Turn off that video game and start working on homework!" quickly teach our children that if they want peace, they will have to stay out of the war zone.

Unfortunately, as parents we tend to drive our kids into their safe places and then we only go to visit them there when we need them to do something. But if we really want to get to know them, we will have to spend some time in there with them, on their home field. Entering the safe zone of our child may feel like an intrusion to us, but to them our visit is probably welcome.

Spending time in the safe zone of others may not be that comfortable to us. We look around and decide exactly how we would do things differently, but it's better off not vocalizing that if we want to be welcome in the long term. We may see that things are not as organized or as clean as we would prefer. We may not like the artwork, music, or smell, but staying put and getting to know the person in charge is a great way to build relationships. We have seen that children and youth are much more likely to open up about their feelings if you go into their place with them. If you can suspend judgement of their place and what they say while you're there, much as one of their friends might, you will find it easier to reach them and have a conversation. It will also build trust. Wouldn't it be nice if we spent so much time in our kids' safe place, that they had to ask us to go outside and play?

Sometimes Just Listen

The goal of entering our child's safe place is to build our relationship with them. When we go onto their turf, so to speak, it's OK to treat them a little differently than you do when you're having to be the parent. Let this time on their ground be a time when you focus on being their friend. Our best friends are there for us. They spend time with us and make spending time with us important to them. They don't "fit us in" on the way to another activity. They listen to us and don't try to solve all (or any) of our problems. They try to feel what we're feeling, and they make us feel good about ourselves by building us up instead of tearing us down. They don't boss us around and they don't think they're in charge of us. They view us as their equals. They seek out and value our opinions and advice. When we share our secrets with them, they don't shout them from the rooftops. In fact, they keep our confidences to themselves.

Yes, parents need to tell their children what to do. But they also need to have a lot of interactions with them when they're not telling them what to do. All those interactions when we're not telling them what to do, is how we build up trust with them. Then on those occasions when we do need to tell them what to do, they won't feel like we're constantly getting down on them for not doing what they should.

If we spend most of our interactions with our children telling them what to do, they probably won't want to come talk to us at other times when they should be talking to us. They rightfully think that every time that they talk to us, we tell them what they should do. As we know, people like to have friends listen to them and just hear their problems and empathize with them rather than solving their problems or telling them what to do.

Conclusion

Don't let yourself get so old and crusty that you can't remember what it was like being young. People like that suck the fun out of life as they pretend they have all the answers and never made the mistakes we make. Remembering what it was like to be a kid means letting them know we hit pitfalls and perhaps they might benefit from hearing about it. Doing so will remind us that we once thought we knew much more than we do now, and our ignorant arrogance lent itself to petulant displays of disgust and impatience with the meaningless dictates of our parents.

Make every effort to enjoy your kids' interests. Be excited with them. Remembering some of the dumb things you were into when in your early years helps to slow down your rush to judgement on the things they like. Teenagism, if not a disease, is at best a disadvantage. Show patience, compassion, and empathy as their budding brain struggles toward full bloom. In the meantime, remind them to live carefully and think through the situations they are faced with. There are plenty of opportunities for young people to learn, and we can provide environments where they can fail safely.

While they may not see a need for some of your cherished religious traditions now, don't lose hope. Things may be tough now, but it's amazing the difference in perspective only ten years will make. There's no huge need to meet out consequences for our kids' dumb mistakes. Life has a way of making sure the consequences are met. To better reach your children and help them through, we need to connect with them in their safe places. We don't have to have an answer for all of the problems they face. Sometimes it's better if we just listen and build trust. Remembering what it was like to be a kid is one of the keys to being a happier parent.

7

SERVICE IN THE FAMILY FIRST

When one prophet quotes the testimony of another prophet, we can be sure that the latter's words were important for our day. When that testimony turns out to be the dying wish of an apostle, we should refocus our attention on the message. This happened in 2015 when Tom Perry gave a regular talk in General Conference and shortly thereafter, we were surprised to learn that it was his last.

So that the importance of his parting witness would not be overlooked, his theme was picked up again by David Bednar six months later. What was the dying message of an apostle that was so important that it was quoted verbatim by another?

"Let me close by bearing witness (and my nine decades on this earth fully qualify me to say this) that the older I get, the more I realize that family is the center of life and is the key to eternal happiness. I give thanks for my wife, for my children, for my grandchildren and my great-grandchildren, and . . . for extended family who make my own life so rich and, yes, even eternal. Of this eternal truth I bear my strongest and most sacred witness."[139] (Bednar, 2015)

There should be no doubt in our minds that family is the key to happiness. This was Perry's "powerful lesson of a lifetime."[140] (Bednar, 2015) To strengthen the family and increase the opportunity we have of achieving that happiness, this chapter will highlight the importance of putting family first when it comes time to give of ourselves in service.

Over the years as we listen to the counsel of our ministers, we begin to understand how important it is to be engaged in acts of service. The Lord has underscored this idea in modern revelation saying we "should be anxiously engaged in a good cause."[141] In our zeal to "bring to pass much righteousness"[142], we may fail to understand what true service is. It is tempting to think of "service" as something you can plan to do. It is an activity you can schedule into your calendar, leave off your normal routine, accomplish it and then return to your regularly scheduled programming. This idea is bolstered by the idea of "service opportunities" we are confronted with at church. These "opportunities" come with a date, time, and duration like any good calendar event.

True service is not an activity, it is a lifestyle. It is not a calendar event; it is an attitude. It is not something you need to leave your normal routine to do; true service is your normal routine. One may fairly ask, How can I participate in service if I never leave my normal routine? And the answer is that unless your immediate family is so buttoned up that they regularly leave their normal routine to help others together, as a family, then you probably have plenty of opportunities for service without ever leaving your normal routine. "Service," clarified Marion Romney, "is not something we endure on this earth so we can earn the right to

---

[139] Tom Perry as quoted by David Bednar in *Chosen to Bear Testimony of My Name*, an address given at the General Conference of the Church of Jesus Christ of Latter-day Saints, October 2015.
[140] Ibid.
[141] Doctrine & Covenants, 58:27.
[142] Ibid.

live in the celestial kingdom. Service is the very fiber of which an exalted life in the celestial kingdom is made."[143] (Romney, 2009)

Celestial Service

"Opportunities to go about doing good and to serve others are limitless. We can find them in our communities, in our wards and branches, and certainly in our homes."[144] (Uchtdorf D. F., The Greatest Among You, 2017) Certainly in our homes. The teachings of Jesus Christ and his disciples show that the main place we serve is in our home. The main people we serve are the people in our immediate family. We serve our spouse, we serve our children, and, if we're celestial, we serve our parents. Parental service may the pinnacle of a Christ-like life. Of course, we serve our spouse. We probably love them more than anything in the world. Serving our children is natural. They are our flesh and blood, and we have an affinity toward them and a maternal instinct to take care of them. But many of us have a blind spot toward our parents. We will never be able to pay them back for all they have done for us, so perhaps we feel like it's not worth trying. If people served their parents more, there wouldn't be such a high demand for elderly care facilities. Those souls who put aside self and do things for their parents deserve special recognition for their love and selfless giving.

A great example of what this celestial service look like was shared by Bonnie Oscarson. During a visit with her grandson Ethan's family one summer, she "observed how Ethan treats his brother and sisters with patience, love, and kindness and is helpful to his parents." Rare indeed is the 17-year-old with this kind of love for members of his family. It is noble, but it doesn't have to be dramatic.

---

[143] Marion Romney, "The Celestial Nature of Self-Reliance," *Ensign*, Mar. 2009, p 65.

[144] Dieter Uchtdorf, *The Greatest Among You*, an address given at the General Conference of the Church of Jesus Christ of Latter-day Saints, April 2017.

Family Love

Fostering love inside the family is the purpose of life here on earth. When we venture out on our own in this cold world, we learn that no one else in the world really cares about us except our parents. This is true forever until and if we are lucky enough to find a spouse who loves us at least as much.

Unfortunately, many cultures have lost sight of the importance of building loving family relationships. We put worldly pursuits and self-satisfaction as a higher priority. But if a soul is not loved in a family, when will she be loved? When will it learn of the joy, peace, security, and power that comes from being loved, from being the most important person to someone?

We are taught in the Bible that the two greatest commandments are to love God and to love our neighbor.[145] In fact, we are to love our neighbors as Christ himself has loved us.[146] And who are our neighbors if they are not the people in our own household? The roots of the word 'neighbor' implies "near inhabitant." Who is an inhabitant more near than your own family?

"Love is the very essence of the gospel, the noblest attribute of the human soul," Thomas Monson says. "Love is the remedy for ailing families, ill communities, and sick nations. Love is a smile, a wave, a kind comment, and a compliment. Love is sacrifice, service, and selflessness. Husbands, love your wives. Treat them with dignity and appreciation. Sisters, love your husbands. Treat them with honor and encouragement. Parents, love your children. Pray for them, teach them, and testify to them. Children, love your parents. Show them respect, gratitude, and obedience."[147] (Monson, As I Have Loved You, 2017)

Notice how in all his examples of love, Monson, is focused 100 percent on members of the family loving each other. It's not that we shouldn't also love our neighbor down the street as much

---

[145] Matthew 22:38-40.
[146] John 13:34-35.
[147] Thomas Monson, "As I Have Loved You," *Ensign*, p 3.

as it is possible, but we will probably never really be able to love them in the way that is being suggested by the prophet. We love those most whom we sacrifice for. We sacrifice most for the members of our own family, not for friends and acquaintances, let alone strangers. Our children and siblings. We don't sacrifice for our family because we love them. We love them because we sacrifice for them. We give up our space to them. We give up our time for them. We give up our money, peace, food, clothes, and shelter for them.

The idea that the main target of our service should be those in our immediate families is supported by the conversation between Peter and Christ about forgiveness. "Then came Peter to him, and said, Lord, how oft shall my brother sin against me, and I forgive him? till seven times? Jesus saith unto him, I say not unto thee, Until seven times: but, Until seventy times seven."[148]

The word that was translated as "brother" in the original Greek is *'adelphos*, the root *delphos* meaning 'womb'. Literally, this word is used to mean a person from the same womb. A flesh and blood brother or sister. While it is generally accepted that the word "brother" in this context is used to mean a member of the same religious community, it is interesting that this word was used by the original Greek authors. It is used elsewhere in the New Testament in contexts that signify references to immediately family members, such as in Luke 8:19 and John 2:12. Think of the power this idea brings to Peter's question to understand that perhaps he was referring to his literal brother, Andrew, who kept sinning against him when he was wondering how forgiving he should be.

David Bednar taught, "Selflessly serving others counteracts the self-centered and selfish tendencies of the natural man. *We grow to love those whom we serve.* And because serving others is serving God, we grow to love Him and our brothers and sisters more deeply."[149] (Bednar, If Ye Had Known Me, 2016)

---

[148] Matthew 18:21-22.
[149] David Bednar, *If Ye Had Known Me*, an address given at the General Conference of the Church of Jesus Christ of Latter-day Saints, October 2016, emphasis added.

The truth that we love those whom we serve partially explains why the love of mothers for their children is so much closer to the love of God. A mother, by day one of their child's life, has very nearly laid down her own life for her child through childbirth. A father must learn to make sacrifices that great and hence must try harder.

Living in such proximity to others as we do in families has a way of trying your patience. You are regularly left with the option of bursting out in rage or choosing to quickly forgive and let offenses roll off. There will never be a better situation for us to learn to love and serve others than in the family. Therefore, we should not think of service as a project on our calendar or something that we take time out of our normal routine to do. True service is our normal routine.

Serving in the Family

Many of our greatest spiritual leaders have recognized that loving and serving is about the neighbors under our own roof. And although we don't seem to hear them when they repeat it often, we find throughout their teachings the idea that serving in our family is most important. Rosemary Wixom teaches that we serve others because of our divine nature. "The divine nature within us ignites our desire to reach out to others and prompts us to act. Heavenly Father and Jesus Christ can help us find the strength to do so. Could the Lord be asking us, "What can be done for this daughter, this brother, this father, or this friend?"[150] (Wixom, 2015)

Two things catch our attention in this statement. The first is that even though we enjoy a divine nature, we still rely on divine help to find the strength to serve others. This tells us that it is no easy task to just try to overlook the unmet expectations we have of others, forgive them, love them, and serve them. The second is that the Lord is asking us to serve those in our family. As a

---

[150] Rosemary Wixom, *Discovering the Divinity Within*, an address given at the General Conference of the Church of Jesus Christ of Latter-day Saints, October 2015.

mother, what can be done for my daughter? As a sister, what can be done for my brother? As a son, what can I do for my father? Only *after* considering those in our own family does Wixom wonder what can be done for a friend.

A church leader was inspired to put together a service project for refugees in Eastern Europe. She worked with many women in her area to make quilts for those suffering the cold of the winters during the 1990s. She was not content to just make quilts for the strangers, but also enlisted her daughter to drive with her in a truck filled with the quilts across Europe from London to Kosovo to deliver them. "On her journey home she received an unmistakable spiritual impression that sank deep into her heart. The impression was this: "What you have done is a very good thing. Now go home, walk across the street, and serve your neighbor!"[151] (Burton, 2016)

This important impression received by a very spiritual woman was a prompting to focus her service more at home. This is not to say that we should not strive to help the suffering around the world, but it is a call to not look past those in need close by only so that we can perform service as a "project" that can be scheduled into our calendar and brush our hands off when we're done. Burton goes on to explain how this woman took to heart the impression and later found she could help people without leaving the walls of her home. There will always be plenty of service to do in your own family. Especially when we define service as the normal sacrifice, we make for those closest to us. Many of us need to simply go home, work within its walls and serve our family. And we should feel just as good about doing that as we would about driving a truckload of quilts across Europe.

Shared DNA, Shared Burdens

We are advocating focusing our service efforts on those closest

---

[151] Linda Burton, *I Was a Stranger*, an address given at the General Conference of the Church of Jesus Christ of Latter-day Saints, April 2016.

to us rather than on strangers. The irony is that many times we find that the members of our own family are strangers to us. Even though we are siblings and grow up with many of the same experiences, normal familial friction, a difference in age, gender, talents and abilities lead us to view life through different lenses. This assertion is regularly borne out by the observation that many siblings are as different from each other as night and day. We all have different tastes and preferences, politics and perspectives. All of these differences must be overcome if we are to love and serve each other.

Sometimes our differences are so extreme that we fail to even understand one another's point of view. We lose empathy for each other and may even harden our hearts toward each other. We cannot let this happen. "No matter what our particular family situation is," Russell Ballard explained, "it is critical that we understand the unique circumstances of each family member. Though we may share DNA, there may be situations and circumstances among us that may make us vastly different from each other and which may require the compassionate collaboration of the family council."[152] (Ballard, 2016)

In his call for family unity, Ballard wisely recognizes how extreme the differences can be between even those that share the same DNA. In a sense we *are* strangers. "For example," Ballard continues, "all the talking and sharing and loving in the world may not solve a medical problem or an emotional challenge that one or more family members may be facing. At such times, the family council becomes a place of unity, loyalty, and loving support as outside help is enlisted in the search for solutions." (Ballard, 2016) No matter how much we love our adopted child, we cannot say that we fully understand what it is like for them to feel like they were abandoned by their birth parents. We may never fully understand the burdens of a sibling who struggles with same-sex attraction or even just low confidence. This is why we will always find plenty of opportunities to act as the Good

---

[152] M. Russell Ballard, *Family Councils*, an address given at the General Conference of the Church of Jesus Christ of Latter-day Saints, April 2016.

Samaritan without traveling the road to Jericho.

There is a need to love and understand the challenges of those who are nearby. As Thomas Monson noted, "I am confident there are within our sphere of influence those who are lonely, those who are ill, and those who feel discouraged. Ours is the opportunity to help them and to lift their spirits"[153] (Monson, Be An Example of Light, 2015) Who will we find that is more within our sphere of influence than the members of our own family? For many of us, there is no one outside our family within that sphere. Monson was focusing our attention where it belongs: on the home.

In truth, we should be making sure we are adequately meeting the needs of those in our sphere before we venture outside the home to look for service opportunities that may come with more recognition. What is a suffering family member to think of us and our faith if we are looking past their trials in an effort to fulfill a scheduled service opportunity for someone else? Would it be wrong for them to feel like they don't matter to us and wonder if our desire to serve comes with a desire to be "seen of men?"[154]

Simple Acts of Service

Perhaps one of the main things that keeps us from serving others is that we think that service will always "take time, intentional planning, and extra energy."[155] (Esplin, 2016) With the new mindset that service is what you do in your own home, it doesn't have to be this way. Many of the acts of service we can do are much simpler than that. "All of us can incorporate some service into our daily living. We live in a contentious world. We give service when we don't criticize, when we refuse to gossip, when we don't judge, when we smile, when we say thank you, and when

---

[153] Thomas Monson, *Be an Example and a Light*, an address given at the General Conference of the Church of Jesus Christ of Latter-day Saints, October 2015.
[154] See Matthew 6:5.
[155] Cheryl Esplin, *He Asks Us to Be His Hands*, an address given at the General Conference of the Church of Jesus Christ of Latter-day Saints, April 2016.

we are patient and kind."[156]

These are things we can and should do in our families, with our siblings, with our children. Saying "thank you" is giving service? Yes! Think how you feel when someone thanks you for your service. How do you feel when someone is patient with you or kind?

These "small" acts of service are not as small as we think. We need to be aware of the necessity of performing them within our family and then give ourselves credit for the efforts we make. These simple acts of service go a long way to healing the souls of those around us. "When we reach out in love and service even in the smallest ways," Esplin taught, "hearts are changed and softened as others feel the love of the Lord."[157] The importance of serving in our family was driven home by James Faust when he taught, "Serving others can begin at almost any age. . . It need not be on a grand scale, and it is noblest within the family."[158] (Faust, 2000)

Love Without Service Is Dead

One father showed to his family his love for them by cleaning up the kitchen after dinner every night. When the meal his wife so lovingly planned, shopped for, and prepared was finished, she and his children could go and relax while he willingly put things away, loaded the dishwasher, cleaned the pots and pans, and wiped down the counters and stove.

This routine had become expected behavior and to some it may have appeared that his children were taking it for granted. Others have raised the objection that he is spoiling his children. The ungrateful youth, they would say, should be put to work and help. But he defended his actions by saying this is a small way he can serve his family every day. It only takes 15-20 minutes, and 6

---

[156] Ibid
[157] Ibid
[158] James E. Faust, "*Womanhood: The Highest Place of Honor*," an address given at the General Conference of the Church of Jesus Christ of Latter-day Saints, April 2000.

people get to relax after dinner. He likes to quote Jose Alonso in his own defense: "Love without service is like faith without works; it's dead indeed." [159] (Alonso, 2017)

Sometimes parents serving children looks strange to others. But this kind of service is so good in the family that it is highly rewarded. We are reminded of the story of Mary Fielding Smith, the tough, faithful widow of Hyrum, who trekked across the plains in the 1840s. This story was related by her son in 1900:

"One spring when we opened our potato pits [my mother] had her boys get a load of the best potatoes, and she took them to the tithing office; potatoes were scarce that season. I was a little boy at the time and drove the team. When we drove up to the steps of the tithing office, ready to unload the potatoes, one of the clerks came out and said to my mother, 'Widow Smith, it's a shame that you should have to pay tithing.' … He chided my mother for paying her tithing, called her anything but wise or prudent; and said there were others who were strong and able to work that were supported from the tithing office. My mother turned upon him and said: 'William, you ought to be ashamed of yourself. Would you deny me a blessing? If I did not pay my tithing, I should expect the Lord to withhold His blessings from me.'"[160] (Oaks, Tithing, 1994)

In the same vein, this father feels indignant that someone would dare to try to deprive him of the blessings of love and healing that will come to his family for his small acts of service. We will be blessed for manifesting more love in our homes. It is about changing your perspective of the tasks you perform and rather than seeing them as a mundane burden, recognizing them for what they are: brilliant acts of service that demonstrate your love for your family.

---

[159] Jose Alonso, *Love One Another As He Has Loved Us,* an address given at the General Conference of the Church of Jesus Christ of Latter-day Saints, October 2017.

[160] Taken from *Tithing,* an address given by Dallin Oaks at the General Conference of the Church of Jesus Christ of Latter-day Saints, April 1994.

It's Not Unfair

Unfortunately, many of us have been conditioned to believe that service is something that is done outside the home. We wait until we are asked to perform service, or we have a "service opportunity" available to schedule onto our calendar. There are many who would never dream of telling their pastor they don't have time to help with a young women's campout, but when it comes to a family camping trip, things are somehow different.

One young father took his family on a camping trip to Bryce Canyon, Utah. He reported that he felt joy in cleaning up camp alone so his family could go and enjoy time by the campground pool. This young man had witnessed spiritual blessings from serving his own loved ones. Rather than thinking it was "unfair" that he did all the "work," he said he viewed it as an opportunity to serve God by serving his children.

We often think of service opportunities as being available only through our callings or assignments at church. But, this father reasoned, "Why should I treat my family any different than I would treat the young women leaders I am asked, or volunteer, to help on girls' camp? Is it because I feel like everyone in my family should have to do their "fair share" of the work? I wouldn't think of telling the youth leaders, 'I'm not setting up one more tent until you have set one up.'"

It's not "unfair" that this father took the lion's share of the work on the family outing. The opportunities to serve in the family are limitless and the blessings that are associated with this service are just as valuable as those blessings that come from serving outside the home, if not more so. "Happiness comes from unselfish service," Harold Lee explained. "And happy homes are only those where there is a daily striving to make sacrifices for each other's happiness."[161] (Williams, 1996)

---

[161] *The Teachings of Harold B. Lee*, ed. Clyde J. Williams (1996), 296.

LOVE AND FAMILY

The Most Important Work

To emphasize this idea that service in the family should always come first, and that it is more important than service outside the family, we need look no further than the teachings of a great prophet, Harold B. Lee. We should be quite familiar with the prophecy of Malachi given in the Old Testament. "Behold, I will send you Elijah the prophet before the coming of the great and dreadful day of the Lord: and he shall turn the heart of the fathers to the children, and the heart of the children to their fathers, lest I come and smite the earth with a curse."[162] This scripture has oft been associated with the need to perform family service for deceased ancestors. But President Lee declared a more significant application in the latter days.

"Today that scripture undoubtedly has a more significant meaning," Lee taught. "Unless the hearts of the children are turned to their parents and the hearts of the parents are turned to their children in this day, in mortality, the earth will be utterly wasted at His coming. There was never a time when so much was needed as today in the homes of the Latter-day Saints and the world generally."[163] (Williams, 1996)

The context of this statement shows that Lee was very much concerned with love inside the home and the need for family members to sacrifice and serve each other. Lee was well-known for preaching the need for this family service. He said, "I have frequently counseled, and I repeat it to you again, to all of you here: "The most important of the Lord's work you will ever do will be within the walls of your own homes." We must never forget that."[164] (Williams, 1996) We do well to take this quote literally and know that not only is the work in your family more important than your career or other worldly pursuits, it's also more important than your service outside the home. Service in

---

[162] Malachi 4:5-6.
[163] *The Teachings of Harold B. Lee*, ed. Clyde J. Williams (1996), 281.
[164] *The Teachings of Harold B. Lee*, 280, as quoted in *Teachings of the Presidents of the Church of Jesus Christ of Latter-day Saints: Harold B. Lee*.

the family comes first.

Happy at Home

Some church volunteers have missed the mark by focusing more time and energy on families other than their own at the expense of the strength of their own family. Those who desire to serve outside the home should first make sure that everything in their own home is in order. "First cast out the beam out of thine own eye; and then shalt thou see clearly to cast out the mote out of thy brother's eye," the Lord advised.[165] While we often receive this teaching in the context of judging others, it is also applicable to the principle of taking care of your own family first.

It is not always easy to see which family members need help. They often seek to hide their needs. And many times, when they do tell us about them, we believe they should be able to help themselves or we don't listen in a way to hear what they are saying. Some families seem solid and well put together. Many of those just seem that way, but in reality, they are not as strong as we would like to think. Other families really are put together. Members of the latter family type are great candidates for serving others outside the home.

Many of us put tremendous pressure on ourselves to do what the Lord asks us to do and when we think He has asked us to serve outside our family, we strive to do so at all costs. Perhaps we remember too clearly the Lord's teaching to those who hesitated in following him. In a story related by Luke and Matthew, several disciples did not put the Lord first. "[The Lord] said unto another [disciple], Follow me. But he said, Lord, suffer me first to go and bury my father. Jesus said unto him, Let the dead bury their dead: but go thou and preach the kingdom of God. And another also said, Lord, I will follow thee; but let me first go bid them farewell, which are at home at my house. And Jesus said unto him, No man, having put his hand to the plough,

---

[165] Matthew 7:5.

and looking back, is fit for the kingdom of God."[166]

It is easy to see how these teachings of Christ could be misconstrued to mean that family service does not come first. Sometimes when we read scriptures like this, we interpret them literally. Other times, when we take them in the context of all the other teachings of Christ and his servants, we realize they cannot possible be interpreted literally. As we have abundantly shown in this work, there is nothing more important than family love and service. And in case any might believe otherwise and confuse the priority, we have the testimony of Boyd Packer.

Packer was known throughout his career as an Apostle of Jesus Christ as a rather stern, no-nonsense individual. Toward the end of his life, some may say, he appeared to soften a little. In what we may believe was an instruction specifically to those who confused the importance of church programs and activities with what is really important in life and perhaps sought to put church work first, ahead of family, President Packer had this to say, "The ultimate end of all activity in the Church is that a man and his wife and their children might be happy at home, protected by the principles and laws of the gospel, sealed safely in the covenants of the everlasting priesthood."[167] (Packer, 2010)

Everything we do in church, all activity, is pursued so that a man and his wife and children might be happy at home. If this happiness is not present, then the point of the entire restoration of the church is not being realized. There is little point in leaving home to serve outside the family if we still have plenty of work to do within the walls of our own home.

In the Service of Your God

To take this idea a step further, let us take a moment to address those who perhaps feel guilty that they are not serving more outside the home. We occasionally hear stories of the families

---

[166] Luke 9:59-62.
[167] Boyd Packer, *The Power of the Priesthood*, an address given at the General Conference of the Church of Jesus Christ of Latter-day Saints, April 2010.

that "give up their Christmas" to go and serve in the soup kitchen. We see others around us devoting way more time to meeting needs of those outside their family. We may even see them meeting the needs of our family. And yet, try as we might, we are unable to do more than what it takes just to survive in our own family. This seems to be especially true for women who have a natural inclination to help everyone they see. And when they compare their offering to that of others, it appears to be meager indeed.

Church leaders are sensitive to this dilemma. Many have spoken to assuage our guilt. Rest assured that this feeling of guilt is unnecessary, unrealistic, and probably inspired by someone who wants to make us feel worse. In a touching sermon from 2010, Jeffrey Holland spent the first 10 minutes expressing gratitude for every conceivable service he'd seen rendered in the Church. But not forgetting those who do their part on the sidelines, he crowned his list by saying, "And to the near-perfect elderly sister who almost apologetically whispered recently, 'I have never been a leader of anything in the Church. I guess I've only been a helper,' I say, 'Dear sister, God bless you and all the 'helpers' in the kingdom.' Some of us who *are* leaders hope someday to have the standing before God that you have already attained."[168] (Holland, Because of Your Faith, 2010)

In her landmark 2016 talk on charity, Cheryl Esplin enlightens about the power of selfless service and cites multiple examples of people serving with Christlike love. Then she recognized, "some of you listening may feel stretched to capacity ministering to the needs of family members. Remember, in those routine and often mundane tasks, you are 'in the service of your God.'"[169] (Esplin, 2016)

This is an important reminder. When you are serving your family, you are serving God. This is the same quality of service as

---

[168] Jeffrey Holland, *Because of Your Faith*, an address given at the General Conference of the Church of Jesus Christ of Latter-day Saints, October 2010.
[169] Cheryl Esplin, *He Asks Us to Be His Hands*, an address given at the General Conference of the Church of Jesus Christ of Latter-day Saints, April 2016.

you would give anywhere else in kingdom. But instead of being a part-time job, service in the family is 24/7. When we learn to understand this and realize how much we are doing for God by striving to bless his children, our brothers and sisters, we should feel less guilt when we are doing all we can.

Less than two years later, Bonnie Oscarson noted the great accomplishments good people had made serving those who had suffered tremendously in an unusually long trend of natural disasters worldwide. But in the same address, she also warned, "What good does it do to save the world if we neglect the needs of those closest to us and those whom we love the most? How much value is there in fixing the world if the people around us are falling apart and we don't notice? Heavenly Father may have placed those who need us closest to us, knowing that we are best suited to meet their needs."[170] (Oscarson, 2017)

We can stop thinking that our call to serve others is always a call to serve outside the home. There are enough opportunities to serve each other in our own families. There is no need to feel guilt that your time, talent, and energy is consumed on those closest to you. You are focused on building the kingdom one family at a time. Often, there may not be enough time to serve anywhere else, at least during this phase of your life.

The Heart of the Plan

If the most important thing to learn and teach in the Church of Jesus Christ is our role in strengthening the family, then you can be sure that the family will be the center of the attack plan of the forces opposed to happiness. The family is at the heart of Heavenly Father's plan because of relationships. The most important thing in this earth life is the human relationship. No matter how much we accomplish in this life, when it comes time to die, if no one cares it is sad indeed. Even the most accomplished and famous people enjoy limelight for a short time

---

[170] Bonnie Oscarson, *The Needs Before Us*, an address given at the General Conference of the Church of Jesus Christ of Latter-day Saints, October 2017.

and then begin to fade from public view. As we approach our final years, many of our fans have passed away, others have forgotten about us, and the younger generations never knew us. It is at that time that one hope is to have people who care to help you through your final days and beyond.

It is in relationships that we learn to love and be loved. "It is not good for man to be alone."[171] The family is designed to force us into relationships so we can get some practice caring and loving. We are all part of Heavenly Father's family and mortality is our opportunity to form our own families and to assume the role of parents. It is within our families that we learn unconditional love, which can come to us and draw us close to God's love. It is within families that values are taught, and character is built. Father and mother are callings from which we will never be released, and there is no more important stewardship than the responsibility we have for God's spirit children who come into our families.

The opposing force wants to tear down families and destroy human intimacy and relationships. Loneliness is misery. Without a relationship, we have, no idea how to love or sacrifice. This is why we see the attacks against marriage. We are taught there is no need to marry, but if we must, we should delay it as long as possible. We are taught that women do not need men and children do not need fathers. We are taught that women are objects of lust and that any consenting group of people may have a sexual relationship, thus stripping away the emotion, sacrifice, and intimacy of humanity's most important relationship. We are taught that adults can enter into sexual relationships with children thus destroying the natural role of caregiver, nurturer, and role model. We are taught that marriage is not sacred, but that any two (or more) people can be married thus destroying the meaning of the word and weakening its purpose. We are taught that mothers should have a right to destroy the fruit of their womb. We are taught our elders should not waste healthcare resources or that it's OK to put them out of their misery near the end of

---

[171] See Genesis 2:18.

their lives.

All of these teachings have a specific purpose: wear down the bonds of family, estrange loved ones from their natural relationships, and destroy the nascent relationships in a family. For if the love of relationships can be destroyed and the family can be eliminated, souls will have no way to learn to love and be loved and the work of God frustrated.

"Let me say again," reiterated Russell Ballard, "that the family is the main target of evil's attack and must therefore be the main point of our protection and defense. As I said once before, when you stop and think about it from a diabolically tactical point of view, fighting the family makes sense to Satan. . . When evil wants to strike out and disrupt the essence of God's work, it attacks the family. It does so by attempting to disregard the law of chastity, to confuse gender, to desensitize violence, to make crude and blasphemous language the norm, and to make immoral and deviant behavior seem like the rule rather than the exception."[172] (Ballard, Let Our Voices Be Heard, 2003)

Everything in this work is describing the types and importance of things that happen within families. Some of us may be estranged from our families for a time, but within is a natural inclination to seek out the love, companionship, stability, and protection that can only come with a family.

The Church and the Family

The Church and the family have had a very symbiotic relationship throughout history. God uses the Church to teach His children and families are the fundamental unit of the church. Good parents want to teach their children the importance of caring for others and loving. We teach them not to "fight and quarrel one with another," but to be kind and treat them as we would be treated.[173] It helps to have the authority of God backing you up

---

[172] M. Russell Ballard, *Let Our Voices Be Heard*, an address given at the General Conference of the Church of Jesus Christ of Latter-day Saints, October 2003.
[173] Mosiah 4:14.

when you are teaching children how to live. At the same time, the Church needs families to accomplish its mission. Gospel teachings are transmitted primarily through the channel of the family. We live the gospel in our homes. We treat our family members as our "neighbor" and minister unto their needs.[174]

"We must remember," reminded Todd Christofferson, "that in the beginning, the Church was the family, and even today as separate institutions, the family and the Church serve and strengthen one another. Neither supplants the other, and certainly the Church, even at its best, cannot substitute for parents. The point of gospel teaching and priesthood ordinances administered by the Church is that families may qualify for eternal life."[175] (Christofferson D. T., Why the Church, 2015)

It is clear that the Church was the family in the beginning. We think that Heavenly Father's plan is to raise up righteous youth and send them out into the world to teach and baptize. In reality, that seems like the backup plan put in place because the original plan fell apart. The original plan is for the father and mother to be the spiritual stewards of the home. They had all the authority necessary to teach, baptize, and ordain their children. But because of lack of faith or shirking of responsibility, families broke down and parents were no longer qualified to administer the gospel in their homes. Thankfully, some people took it upon themselves to continue to transmit the gospel virtues to individuals and families seeking truth, love, and happiness so that all would not be lost.

"Beginning with Adam," Christofferson taught, "the gospel of Jesus Christ was preached, and the essential ordinances of salvation, such as baptism, were administered through a family-based priesthood order. As societies grew more complex than simply extended families, God also called other prophets, messengers, and teachers."[176] (Christofferson D. T., Why the Church, 2015)

---

[174] See Luke 10:29-37.
[175] D. Todd Christofferson, *Why the Church*, an address given at the General Conference of the Church of Jesus Christ of Latter-day Saints, October 2015.
[176] Ibid

Love at Home

Some reading this may bristle at the idealization of the family in these pages, having come from a broken home or an abusive situation, wondering if it is real. Does this type of family exist? Many have never felt the warmth and security spoken of in these pages and instead have suffered only abuse and hatred. Our heart aches for you.

Yet we signal that it is true and possible, but it may take many generations of correct thinking and behavior to overcome the entropy of the Fall that tends to tear away at the ideal family. We must first understand what is possible, we can then strive for the ideal. While we may go astray and be lost for a time, we can ever find our way back through the teachings of Jesus Christ and his apostles.

Listen to this poetic wisdom from a prophet and disciple of the Prince of Peace as he speaks about the importance of love in home and family: "I have since come to know that love is more than a paper heart. Love is of the very essence of life. It is the pot of gold at the end of the rainbow. Yet it is more than the end of the rainbow. Love is at the beginning also, and from it springs the beauty that arches across the sky on a stormy day. Love is the security for which children weep, the yearning of youth, the adhesive that binds marriage, and the lubricant that prevents devastating friction in the home; it is the peace of old age, the sunlight of hope shining through death. How rich are those who enjoy it in their associations with family, friends, church, and neighbors."[177] (Hinckley, 1984)

The beauty that arches across the sky on a stormy day. What a wonderful metaphor. The rainbow is the beauty that arches across the sky on a stormy day. The rainbow is love. A full rainbow is a circle. You must be above the ground to see that;

---

[177] Gordon B. Hinckley, "And the Greatest of These Is Love," *Ensign* March 1984, 3.

therefore, we normally only see a portion of it. The circle is eternal like love. As the storms swirl around us daily, love is there reminding us of hope. It gladdens the heart and is exhilarating and rare. Let that love be in our home and be the center of our family. Let that love be there for our children to be drawn to and encouraged by. Let its nature be eternal, without beginning and end, a constant in the lives of those around us.

Conclusion

This chapter highlights how important it is to serve in our families first. Serving outside the home is important and valuable, but not at the cost of our own family strength. Serving in the family seems to be more of a challenge because we tend to overlook the needs of those closest to us. But for those who serve in the family, they learn what charity is and could even learn one of the highest forms of service, that of a child for a parent.

We are so conditioned that our neighbor is a stranger like the person who received the anonymous help of the Good Samaritan, we forget that neighbor literally means "near inhabitant." We have seen how just because we are under the same roof, we do not always see or understand the challenges those closest to us are facing. Though we share the same DNA, our diverse life experiences can have an alienating effect.

Don't accept the idea that service should be something dramatic and recognizable (or recognized by others) to be of value. The daily, mundane tasks we perform for others in our sphere of influence are acts of service to God. Without the evidence of this daily toil, we can hardly make the case that we love our family. Love without service is dead. Don't allow yourself to feel used or to feel that everyone in the house must perform their "fair share." Again, teaching the virtue of work is important, but teaching the divine work of serving loved ones is more so.

The importance of family cannot be overstated and the work we do to build the kingdom at its foundation is the most important work we will ever do. Everything we do in our church is to bring happiness into the home and happiness cannot be had without service one to another. Serve your family first and in so doing you will be in the service of your God.

8

SEEING OTHERS AS GOD SEES THEM

Through a Parent's Eyes

In Chapter One we talked about the importance of being able to feel what others feel. This type of empathy comes from being able to see others as God sees them. While we may not be able to do that straight out of the gate, we can begin by seeing others the way a parent sees them. A beautiful example of learning to do this was related by Dale Renlund in a story he told from his medical career.

"In 1986 a young man named Chad developed heart failure and received a heart transplant. He did very well for a decade and a half. Chad did all he could to stay healthy and live as normal a life as possible. He served a mission, worked, and was a devoted son to his parents. The last few years of his life, though, were challenging, and he was in and out of the hospital frequently.

"One evening, he was brought to the hospital's emergency department in full cardiac arrest. My associates and I worked for a long time to restore his circulation. Finally, it became clear that Chad could not be revived. We stopped our futile efforts, and I declared him dead. Although sad and disappointed, I maintained a professional attitude. I thought to myself, 'Chad has had good care. He has had many more years of life than he otherwise would have had.' That emotional distance soon shattered as his parents came into the emergency room bay and saw their deceased son lying on a stretcher. In that moment, I saw Chad through his mother's and father's eyes. I saw the great hopes and expectations they had had for him, the desire they had had that he would live just a little bit and a little bit better. With this realization, I began to weep. In an ironic reversal of roles and in an act of kindness I will never forget, Chad's parents comforted me."[178] (Renlund, Through God's Eyes, 2015)

It is hard not to have compassion on your own child and imagining others through this lens brings a measure of softening to an otherwise hard heart. Please allow this short indulgence as I illustrate this principal from personal experience. From youth I was taught to avoid speaking with strangers and to avoid even eye contact with homeless people. If you don't look at them, went the reasoning, they will not approach you begging. As an adult, it has been uncommon for me to meet homeless people given where I live, but on one such encounter I saw a man who was probably in his 40s but appeared much older. I routinely walked past him without looking, but was struck by the thought, "What if that man were your son?"

I imagined my second-born son, Jonah, whom I dearly love, and that somehow his life had gone off the rails and that he had ended up in the street like this homeless man. My heart welled up and tears began to flow. If I knew my Jonah was out there on the street and we had somehow lost contact with him over the years, I wished and prayed that whoever met him would have compassion on him and reach out to him and offer help. My heart was instantly melted from callousness to empathy simply by imagining that the object of my indifference was my own child. There is little doubt that our Heavenly Father feels the same as he contemplates us in our miserable state.

This type of envisioning is a powerful tool to discard

---

[178] Dale Renlund, *Through God's Eyes*, an address given at the General Conference of the Church of Jesus Christ of Latter-day Saints, October 2015.

judgement and feel compassion. Seeing others through the eyes of their mother or father is often what it takes to have empathy for their struggles. But sometimes this is challenging, even for us to see our own children this way. Nevertheless, "to effectively serve others we must see them through a parent's eyes, through Heavenly Father's eyes. Only then can we begin to comprehend the true worth of a soul. Only then can we sense the love that Heavenly Father has for all of His children. Only then can we sense the Savior's caring concern for them."[179] (Renlund, Through God's Eyes, 2015)

Wind in Our Sails

If we were better at pausing to feel the compassion required to see others through God's eyes, we would do more to help them through their trials. We would be happier for their successes. "Our genuine concern should be for the success of others."[180] (Hunter, 1984) Too many of us seem to think that life is a zero-sum game in which each participant's gain is exactly balanced by the losses of the other participants. In reality, when other people win, we win too. We can be happy when others succeed, and it doesn't make us any less successful. In fact, it's the opposite. Being happy for others' successes *makes* us more successful. Being envious, less so.

Congratulations and approval of others are powerful tools for building them. Jean Bingham related a story that illustrated the power of having the wind at her back as she and a group of young women took canoes across a large lake. It lifted them and assisted them and refreshed them. "How like that glorious wind can be the sincere compliment of a friend, the cheerful greeting of a parent, the approving nod of a sibling, or the helpful smile of a co-worker or classmate, all supplying fresh "wind in our sails" as

---

[179] Ibid.
[180] Howard Hunter, *The Pharisee and the Publican*, an address given at the General Conference of the Church of Jesus Christ of Latter-day Saints, April 1984.

we battle the challenges of life!"[181] (Bingham, 2016)

As a parent, do you realize the power of a "cheerful greeting" to your child? As a brother, do you understand the significance to your sister of your approval? We often overlook the difference we can make in others' lives through something as simple as a nod. You are not the only one being worn down by the "challenges of life." We all are. And apparently the slightest effort by someone in our family can invigorate and refresh us to continue he battle.

Beyond making the slightest effort, it may be that the most kindness we can show requires neither words nor deeds. "One of the most significant ways we can develop and demonstrate love for our neighbor," Bingham noted, "is through being generous in our thoughts and words. Some years ago, a cherished friend noted, 'The greatest form of charity may be to withhold judgment.'"[182] (Rogers, 1996)

The simplicity of this statement is hard to grasp at first. *The greatest form of charity may be to withhold judgment?* The greatest form of charity, which is the greatest form of love, is to withhold judgment? There is no greater way to show our love for our parents, spouse, or siblings than to simply refrain from judging them? Think about that. While it seems simplistic on the surface, what underlies that statement is that withholding judgment must be a lot more difficult than we think.

What paying attention in life shows us is that we are in a constant state of judgment. We regularly and frequently try to discern the intent behind the words and actions of everyone we interact with. And guess what? All too often we are not very charitable when we judge others' intent. Often, we judge that others acted with malintent.

"If your complaint about other people," Scott Adams said, "involves your belief that you can deduce their inner thoughts,

---

[181] Jean Bingham, *I Will Bring the Light of the Gospel into My Home*, an address given at the General Conference of the Church of Jesus Christ of Latter-day Saints, October 2016.
[182] Ibid. Quoting Sandra Rogers, "Hearts Knit Together," in *Hearts Knit Together: Talks from the 1995 Women's Conferenc*e (1996), 7.

you might be in a mental prison. We humans think we're good judges of what others are thinking. We are not. In fact, we're dreadful at it. But people being people, we generally believe we're good at it while also believing other people are not."[183] (Adams, 2019)

This can be, according to psychologist Scott Braithwaite, because we like to develop simple stories in our minds. "When we live life," Braithwaite says, "we typically have a few facts and then we have to fill in the blanks."[184] (Braithwaite, 2018) Unfortunately, we're not very creative when filling in the blanks and so we develop these stories to explain our experiences, and from these stories we draw our conclusions about the intent of others.

"Usually, the story that we tell ourselves," continues Braithwaite, "is really simple. It's a clean, neat, tidy story with good guys and bad guys. Usually, we're the good guy and the other people who have aggrieved us are the bad guy and we kind of run with it. And we believe the whole thing. It's almost like we don't realize that we filled in the blanks. We just believe that that story is the truth."[185]

Braithwaite relates the example of two people walking down the hallway toward each other at church. The one smiles and says hello. The other walks by without acknowledging the greeting. The person that smiled and said "hi" is hurt because they feel like they were snubbed and instantly form a simple story to explain why the other person ignored them. Many times, a story like this arrives at the conclusion that the reason the other person didn't respond is because they are a jerk. In reality, they were, perhaps, deep in thought about a text they just received about their mother being diagnosed with cancer and were hurrying to their car to drive to the hospital. But because we can't read their minds and

---

[183] Scott Adams, *Loserthink: How Untrained Brains Are Ruining America*, Chapter 3, The Mind Reading Illusion, Audible Edition, 2019.
[184] Scott Braithwaite, PhD., *What Every Leader Needs to Know About Faith Crisis – An Interview with Scott Braithwaite*, a podcast published by LeadingSaints.org, October 14, 2018.
[185] Ibid.

we don't have all the facts; we're left to run with our simpler explanation. And because of our uninformed conclusion, we judge the intent of the other person uncharitably.

This type of simple explanation and self-justification seems to happen regularly with most of us in almost all areas of our life. It seems to be some kind of natural defense mechanism, but it rarely fails to result in our concluding in judgment of others. Realizing this helps explain why developing the ability to forbear and withhold judgement may be the greatest form of charity. We must overcome the natural man to do so.

The Rich Young Man

It may be necessary for us to go through some type of spiritual transformation to find the place where we can view others the way God views them. Just because the necessity of this achievement is being casually discussed here does not mean it is going to be casually obtained. In the same talk that was quoted earlier, Mark Palmer shares his conversion experience when he was given the transformative gift of seeing others as God seems them.

Frustrated with the attitudes of some of the youth that he was called to lead and watch over, he diligently sought insight into how he could reach them. While pondering his predicament on a drive through the country in the Western United States, he heard the story of the rich young man as related in Mark 10. For the first time ever, he reports, he heard the words, "And Jesus beholding him, loved him."[186] He was struck with the words "beholding" and "love" and understood that when he looked at the youth in his charge, he must see them differently and by doing so increase in his love for them. And the way that he needed to behold them was the same way that Christ beheld the rich young man: with love. "The question no longer was 'How does a frustrated mission president get a struggling missionary to behave better?'" Palmer realized. "Instead, the question was 'How can *I*

---
[186] Mark 10:21.

be filled with Christlike love so a missionary can feel the love of God through me and desire to change?' How can *I* behold him or her in the same way the Lord beheld the rich young man, seeing them for who they really are and who they can become, rather than just for what they are doing or not doing? How can I be more like the Savior?"[187] (Palmer, 2017)

From that time on, he was able to sit with his challenging missionaries and look into their eyes and feel Heavenly Father's love for them. Rather than seeing them as people struggling to obey, he could see them as a person with a desire and the faith to serve a mission and doing their best given all of the circumstances and their experiences that culminated in this moment. Palmer was blessed with the gift to see others the way God does, and it made all the difference in the work he was asked to do.

"Seeing others as God does is a gift."[188] For anyone who has felt this love, you know it comes from God and it is a gift. It is a gift to feel Heavenly Father's love for another person, no matter how pathetic they may look to the natural man. It is an important gift. It is a powerful gift. It is the gift of charity. It is a gift that enables us to withhold judgment. It comes from God and it is to be prayed for "with all the energy of heart, that ye may be filled with this love, which he hath bestowed upon all who are true followers of his Son, Jesus Christ; that ye may become the sons of God; that when he shall appear we shall be like him, for we shall see him as he is; that we may have this hope; that we may be purified even as he is pure."[189] (Holmes D. D., 2020)

Stephen Richards said, "The highest type of discernment is that which perceives in others and uncovers for them their better natures, the good inherent within them."[190] (Richards, 1950)

---

[187] Mark Palmer, *Then Jesus Beholding Him, Loved Him*, an address given at the General Conference of the Church of Jesus Christ of Latter-day Saints, April 2017. Italics added.

[188] Douglas Holmes, *Deep in Our Heart*, an address given at the General Conference of the Church of Jesus Christ of Latter-day Saints, April 2020.

[189] Moroni 7:48.

[190] Stephen Richards, in *Conference Report*, April 1950, 162, from David A. Bednar, "Quick to Observe," *Ensign*, December 2006, 35.

A Great Person

Part of seeing others the way God sees them is to not see them as they are but to see them as they have potential to become. Every person in this world is a child of God. This means they have the potential to become like God. Not just to become a god, but to become *like* our Father in Heaven. A baby dog is called a puppy. It will grow up to be a dog like its parents. It will not grow up to be a cat or a giraffe or anything else. An acorn is an oak tree in embryo. If it is planted and nourished, it will become a mighty oak. It will not become a pine tree or a redwood. Each creation has seed in itself to bring forth after its own likeness.

God also has seed in Himself. His seed are his children, and they will grow up to be like Him. The big difference between the seed of God and the seed of all of His creations is that His seed has moral agency, unlike His other creations. His seed must *choose* to become like Him. Or they can choose to be something less, but it is always choice. When Heavenly Father beholds us, He sees all our potential and divinity. He sees our greatness and knows what we can become if we so choose. This is what it means to see others the way God sees us. We see in others their greatness and potential.

Sometimes we look at others and their behavior is a big deterrent to our seeing them as a child of God. They may be rebellious, sloppy, disobedient, lazy, arrogant or criminal. They may not yet know how to bridle the tongue. They test us and try us and trigger us, but we must somehow overcome the outward appearance and look on the heart.

Henry Eyring recalled a moment as a young father when he almost failed to see the divinity within his rambunctious son. "I remember once a seven- or eight-year-old son of ours jumping on his bed hard enough that I thought it might break. I felt a flash of frustration, and I moved quickly to set my house in order. I grabbed my son by his little shoulders and lifted him up to where our eyes met. The Spirit put words into my mind. It seemed a quiet voice, but it pierced to my heart: 'You are holding a great person.' I gently set him back on the bed and apologized. Now he has become the great man the Holy Ghost let me see 40 years ago."[191] (Eyring, My Peace I Leave With You, 2017)

In another context, Eyring explained to a collection of professional educators that the importance of their work lay not so much in helping young people master a certain subject, but in showing them their true nature and worth. One might be tempted to believe that university professors should focus on subject mastery and leave the building up of confidence to the students. But any leader (or parent) who has influence in the life of another has the right and obligation (if they have the gift) to reveal the true nature of those in their charge. "What will matter most is what they learn from us about who they really are and what they can really become. My guess is that they won't learn it so much from lectures. They will get it from feelings of who you are, who you think they are, and what you think they might become."[192] (Eyring, Teaching Is a Moral Act, 1991)

We may object that there are some people who don't seem to have any divinity in them at all. For example, take the beautiful young woman who had so many differences with her parents she left home at an early age to work making adult films. She now has plenty of money to spend on a degraded lifestyle filled with parties, drugs, and sexual relationships with many partners. Surely, we cannot be expected to see such a degenerate as a child of God. Some may look at her and label her as a slut or a whore and work to keep her away from their children.

Time has shown us that really there is no such thing as a slut or a whore. There is only a beautiful daughter of God who has lost her way. She has not chosen to fulfill her potential . . . yet. But the end of the story has not yet been written. Who knows what but that she may come to herself and seek out the more

---

[191] Henry Eyring, *My Peace I Leave with You*, an address given at the General Conference of the Church of Jesus Christ of Latter-day Saints, April 2017.
[192] Henry Eyring, *Teaching is a Moral Act*, an address during the BYU Annual University Conference held August 1991.

lasting security of her Heavenly Father's love? When that time comes, will God be willing to forgive her and accept her and exalt her the same as the most obedient saint? Of course, he will. And to certify that, Christ told multiple parables including the lost sheep which ends, "I say unto you, that likewise joy shall be in heaven over one sinner that repenteth, more than over ninety and nine just persons, which need no repentance."[193]

Abandon Outward Appearances

In one of our favorite Old Testament stories, Samuel the Prophet is commanded by the Lord to go to Bethlehem and anoint a new king for Israel. The current king, Saul, was off the rails and the Lord would no longer forbear with him. Samuel was scared because, he said, "How can I go? If Saul hear it, he will kill me."[194] But the Lord ignored Samuel's concern and sent him to the house of Jesse who had eight sons, David being the youngest.

After Samuel and Jesse met and had offered sacrifice, Samuel saw Eliab, Jesse's firstborn son. He was a soldier and fought for Israel in Saul's army. Apparently, there was something about Eliab that made him look like a king. Eliab must have been impressive, for when Samuel saw him, he judged, "Surely the Lord's anointed is before him."

In what seems like a gentle correction, the Lord explained to Samuel, "Look not on his countenance, or on the height of his stature; because I have refused him: for the Lord seeth not as man seeth; for man looketh on the outward appearance, but the Lord looketh on the heart."

Man looks upon the outward appearance, but the Lord looks on the heart. Only the Lord can see into a person's heart, but to see others as God sees them, we must try to look upon the heart.

On the topic of looking not on the outward appearance, but rather on the heart, we have noted numerous poignant stories from people who have failed in this regard. It is a humiliating

---

[193] Luke 15:7.
[194] 1 Samuel 16:1-7.

experience when we realize we have been sitting in unrighteous judgment of another person. Especially when we have been trained to know better. And even worse when the defendant is a member of our own family. Robert Gay related one such a tale which stirs emotion every time it is heard.

"A few years ago," he remembers, "my older sister passed away. She had a challenging life. She struggled with the gospel and was never really active [in her church]. Her husband abandoned their marriage and left her with four young children to raise. On the evening of her passing, in a room with her children present, I gave her a blessing to peacefully return home. At that moment I realized I had too often defined my sister's life in terms of her trials and inactivity. As I placed my hands on her head that evening, I received a severe rebuke from the Spirit. I was made acutely aware of her goodness and allowed to see her as God saw her—not as someone who struggled with the gospel and life but as someone who had to deal with difficult issues I did not have. I saw her as a magnificent mother who, despite great obstacles, had raised four beautiful, amazing children. I saw her as the friend to our mother who took time to watch over and be a companion to her after our father passed away. During that final evening with my sister, I believe God was asking me, 'Can't you see that everyone around you is a sacred being?'"[195] (Gay, 2018)

This is a bittersweet tale. On the one hand, Robert was rebuked and made to realize that he had been wrong for much of his life in the way he judged his sister and in the conclusions he had drawn about her. Especially given that he had not yet had the chance to walk in her shoes and face her difficult issues. Yet God, in His mercy, still granted him the gift to "see her as God saw her." Through this wonderful inspiration he finally saw her as the magnificent, hard-working mother that she was. Unfortunately, that moment did not come for him until the last day of his sister's

---

[195] Robert Gay, *Taking Upon Ourselves the Name of Jesus Christ*, an address given at the General Conference of the Church of Jesus Christ of Latter-day Saints, October 2018.

life.

Let's not allow ourselves to sit in judgment of our family members for our entire life when we have the option to begin to see them for the glorious beings they are. Won't our lives be immeasurably better if we can rejoice in each other's divinity, despite our faults.

Personal Witness

At the risk of making this too personal, I want to add my testimony to all of the others about this topic of seeing others as God sees them. I've worked hard to be able to see all people as beloved children of God. When I remember to do this, I can feel God's love for them. I know what this feels like, and I recognize it when I hear about it. A good young man I know met David Bednar and said that Elder Bednar looked into his eyes. The young man said he could feel God's love through Bednar. This was an apostle looking at the young man the way God does. He beheld him, and he loved him.

During my years serving as a bishop, I had opportunities to sit quietly with a few of God's children as they poured out their hearts to the Lord. I felt the Lord's love for these people. I don't know if they could feel what I was feeling, but I hope they could and that they were lifted knowing God's empathy, love, and concern for them.

It's hard to keep this feeling with all the mundane distractions. For me, it requires looking at all people, no matter how humble, as someone who can teach me, someone who has valid spiritual experiences. In a testimony meeting, an older woman who appeared to have limited formal education and means, told the story of seeing Jesus Christ appear to her on the banks of a river, as she wondered about truth and the path she should take. This story was repeated regularly and to the outward appearance, she looked a little crazy. But in her heart was an experience that strengthens my faith. One of the first steps toward seeing others through God's eyes is to begin seeing others as our equal. We are all equal in the sense that we are all children of our Heavenly Father. This is the most basic truth of religion, and it was taught to us by the Savior in the most basic prayer: Our Father who art in Heaven. Yet this most basic truth seems truly elusive to most of Heavenly Father's children.

One other technique I use is looking at someone for a while. I've noticed many times that my first judgement is harsh, but my considered judgement is more mellow. You can try this on pictures of people's faces. (It also works for me if I look at their face, but that can be uncomfortable for them.) When I first look at someone and I have a thought like, ugly, strange, weird, or whatever it may be that first comes into my mind, I find that if I look at the person's face for longer, I begin to see them in a different light. The things that bothered me at first start to fade away. I begin to see softer features and find more of the good. It is an interesting phenomenon for me, and I don't know if it works for others, but it might be worth trying if you find yourself making snap judgments about people's looks.

Conclusion

In this chapter, we have expanded on the idea mentioned in the first chapter that seeing others the way God sees them is a powerful way to feel love for them. It is a divine gift when you feel Heavenly Father's love for his children in your own heart. We discussed how, in the absence of this gift, you can begin to prepare to receive it by looking at others as if they were your own child. That technique worked for Dale Renlund, and it worked for me.

We touched on the idea that the simplest acknowledgement of the good in others acts as a refreshing wind to their soul and explored in depth the notion that withholding judgment is a supremely charitable act. We learned how this gift from God can be fleeting and must be sought after in earnest prayer. We can cultivate this gift and when we do, we are choosing to be like our Heavenly Father. Our agency, our ability to choose to be something more, is what separates us as children of God from all of His creations. Once we begin to experience this and see others this way, we realize that people are good, even if they're temporarily lost. To see others as God sees them, we must remember to look at their heart.

9

TEACH CORRECT PRINCIPLES

In the 1840's, Joseph Smith established a city and named it Nauvoo. Since the Saints at the time could only inherit land that absolutely no one else wanted, they drained a swamp by the Mississippi River so that they could build their city. Since they were starting from scratch, they had the opportunity to plan out every detail about how they wanted the town to be. It was a well-organized place with its own charter, government, and militia. Visitors to Nauvoo marveled that a man with the equivalent of a 3rd grade education could establish a religion, attract tens of thousands of followers, build a temple, organize a government, and stand at its head. This while mayors and governors across the young country were struggling with a frontier mentality and the law of the wild west. What kind of mind control did Joseph have over his followers that he could get them to do his every bidding?

"The question was asked," remembered Brigham Young, "a great many times of Joseph Smith, by gentlemen who came to see him and his people, 'How is it that you can control your people so easily? It appears that they do nothing but what you say; how is it that you can govern them so easily?'"[196] (Smith J. , Teachings

---

[196] Brigham Young, *Teachings of Joseph Smith*, Chapter 24: Leading in the Lord's Way.

of Presidents of the Church: Joseph Smith, 2007)

John Taylor reported the same thing. "Some years ago, in Nauvoo, a gentleman in my hearing, a member of the Legislature, asked Joseph Smith how it was that he was enabled to govern so many people, and to preserve such perfect order; remarking at the same time that it was impossible for them to do it anywhere else. Mr. Smith remarked that it was very easy to do that. 'How?' responded the gentleman, 'to us it is very difficult.'"[197]

What was Joseph's secret? And if he has a secret, could he please share it? And whatever it was, could it be used by other governments and employers? Even parents would benefit if they could learn how to just keep their children in line. Joseph remarked that it was very easy to do. In fact, he said, "I do not govern them at all."[198] On one such occasion he replied, "I teach them correct principles, and they govern themselves."[199] This revelation must have come as a shock to the listeners. Could anything be as simple as that? The response begs the obvious question: Which principles are correct? We've tried any number of things and none of them really seem to work for long.

The principles that Joseph Smith was referring to are the principles of the Gospel, but it's unlikely that answer would be accepted by the outside world. It goes against their whole way of doing things. "The Lord works from the inside out," Ezra Taft Benson taught. "The world works from the outside in. The world would take people out of the slums. Christ takes the slums out of people, and then they take themselves out of the slums. The world would mold men by changing their environment. Christ changes men, who then change their environment. The world would shape human behavior, but Christ can change human nature."[200] (Benson, 1985)

This idea should be the main force behind parenting. Why not?

---

[197] Ibid.
[198] Ibid.
[199] Ibid. As quoted from, John Taylor, "The Organization of the Church," *Millennial Star*, Nov. 15, 1851, p. 339.
[200] Ezra Taft Benson, *Born of God*, an address given at the General Conference of the Church of Jesus Christ of Latter-day Saints, October 1985.

It's the way Heavenly Father parents. Heavenly Father teaches his children through the scriptures and other inspired people, and then He leaves it up to them to choose to follow his teachings or not. God does not force us to obey his teachings. "He teaches us step by step and guides us, never forcing."[201] (Eyring, He Goes Before us, 2020) Obedience means nothing if we are forced to obey. Obedience is only rewarded when it is a choice. Agency is the grand key. Heavenly Father wants us to *choose* to become like him. And as parents, assuming we are setting a good example to our children, we most certainly want them to choose to follow in our footsteps.

This theme underlies the premise of this entire work. The idea that we can teach, love, and build up the members of our family and support them when their choices bring them hardships. This is not to say that if you make all the right choices (you won't) that you won't have any hardships (you will). It is to say that no matter what our family members do or become, we must love them. If they are lost at sea, we must be their lighthouse. If they are across the chasm, we must be their bridge home. Ridicule and shame have no place in bringing our loved ones back to us. They don't work.

So, we will teach them correct principles, and let them govern themselves. This chapter outlines, in no particular order, a few of the correct principles we should be teaching.

Teaching Humility

As a young woman graduated from high school and headed off to college, her father realized that it wouldn't be long until she showed up with a young man that she wanted to marry. He desired to give her counsel about the type of young man she should wait for, but he wondered what he should say? What were the qualities in a man that this anxious father would want his daughter wedded to? As he pondered that question, three broad

---

[201] Henry Eyring, *He Goes Before Us*, an address given at the General Conference of The Church of Jesus Christ of Latter-day Saints, April 2020.

categories came to mind. She should wait for someone who is hard-working, faithful, and humble.

He was somewhat surprised that humility was at the top of the list, but too many times he had seen people who were hard-working and successful treat their loved ones poorly because of their pride. Elsewhere in this work we have treated at length the principles upon which parental and spousal authority should be exercised and the core of these principles is humility. Teaching children to take humility as a companion will facilitate better parenting in their later years.

Humility is a godly attribute. We want to find it in ourselves, and we want to teach it to our children. It is also an attribute that cannot easily be taught. More likely it must be caught. And this by others seeing our example. Anger has no part in humility, and when our children see us angry or unkind, they are not learning it. In our interactions with our children, especially in our discipline, we need to promote kindness and mildness.

"As we raise our own children," Steven Snow taught, "we need to help them remain humble as they mature into adulthood. We do not do this by breaking their spirit through unkindness or by being too harsh in our discipline. While nurturing their self-confidence and self-esteem, we need to teach them the qualities of selflessness, kindness, obedience, lack of pride, civility, and unpretentiousness. We need them to learn to take joy in the successes of siblings and friends."[202] (Snow, 2016)

It's easy to believe that a big part of pride is low self-confidence. Pride takes joy in putting oneself ahead of another. Why would one feel the need to do this unless they felt inferior? "Pride gets no pleasure out of having something," observed C.S. Lewis, "only out of having more of it than the next man. . . It is the comparison that makes you proud: the pleasure of being above the rest. Once the element of competition is gone, pride is

---

[202] Steven Snow, *Be Thou Humble*, an address given at the General Conference of the Church of Jesus Christ of Latter-day Saints, April 2016.

gone."[203] (Lewis, 1996) This is why the strategy of building them up and strengthening their confidence is so important. If we can teach our children to eliminate the need to defeat others as a means of making ourselves feel better, they can replace it instead with the true joy of seeing others succeed.

This is not to say that our children shouldn't be competitive and strive to win. Winning is the culmination of doing your best. Champions in all areas focus other's attention on the work they and their team performed to reach the pinnacle rather than the weaknesses and inferiority of the competition.

Teaching Repentance

Repentance may be the single most incorrectly taught gospel doctrine of all time. For a concept so simple, it could take years to understand its meaning given the prevailing misconceptions about it. Nevertheless, we need to learn it for ourselves and transmit its meaning to our children. Let's take a side trip to understand some of the things that repentance is not.

Millennia ago, the idea of repentance got into a rough patch in the New Testament. "In those days, came John the Baptist, preaching in the wilderness of Judea, and saying, Repent ye: for the kingdom of heaven is at hand."[204] The narrator of Matthew informs us that John was he that was spoken of by Isaiah, saying, 'The voice of one crying in the wilderness.' "And the same John had his raiment of camel's hair and a leathern girdle about his loins; and his meat was locusts and honey."[205]

Straight out of the gate we associate the idea of repentance with a primitive prophet wearing animal skins and eating locusts, screaming in the wilderness for people to repent. In a way, it seems surprising that John ever picked up any followers. When the religious leaders of his church approached him, he called

---

[203] C.S. Lewis, *The Joyful Christian* (1996), 164, Simon and Schuster, as quoted on AZ Quotes: https://www.azquotes.com/quote/353655
[204] Matthew 3:1-2.
[205] Matthew 3:4.

them a "generation of vipers."[206] Sensitive modern souls recoil at this image and, unfortunately, we seem to have recoiled from repentance as well.

Somehow, we have associated the idea of repentance with only the most grievous sin. We have been taught that if we ever mess up really badly, we can always repent. We have been taught to "be perfect," even though we have been simultaneously taught that there has only ever been and ever will be one perfect person or Earth. We have been taught that there is joy in heaven over the 99 righteous people who need no repentance and we long to be in that group and not the one lost sheep. We have been taught that repentance is a process, not a one-time event. And that there are five "R's" of repentance[207] (Hodge, 2014), or was that six[208] (Keen, 2020), or seven?[209] (Critchlow, 2003) Suffice it to say that we have tried hard to break it down into something we could understand. Instinctually, we knew it was important, but we have just not been able to understand exactly what "it" is.

It's no wonder we struggle so hard with this principle. Despite all these logical contortions and mnemonic devices, we have never really seemed to get to the core of it. It's so bad that, at the time of this writing, two centuries after the restoration of the gospel began, Russell M. Nelson had just focused his keynote General Conference address on the topic and made this clarifying statement: "Too many people consider repentance as punishment—something to be avoided except in the most serious circumstances."[210] (Nelson, 2019) As a sort of anti-John,

---

[206] Matthew 3:7.
[207] Bryan Hodge, "The Five R's of Repentance," posted September 19, 2014, https://bryanhodge.net/2014/09/19/the-five-rs-of-repentance/ accessed June 7, 2020.
[208] James Keen, "6 R's of Repentance – Part 1," from a talk given October 1, 2017, https://www.sermonaudio.com/sermoninfo.asp?SID=107172212126 accessed June 7, 2020.
[209] William J. Critchlow, Jr., "The Seven R's of Repentance," posted January 3, 2003, http://mormonmomma.com/the-seven-rs-of-repentance/ accessed June 7, 2020.
[210] Russell M. Nelson, *We Can Do Better and Be Better*, an address given at the General Conference of the Church of Jesus Christ of Latter-day Saints, April 2019.

Nelson quietly and calmly helps us understand that the meaning of repentance is "change." Particularly, change for the better.

No prophet put it in more amiable terms than Gordon Hinckley. In what may be his most famous Internet quote, he said, "Do your best, and be a little better than you are."[211] This is the best explanation of repentance we can find. It's about being a little bit better each day and the driving factor of this effort many of us learned (and later forgot) in Cub Scouts. The whole idea of repentance can be reduced to the Cub Scout motto. Any child should be able to understand this: Do your best![212] (Bryan, 2020) This is what repentance really boils down to and in case that's not simple enough, Hinckley explained it in more detail when he said, "Let us return to our homes with resolution in our hearts to do a little better than we have done in the past. We can all be a little kinder, a little more generous, a little more thoughtful of one another. We can be a little more tolerant and friendly to those not of our faith."[213] (Hinckley, Thanks to the Lord for His Blessings, 1999) We can only repent of one sin at a time. If we could repent of all our sins, we would be perfect.

Teaching your children this understanding of repentance takes the scary away from it. Deep down inside, who doesn't want to be the best person they can be? We all do. We all want to be kinder and more generous. It's just we can't go from being a mean, selfish person to something much better overnight. That's why we're taught to just chip away at it. Don't try to fix everything in one day. Just try to be a little better than you were . . . each day. There's always going to be one more thing you can repent of. There's always going to be one more thing you can do better. Repentance simply means caring. Caring about who you are and caring enough to make yourself better. When you catch yourself taking shortcuts, being mean or caustic, impatient, rude, lazy,

---

[211] Gordon B. Hinckley, *Quotes*, Goodreads, (Hinckley, Quotes, 2020), accessed June 7, 2020.
[212] Bryan on Scouting, *Cub Scout Motto*, https://blog.scoutingmagazine.org/tag/cub-scout-motto/ accessed June 7, 2020.
[213] Gordon B. Hinckley, *Thanks to the Lord for His Blessings*, an address given at the General Conference of the Church of Jesus Christ of Latter-day Saints, April 1999.

selfish, dishonest, arrogant, or whatever it is, care about it. Care enough to make it better. Try a little harder to be a little better. That's repentance. That's the principle we need to embrace for ourselves and transmit to our children and doing so will increase the likelihood that they will be a productive and contributing member of the community.

Teach Accountability

There is hardly anyone left that will not confess that there is a certain rot that has been eating away at our culture and it seems to be getting worse. It manifests itself in new employees in the workplace who expect to be given accolades for each contribution they make. It is manifest in the bewildered look of young people who have a run-in with the law and are shocked that there are consequences for their actions. We see it in teenagers who should be well on their way to taking responsibility for their actions when they look to their parents to bail them out of a mess they have gotten themselves into. This rot comes from a failure to understand one part of the choice and accountability equation. And guess which part they don't understand?

Wendy (names have been changed) had her fourteen-year-old daughter, Jessica, invite her friend Sarah over for the weekend. During their time together, Jessica and Sarah walked over to Walmart to kill some time. A few hours later, Wendy received a call from the Sarah's mother. Wendy received an earful about how Sarah had worked very hard for some money she brought over for the weekend and now she was complaining that Jessica had talked Sarah into spending half of it on her. Wendy was very cordial and polite to the calling mother and promised to rectify the situation.

When she hung up the phone, her husband, who was riding along in the car and overheard the conversation and asked, "What would we have done if the roles were reversed? What if our daughter was the one who had earned the money and her friend had talked her into spending it?"

"We would have said, 'Tough!', replied Wendy. 'Don't let people talk you into things you don't want to do.' We would have let it be a life lesson." Her husband grinned and kept on driving.

In this work, we have taken a stand against helicopter parents. We have alerted you to the dangers of getting between your children and the consequences of their choices. We have advocated for letting your children fail safely. This incident would have been a perfect opportunity for Sarah's mother to shrug her shoulders and let Sarah own the responsibility for her actions. Instead, she chose to intervene, shield her daughter from the consequences of her choices, and figure out a way to get some of her money back. This type of parenting is a huge disservice to young people. It does not prepare them for the real world. If you make a choice as an adult that costs you a lot of hard-earned dough, there's nobody but nobody that's going to be there to help you get it back.

Now poor Sarah will continue to rely on her mother to intervene. If it continues to work for Sarah, her mother will find it progressively harder to extract herself from the cycle of protecting her child. The first time you show tough love to a kid can be pretty hard on you. It seems that it's much harder on us than it is on the kids. It is usually so easy to step in and help out in the early years, and the kids seem so innocent and vulnerable, it's tough to make the transition to letting them go it alone. When the child first doesn't get their way and they realize that they are going to have to live with the consequences of their choices, it can lead to tantrums and feigned sadness. You could be accused of not loving them or appear indifferent to their feelings.

The next time the child makes a mistake, and they go to their parent for reparations, they will already half expect that they won't get satisfaction and so the objections won't be so strenuous. Soon enough they will learn that asking their parents to intervene is a waste of time. At that point, they begin to live more carefully.

"Clearly," says Stephen Covey, "in the Christ-centered home the atmosphere is one of love. Love is kindness, patience, affirmation of the other person's worth. In saying this, however, we are not saying that love is permissiveness, softness, 'nice-guyness' . . . The criterion or essence of divine love is the growth and development of the person loved, not his temporary pleasure or one's own popularity. Sometimes the kindest thing we can do is to hold another to the responsible course while he is condemning us for doing so, or to allow natural and logical consequences to teach him accountability and responsibility. This 'tough love,' as some call it, communicates that we care more for and believe more in that person than he does in himself. We are saying we know he can do it, and that we will neither give up on him nor give in to him."[214] (Covey, 1982)

This is not to say that we should never help out those we love when they get into a predicament. Sometimes others do their best, make good choices, and still things go poorly for them. But when we hear their story and we think to ourselves that the mess they are in could have been avoided if they had made a smarter choice or been a little less lazy or not been so concerned about how they look to others, perhaps it's a good time stand down and let life teach them.

Choice and accountability is one of the equations that holds a key to happiness. The sooner I learn that I, and only I, am accountable for my life and actions, the sooner I will be off the road to victimhood and on the road to happiness. Being accountable for all you do is a liberating mindset. Sometimes it is difficult to admit you are wrong. We are often tempted to blame our failures on surrounding circumstances, but there is little in life that is more attractive than an adult who owns the responsibility for their work. Sometimes we just have to admit that we made a mistake.

Teach Obedience

Being accountable makes us a productive member of society.

---

[214]Stephen R. Covey, *The Divine Center*, R.R. Donnelly & Sons, Harrisonburg, VA, 1982, 116.

Owning our outputs makes us an asset to our employer. Being mature enough to admit our mistakes makes us a better parent. The process of learning accountability teaches us that life is set up with guardrails that will lead us to more happiness if we're on the right road. These guardrails are sometimes called rules or laws. Following the law is called obedience. Obedience is smart. When you are obedient it shows that you understand the system of rules and rewards that is in place to help you achieve your life goals.

Teaching obedience is tricky. The last thing we want to do is force others to be obedient. This accomplishes nothing. Forcing others to be obedient means asserting our will over theirs. This tactic is satanic. Forced obedience robs a person of their agency. When a person has no agency or choice, they are no longer accountable for their outcomes. In this sense, forcing others to obey also robs them of their accountability. In teaching obedience, we do well to take our instruction from the way God teaches obedience. "Our Heavenly Father's goal in parenting is not to have His children *do* what is right; it is to have His children *choose* to do what is right."[215] (Renlund, Choose You This Day, 2018) Pleasure in obedience comes only when you choose to obey.

As we have seen, Joseph Smith was able to govern so large a group of people and make it look easy by teaching correct principles and letting his followers govern themselves. We best teach obedience through a loving example and by clearly reviewing the options and consequences for each course of action. We let other see that our obedience doesn't interfere with our happiness the way that so many believe and teach who object to the notion. Hoping others will choose the best course of action requires a lot of patience and love.

"As much as we love a child, an investigator, or our friends," observes Henry Eyring, "we cannot force them to keep the commandments so that they qualify for the Holy Ghost to touch

---

[215] Dale Renlund, *Choose You This Day*, an address given at the general conference of the Church of Jesus Christ of Latter-day Saints, October 2018. Italics in original.

and change their hearts. So, the best help we can give is whatever leads those we love to watch over their own choices."[216] (Eyring, Happiness for Those We Love, 2016) The key here is to get them to watch over their own choices rather than us watching over their choices for them.

We notice in ourselves and others a couple things that tend to get in the way of obedience. One is the rebellious instinct of the natural man, and the other is low confidence. Being born into a fallen world, we all seem to have within us, to some degree, a rebellious streak that bristles at the thought of being told what to do. This is natural and "the natural man is an enemy to God."[217] The good side of this rebellious streak is the spirit of independence. Not taken to the extreme, it can be an asset that helps us try to do and accomplish things on our own. This is a good trait when trying to survive in this world. Likely this characteristic in President Herbert Hoover led him to coin the term "rugged individualism," or "the belief that all individuals, or nearly all individuals, can succeed on their own."[218] Fostering this kind of individual strength and balancing it with the humility required to follow the rules can be challenging. Helping others overcome their rebellious nature can be done by helping them build confidence.

Building confidence in others is important because low confidence can lead to disobedience. Especially in youth, there is constant peer pressure to experiment with new things and discover the boundaries in life. People with low confidence are more susceptible to negative pressure because of their heightened desire for acceptance. Being mocked for obedience is the oldest trick in the book when it comes to negative influences in our life. Who isn't repelled at the notion of being mocked as a 'Goody Two Shoes' or a 'Molly Mormon'? We all must be able to stand up to this type of pressure if we are to be happy, but in order to do so we must feel accepted and approved by those who love us

---

[216] Henry B. Eyring, "Happiness for Those We Love," *Ensign*, January 2016.
[217] Mosiah 3:19.
[218] See Dictionary.com.

most.

This is another reason why forcing loved ones to be obedient never works. It is not uncommon to see mockery being used to keep in line those who do not conform to our wishes, whether we be a peer or a parent. This tactic never results in the person being made fun of feeling more loved and approved. This can lead to the low-confidence person seeking approval from those who think following rules is for weaklings.

"Sometimes I think we misunderstand obedience," noted Dieter Uchtdorf. "We may pound the metaphorical hammer of obedience against the iron anvil of the commandments in an effort to shape those we love, through constant heating and repeated battering, into holier, heavenly matter. Maybe obedience is not so much the process of bending, twisting, and pounding our souls into something we are not. Instead, it is the process by which we discover what we truly are made of. We are made of supernal material most precious and highly refined, and thus we carry within ourselves the substance of divinity."[219] (Uchtdorf D. F., He Will Place You On His Shoulders and Carry You home, 2016)

These words from Uchtdorf underscore the importance of confidence in obedience. If we could recognize our true selves, the "substance of divinity," we would not need to seek out approval of others. We could rely on the approval of our Heavenly Father to motivate us to be obedient.

Teach Compassion

The same natural man that resists being told what to do can also be a swift and harsh judge who ridicules others for failing to do what he thinks they should do. "The natural man and woman in each of us," noted Robbins, "has a tendency to condemn others

---

[219] Dieter Uchtdorf, *He Will Place You on His Shoulders and Carry You Home*, an address given at the General Conference of the Church of Jesus Christ of Latter-day Saints, April 2016.

and to judge unrighteously, or self-righteously."[220] (Robbins, 2016) For many of us, finding fault in others is a misguided attempt to make ourselves look better in our own eyes. If we cannot succeed ourselves, we think, often subconsciously, then let us hedge up the way against those who are and hinder their success. We are often like so many crabs preventing our comrades from succeeding. "If you have a number of crabs in a bucket, and one of them attempts to escape by crawling out, the other crabs that remain in the bucket will prevent that crab from escaping by dragging them back down into the bucket."[221] (Duperouzel, 2020) This observed phenomenon feels so familiar that we have incorporated the idiom into our language.

Instead, we should be more empathic. Not only should we "mourn with those that mourn, and comfort those who stand in need of comfort," but we should rejoice with those who rejoice and celebrate with those who celebrate.[222] Empathy and compassion are closely linked. Being able to feel the pain (and joy) of another is a talent that helps put ourselves in their shoes. If we can understand how others feel, we are less likely to be that harsh judge of their failures.

We do well to teach compassion to our children using the same principles taught to bishops whose role it is to be a judge of others' moral failures. In guidance that may come as a surprise to those who thought that the role of the priesthood leader was to correct behavior, we learn from a Church authority that a higher purpose of those with the priesthood is to help us get in touch with the love of God. After relating the story of James and John asking permission to call down fire from heaven upon the heads of those who treated the Savior disrespectfully, Lynn Robbins taught, "Bishops and branch presidents should avoid any similar impulse to condemn. A righteous judge would respond to

---

[220] Lynn Robbins, *The Righteous Judge*, an address given at the General Conference of the Church of Jesus Christ of Latter-day Saints, October 2016.
[221] Dr. L. Christian Duperouzel, "Finding Compassion for the Crabs," https://drlchristianduperouzel.wordpress.com/2020/06/19/finding-compassion-for-the-crabs/, accessed July 5, 2020.
[222] Mosiah 18:9.

confessions with compassion and understanding. An erring youth, for example, should leave the bishop's office feeling the love of the Savior through the bishop and enveloped in the joy and healing power of the Atonement – never shamed or held in contempt."[223] (Robbins, 2016)

To hear that those who sin should never be shamed by the person who is charged with teaching them how to live may come as a shock to some. To shame someone is to make them feel guilt for their behavior. Feelings of guilt that come from within may be our spirit's way of guiding us to the right path, but when the shame and contempt are placed upon us from the outside, we generally esteem the person shaming us as our enemy. This is why inspired counsel for exercising priesthood authority teaches us to show forth an "increase of love" for those we have reproved.[224]

As noted earlier, most of us don't need someone to tell us when we're making mistakes. "Always allow other people the luxury of being mistaken. They will find out for themselves soon enough."[225] (Chambers, 1952) Mistakes are painful and we're usually acutely aware that the pain is self-inflicted. Robbins also shows us how "the Book of Mormon teaches us that when we willfully sin, we become our "own judges" (Alma 41:7) and consign ourselves to spiritual prison."[226] (Robbins, 2016) In this same address, Robbins reminds us of the story of when Joseph Smith lost the 116 manuscript pages of the Book of Mormon. This is a terrifying story of disobedience that poignantly highlights how the person that owns their mistakes feel the most pain.

Joseph Smith was first given the knowledge of the gold plates containing the inscriptions that he would translate as the Book of Mormon in September 1823, though he was not permitted to

---

[223] Lynn Robbins, *The Righteous Judge*, an address given at the General Conference of the Church of Jesus Christ of Latter-day Saints, October 2016.
[224] Doctrine & Covenants, Section 121:43.
[225] Whittaker Chambers, Witness, Regnery History, Washington, DC, 1952, https://www.goodreads.com/work/quotes/748601-witness
[226] Lynn Robbins, *The Righteous Judge*, an address given at the General Conference of the Church of Jesus Christ of Latter-day Saints, October 2016.

retrieve them at that time. Rather, he was instructed to return to the same place on the same date once a year for the next 4 years. After much trial and hardship, he obtained the plates in September of 1827. Joseph related, "No sooner was it known that I had them, than the most strenuous exertions were used to get them from me. Every stratagem that could be invented was resorted to for that purpose. The persecution became more bitter and severe than before, and multitudes were on the alert continually to get them from me if possible."[227]

By some miracle Joseph was able to maintain possession of the plates and over the course of the next several months he and his companion, Martin Harris, worked on the translation until they had produced 116 manuscript pages. The wife of Martin Harris was not a believer in the plates and seemed resentful toward her husband for the time he spent with Joseph. To show her the truthfulness of the work, Martin importuned Joseph to take the manuscript to show to his wife. Joseph inquired of the Lord and was twice refused. Unsatisfied, Martin pressed harder until Joseph made a third inquiry of the Lord. This time permission was granted.

During this dark time, Joseph's wife, Emma, and newborn child were ill and the child passed away. After Martin had been gone with the manuscript for three weeks, Joseph became extremely worried. Emma gave him leave to return to Palmyra, NY, from Harmony, PA, so Joseph traveled all night to his parents' home arriving at daybreak. Once he had recovered a little, the family sent for Martin Harris who was uncharacteristically slow in responding to their summons. After several hours of waiting with breakfast on the table, Martin finally arrived. The following interactions, related by Joseph Smith's mother, Lucy Mack Smith, rend heartstrings as we imagine the sorrow these two young men felt.

"[Martin] took up his knife and fork as if he were going to use them, but immediately dropped them. [Joseph's brother] Hyrum, observing this, said, 'Martin, why do you not eat; are you sick?'

---

[227] Joseph Smith Jr., Joseph Smith – History 1:60.

Upon which Mr. Harris pressed his hands upon his temples, and cried out in a tone of deep anguish, 'Oh, I have lost my soul! I have lost my soul!'"

"Joseph, who had not expressed his fears till now, sprang from the table, exclaiming, 'Martin, have you lost that manuscript? Have you broken your oath, and brought down condemnation upon my head as well as your own?'

"'Yes, it is gone,' replied Martin, 'and I know not where.'

"'Oh, my God!' said Joseph, clenching his hands. 'All is lost! All is lost! What shall I do? I have sinned – it is I who tempted the wrath of God. I should have been satisfied with the first answer which I received from the Lord; for he told me that it was not safe to let the writing go out of my possession.' He wept and groaned and walked the floor continually.

"'Then must I return with such a tale as this? I dare not do it. And how shall I appear before the Lord?' Joseph asked. 'Of what rebuke am I not worthy from the angel of the Most High?'"[228] (Smith L. M., 2000)

It is doubtful we can imagine in the least part the anguish of Joseph's soul. He willfully ignored the counsel of the Lord. He lost months' worth of priceless work. For all he knew, the angel would take back the plates and find another, more obedient prophet. Or perhaps the great restoration of the gospel which was about to burst forth would be shut down for some unknown length of time and countless souls denied the light of the additional scripture. Not surprisingly, the angel reclaimed the plates from Joseph, and he was placed on a sort of probation. Very few of us have made mistakes of this magnitude through simple disobedience.

But the point of this story being related in this work is to illustrate how we know when we have done wrong. Joseph did not need his mother to reprimand him for this awful mistake, nor do our children need a parent who is a travel agent for guilt trips. We are better off to let life's consequences be the teacher.

---

[228] Lucy Mack Smith, *The History of Joseph Smith by His Mother*, Covenant Communications, 2000, 126-127.

After enduring a painful period without the plates or the right to translate, both were returned to Joseph by the angel. It is interesting to note that when these things were restored to him it was not with warnings and dark forebodings, but rather, "The angel was rejoiced when he gave me back the Urim and Thummim and said that God was pleased with my faithfulness and humility, and loved me for my penitence and diligence in prayer."[229] (Smith J. , Teachings of Presidents of the Church: Joseph Smith, 2007) No doubt Robbins bases his guidance on observations of the way the angel handled Joseph's return to the good graces of God. The angel rejoiced in Joseph's happiness and success and made sure that he knew that God loves him. "The proceedings of a righteous judge are merciful, loving, and redemptive, not condemning. To effectively teach a child is the very essence of good parenting, and to lovingly discipline is the very essence of being a righteous judge."[230] (Robbins, 2016)

One can only teach compassion by demonstration. We show others compassion by being there for them during the hard times and not judging. We seek to build them up when they are down. We try to empathize with their struggles, and we rejoice with them in their successes.

Between God and Me

Sometimes despite our best efforts, we fail to convey the power of these important principles. Everyone has to make their own way in life and many times that means learning with sadness. Through a combination of complex factors, some individuals pass beyond the question of obedience and embrace life choices that bring themselves and those who love them tremendous amounts of pain. There are many behaviors we are free to choose from which will lead us into a trap of addiction and dependency. Unchecked behaviors can lead to abuse of self and others. The

---

[229] *Teachings of Presidents of the Church: Joseph Smith* (2007), 71
[230] Lynn Robbins, *The Righteous Judge*, an address given at the General Conference of the Church of Jesus Christ of Latter-day Saints, October 2016.

principle of giving others freedom to make mistakes and learn from them may require a great deal of faith and trust that there is a power higher than our own that is actually the primary teacher and is ultimately responsible for the life and well-being of all of us.

With this faith and trust, we can learn to "let go" of the ownership of another's mistakes. Letting go is much preferred to attempts at control through anger, stubbornness, hatred, and yelling. "Detaching from the chaos and negative emotions of an addict is essential in developing a strategy [to deal with them]. The key to detaching from the addict is to 'attach' oneself to a higher power (God). Getting angry and being resentful about someone else's behavior ought to remind us that 'this isn't between the addict and me, but rather between God and me.' When your spouse eats more sweets than you would like or your son is more sexually active before marriage than he was taught to be, anger should not result. If threats, yelling, or hate results because of someone else's behavior, then codependency has occurred, and powerlessness has set in. You have now committed a sin. Your behavior including your temper, lack of patience, and inability to love your enemy are issues that should be dealt with between God and you."[231] (Hidden Treasures Institute, 1994)

The freedom that comes with letting others own their own mistakes enables you to love them unconditionally. This is exactly what we need in our darkest hours: someone who is waiting up for us to come home. Teaching obedience is a necessary first step, but there is only so much you can do. After the lesson is over, the desire to embrace the principles must come from within the individual, it cannot be imposed from the outside. A person usually cannot be shamed into correcting their behavior.

Change from Within

So, what *can* we do when an older child is late for church every

---

[231] Hidden Treasures, "Hold on To Hope: Suggestions for LDS Co-Dependents," 1994, p. 122.

week? We have taught them the importance of being on time to their engagements. What do we do when a teenager isn't listening in church? Should we simply be grateful that they have chosen to be in church? Or should we punish them and take away privileges? When an adult child has a problem, you can seek answers on their behalf, but you cannot impose your solution.

Changes in character have to come from the inside. Correct principles can be taught and re-taught from the outside, but imposing your will is not in accordance with God's plan. Instead, it can ignite in the other a spirit of hatred, which is the spirit of the devil. Exercising the spirit of the devil to impose your will engenders the spirit of rebellion. Helping mold and encourage and build up through the spirit of love must also engender the spirit of love in the other. When they feel the spirit of love, the change will begin to come from within. We don't really need to tell people to repent, but we can let them know when they come to themselves and they have a desire for forgiveness, repentance is the way for them to receive it. The gift of repentance is the path to the blessings of the atonement, to have our guilt lifted, to have our burden removed. It is cause for celebration, intended to bring joy. "Behold, he who has repented of his sins, the same is forgiven, and I, the Lord, remember them no more."[232]

Conclusion

Teaching correct principles is essential at any age. We must always strive to learn what the principles are underlying the experiences we have and hear about in this life. In this chapter, we learned that letting people govern themselves when they are in possession of correct principles is the best we can do. It is the way God teaches us.

A few of the correct principles that have guided us through life are humility, repentance, accountability, obedience, and compassion. These are all Gospel principles that are at the core of being like Christ. Living them is not easy. Teaching them is

---

[232] Doctrines & Covenants, 58:42.

even harder. Humility is taking joy in the success of others. Repentance is trying to do a little bit better each day. Accountability mean owning the outcomes of our choices. We cannot force others to obey; this is not God's way. And compassion is permitting others the luxury of being mistaken. We don't need to highlight to others their errors, and we remember that change must come from within.

10

RELATIONSHIPS ARE THE KEY

One of the driving factors for this work was the realization that there is nothing more important in this life than human relationships. Relationships are all we have to keep us from being alone. We all need to feel close to someone. Relationships give us the opportunity to improve ourselves as we often see our own weaknesses in others. Some wise people have stared death in the face and confessed that their biggest regret is not spending more time with their loved ones in this life. Have you ever heard of someone at the end of their life on this earth regretting that they didn't get a certain promotion or make enough money?

"We sometimes forget the importance of relationships," noted Douglas Holmes. "With ever-increasing secular forces pulling at us, we need the strength that comes from loving relationships. We need love and support from parents, other family members, friends, and leaders who are also walking the path. These kinds of relationships take time. Time to be together. Time to laugh, play, learn, and serve together. Time to appreciate each other's interests and challenges. Time to be open and honest with each other as we strive to be better together. These relationships are one of the primary purposes of gathering as families. . ."233 (Holmes D. D., 2020)

Don't Ruin Relationships

Earlier in this work we related the story of the father who realized with his oldest son that maintaining a good relationship was far more important than the grades his son received in junior high school. When those we love are unwilling to meet our expectations, we should re-evaluate our expectations, and put our relationship with our loved one above all else. It is only with a true, loving relationship that we can ever hope to have any influence in the life of another.

So many times, we have seen others who sacrifice the relationship because they don't get their way or don't agree with a lifestyle choice. Nothing in this life is worth ruining a relationship with a loved one over. We all have a deep inner need to feel approval and acceptance from those in our sphere. We often don't see how our choices affect others and think we are more independent than we really are. It can be difficult when a person we love seems to be going down a path that will cause them harm, but the best thing to do is to wait for them to ask advice and support them the best we can while at the same time not supporting the decisions we disagree with. In fact, the topics of disagreement rarely need to come up. As we have shown, we all understand when someone doesn't agree with something we have done or said. We do not need them to point it out to us over and over.

Keeping relationships hallowed and strong can be difficult work. It demands that we overlook many areas of disagreement. But if we genuinely want to be there for someone, we have to meet them on their ground. We can't expect them to change their life choices just to be with us. For many of us, our most important relationship is our marriage. There are many things we can do to

---

[233] Douglas Holmes, "Deep in Our Heart," from an address given at the General Conference of the Church of Jesus Christ of Latter-day Saints, April 2020.

keep our relationships strong. One is to make sure that we don't feel entitled to everything we expect from others.

Don't Feel Robbed

Gordon Hinckley quoted one of the most helpful, timeless observations when he spoke to a group of young adults many years ago. "Marriage," he said, "requires a high degree of tolerance, and some of us need to cultivate that attribute. I have enjoyed these words of Jenkins Lloyd Jones, which I clipped from the newspaper some years ago. Said he:

"'There seems to be a superstition among many thousands of our young [men and women] who hold hands and smooch in the drive-ins that marriage is a cottage surrounded by perpetual hollyhocks to which a perpetually young and handsome husband comes home to a perpetually young and [beautiful] wife. When the hollyhocks wither and boredom and bills appear, the divorce courts are jammed.

"'Anyone who imagines that bliss [in marriage] is normal is going to waste a lot of time running around shouting that he has been robbed. [The fact is] most putts don't drop. Most beef is tough. Most children grow up to be just people. Most successful marriages require a high degree of mutual toleration. Most jobs are more often dull than otherwise . . . Life is like an old-time rail journey: delays, sidetracks, smoke, dust, cinders and jolts, interspersed only occasionally by beautiful vistas and thrilling bursts of speed. The trick is to thank the Lord for letting you have the ride.'"[234] (Hinckley, A Conversation with Single Adults, 1997)

Minimizing our false expectations of others will do more than anything in helping us form and maintain a feeling of love and gratitude for the people in our lives. Understanding that "most children grow up to be just people" is a great realization for many parents who are trying to boost their children above their natural

---

[234] "Big Rock Candy Mountains," *Deseret News*, 12 June 1973, A4, quoted by Gordon Hinckley.

capacity to achieve and in the process engender feelings of hatred for not recognizing the areas of interest and skills that their children do have. We have to help others find their interests and support them in pursuit of those even if they are not what we had envisioned or hoped for.

It is important to note that we are advocating for lowering our *false* expectations of others. This does not mean that we should not help others set high goals for themselves and support them in pursuit of those. It means that we should be focused on helping them find their own goals in their own areas of interest and help them achieve there rather than where we falsely hope they will achieve.

The Triad of Marriage

While on the topic of marriage, let's explore some observations on building and preserving a strong relationship between spouses. We have found that there are three essential ingredients that help build a marriage relationship on a foundation that cannot be shaken. All three of these are required and if any one of them is missing, we will never even achieve the high degree of mutual toleration we are seeking, let alone be able to sustain our marriage through its most difficult trials. These three ingredients are charity, intimacy, and security.

We have discussed charity, or unconditional love, in this work extensively. Charity means loving someone for who they are inside, a son or daughter of God, and not for all of the worldly attributes that are easier to see on the outside. We must see past their shortcomings and annoying personality traits, see them with the eyes of God and love them in the way that He does. Doing this not only requires a high degree of toleration, but it also takes a lot of patience, forgiveness, repentance, empathy, and compassion. It is an extremely high bar. It is a gift from God, and we should "pray unto the Father with all the energy of heart, that ye may be filled with this love."[235]

---

[235] Moroni 7:48.

Intimacy is essential in a marriage. When we hear about intimacy in marriage, it commonly refers to the sexual relationship in a marriage. And while that aspect is super-important, there is another form of intimacy that is equally valid. This is the type of intimacy that takes place without sex. It is touching, kindness, compliments, encouragement, being close physically, supporting and listening intently. It means being a shoulder to cry on, not a judge. It is the type of intimacy that Russell Ballard was referring to when he pleaded with his listeners, "Please do not miss an opportunity to look into the eyes of your family members with love."[236] (Ballard, Giving Our Spirits Control Over Our Bodies, 2019)

We often find that we are living with others, and we can barely even look them in the eye. Because of disagreements or hurt feelings, we tend to avoid the powerful glance into another's soul that takes place when we look them in the eye. When was the last time you looked deep into the eyes of one of your family members with love? Of course, when asked, we say that we love our family members. And yes, we do love them in the abstract. But have we looked into their eyes with love? This is an intimate act. It requires a break from all the distractions in the home. It requires that we settle down. It requires that we already have a particularly good relationship with someone. The eyes are a window into the soul, and it requires a great deal of trust to permit someone to look into ours. This type of trust comes from charity. When we feel that someone loves us unconditionally, we trust them enough to allow them to be intimate with us.

Intimacy leads to security, the third pillar in the triad of marriage relationship essentials. By security, we are not referring to financial security, although that is important to a strong marriage. It is very comforting to not have to worry that you will always have a roof over your head and a place to sleep and food to eat. Nor do we refer to physical security. While it is also

---

[236] Russell Ballard, *Giving Our Spirits Control Over Our Bodies*, an address given at the General Conference of the Church of Jesus Christ of Latter-day Saints, October 2019.

important that we feel safe from threat in our home, the type of security that is essential to a marriage is the security that comes from knowing that someone will always be there for you no matter what.

Many of us are not confident in our abilities or our person. We are often brash, short-tempered, and rude. We're well aware that those closest to us bear the brunt of our impetuousness. In moments of insecurity, we wonder why anyone puts up with us. Many of us were mistreated and abused as a child by the people who were supposed to be watching out for our best interests and protecting us. Trusting others is hard. If we've never been loved much, we wonder if we are even lovable. If our relationship with our parents is worn out or gone or was never there to begin with, there is no one left in the world who really cares about us and what happens to us.

Somehow, we hide all these insecurities and make our way through life. We put on a tough face for the world to see or a happy face. Or we fill our lives with distractions and superficial friends to keep our mind occupied. Some of us turn to God to try to fill this need and lucky are we if we can fill it. But no matter how strong we appear on the outside, we need to know that someone on this earth is there for us. We need to know that someone will love us for who we are, shortcomings and all. We need be able to trust someone with our burdens who will take them without judging us or giving us their solution. We need to know that they will always be there for us, no matter what.

Sometimes we have a person like that in our lives, but because we feel so unlovable, we try to push them away to prove our point that we are unlovable. This type of ironic resistance from the object of our love is one reason having unconditional love for another human is such a challenge. Being that person who is there for another requires that we have charity, and when we do, we provide the type of security that is essential to building an enduring relationship.

Establishing this type of trust is even more difficult in an age when the solution for the friction that inevitably arises in a marriage is to remove the resistance. Unfortunately, many cultures have made it acceptable to divorce and try again when the slightest bit of difficulty arises. Sometimes divorce is the best answer for the differences between two people, but others could be avoided if the partners had been trained in the type of selfless love that is required to make a marriage work. To establish this type of marriage, we must love unconditionally, be physically close and kind, and convince those we love that we will always be there for them.

Surprisingly, there was a pop song written about this type of love in the early 1980s. Howard Jones, an English musician, at only 28 years of age, had some deep insights into the nature of unconditional love and providing the type of security we all need in our relationships. He observed that charity "seeketh not her own," in other words, a loving person does not look to see if their love is reciprocated.[237] He notes that charity requires us to love someone regardless of what they choose to be, and to have this love for another is not always enough to make them feel lovable and stop questioning your love. The lyrics to that song are highly recommended listening.[238] (Jones H., 2021)

Charity, intimacy, and security are the triad of marriage. Each ingredient is precious enough on their own, but to find all three in the same relationship is as rare as a diamond. Striving for them is a requirement if we are to hope of forging relationships that will last beyond this life.

---

[237] From 1 Corinthians 13:5.
[238] Howard Jones, "What is Love?," published by WEA/Elektra, 1984. Ironically, at the time, Don Watson of NME was extremely critical of Jones, writing in a scathing review, "It's as hard to distinguish his music as it is to distinguish it from your carpet; conveniently, though, the lyrics are printed on the inner sleeve so that we may fully appreciate the complete lack of any novel observation in the songs... What's so amusing about Jones's songwriting is the glib manner in which he brandishes threadbare platitudes as unique insights." Apparently, Watson wasn't paying close attention. (https://en.wikipedia.org/wiki/Human%27s_Lib)

Eternal Relationships

It is confessed that the primary audience this work is intended for consists of people who have lived a common life, without extreme abuse by another. We fully acknowledge that there are many people in this world and throughout time who have been born into a hell where they were abused from an early age. We understand that in many cases, this abuse was perpetrated by those who were supposed to be their guardians, their parents. Often the perpetrators are damaged people who themselves were abused and have grown up without love in their life. It is an awful cycle that continues in the dark corners of all cultures. The author is fully unqualified to speak to or counsel those in situations like this and our heart goes out to you, and we pray for you and hope that you will be healed. These poor souls do well to escape the relationships that are hurting them. Frequently, these relationships cannot be healed in the normal course of events. This is not to say that they cannot be healed by the power of the atonement of Jesus Christ, but that there are very many complex layers that will require miracles and the power of God to unravel. For these souls, the thought of an eternal relationship with a family member raises the specter of hell in their heart and rightfully so.

For those who are in relationships of love, whether they be strong or messy, a desire often exists to continue that relationship for as long as possible. To do so requires effort from both members of the relationship. It is not something that can easily be sustained by the efforts of one person. Nevertheless, we must try and the way we begin to attempt to heal and strengthen these relationships is by serving the other person. This is why we have made the case that service is better placed in the home than outside it.

"Begin your service in your own homes and within your own families," taught Bonnie Oscarson. "These are the relationships that can be eternal. Even if—and maybe especially if—your family situation is less than perfect, you can find ways to serve, lift, and strengthen. Begin where you are, love them as they are, and prepare for the family you want to have in the future."[239] (Oscarson, 2017)

No one has a family situation that is perfect no matter how good it looks from the outside. Do not allow yourself to use the excuse that because this person was rude or selfish, it justifies you in withholding your service from them. There is nothing that increases one's love for another more than time voluntarily spent in their service. This can be challenging, especially when our love and service is not reciprocated or our loved one is choosing to live in a way that is not in accordance with our desires, but it is this type of self-sacrifice on behalf of another that will begin to forge a bond in the relationship that will endure beyond death. If we desire to live the gospel and follow Jesus Christ, it is required that we set the example by our acts of service, following his commandments, and our unconditional love of those we seek to be with eternally.

Love and Law

In our struggle to forge eternal bonds, we are often faced with the contradiction of loving the sinner and hating the sin. Throughout time, Christians have been called on to make the choice between following the Savior and living in the world. It seems difficult for many of us to separate the child of God from their actions. This becomes even more challenging when their actions contradict our morals and values or, even worse, are straight up criminal or perverted.

It is difficult to sort out how we will defend the faith and maintain the relationship. And for those who are not strong enough, perhaps taking a break from the relationship is the ideal situation. But we must strive harder to understand that loving someone does not require that they be perfect. It does not require them to be very good, nor even good at all. We do not have to

---

[239] Bonnie Oscarson, *The Needs Before Us*, an address given at the General Conference of the Church of Jesus Christ of Latter-day Saints, October 2017.

compromise our own faith and virtue to reach out to them and be their friend.

A common example of where this teaching is beneficial is when someone we love chooses to live in a way that is incompatible with our understanding of the gospel. For example, how does a brother treat his sibling when they confess their same-sex attraction? We fully understand that there is no divine approbation for homosexual relationships. They are contrary to the principles set forth in the "Family, A Proclamation to the World." Will we not be condoning their behavior if we accept our gay brother into our heart? We know that heaven cannot look upon sin with the least degree of allowance.[240] At the same time we are told to judge others as we would be judged.[241] We are informed that we should not judge and, simultaneously, that we should judge righteous judgements.[242] It can be a perplexing conundrum to know what to do in some situations.

"I have been helped," reports Dallin Oaks, "by thinking of the dual obligations of love and law as a two-sided coin: keeping the commandments is one side of the coin and loving others is the other side. We should keep each side in mind and not pursue or teach either side in a way that displaces or ignores the other."[243] (Oaks, We Must Both Live God's Law and Love Those Who Don't, 2018) There is much more available to help resolve this conflict in his full address and also in another talk given in October 2009.[244] (Oaks, Love and Law, 2009) The gist of these messages is what we need to understand before we can fully love others when we don't understand their choices. The bottom line is that we must continue to love, no matter what.

---

[240] Alma 45:16.
[241] Matthew 7:1-2.
[242] John 7:24.
[243] Dallin Oaks, *We Must Both Live God's Law and Love Those Who Don't*, an address given at Brigham Young University – Idaho, October 30, 2018.
[244] Dallin Oaks, *Love and Law*, an address given at the General Conference of the Church of Jesus Christ of Latter-day Saints, October 2009.

People Before Principles

If the reader will forgive the personal indulgence, let us consider a life lesson that perfectly illustrates the power of love in relationships and the destructive forces present when it's missing. I was introduced to the gospel by an Englishman. In the late 80s, I was a religious non-Christian. A friend of mine invited me to attend an adult religion class sponsored by the Church of Jesus Christ of Latter-day Saints. Having had religion and philosophy as a major life theme for over a decade, I thought it an easy task to attend, listen to the teachings, and highlight for my friend why they were false. The adult religion class took place in a church meetinghouse one night a week.

During my first visit, I was blown away by the doctrine of Christ. The teacher taught with power and authority and an interesting British accent. He did so with a smile. He taught about the power of the atonement and the need for repentance. His teaching set me on a course that would eventually lead to my baptism. The teacher was a professional seminary teacher for the church and became a friend of mine. He used to host small groups in his home with his family to which I was invited, and he would dazzle us with his seemingly unlimited knowledge of the doctrine. One of the things that attracted me to him was that he made everything seem so black and white. He was not about the emotional, sappy side of the gospel, and that fit quite well with me.

He once related the story of a teenager in one of his classes. The teen told a story to the class about how he had gotten caught stealing something small. When he was confronted about it, the young man confessed and admitted that he had done it. The student related this experience to the class and seemed to be seeking approbation for admitting his misdeed. When my friend heard the story, he questioned the teen in front of his classmates about whether he should be proud of him because he only steals but doesn't lie. It was not the response the teenager was hoping for.

We had a laugh about it when he told the story to his adult religion class. For those of us that found the temptation to lie and steal easy to overcome, it was quite a humorous anecdote. But what I didn't realize at the time is that the story was one in a pattern of the teacher making young students feel bad because of their shallow understanding of the gospel.

Over the next few years, this great teacher was placed on probation and ultimately relieved of his teaching position by the Church Educational System. This came a shock to me because I always thought of him as one of the most knowledgeable and inspiring teachers I'd ever heard. I even wrote a letter in his defense, suggesting that those who were against his teaching were against Christ because his teachings were so Christ-centered. He left no grey area when teaching the doctrine.

Time and circumstances caused us to drift apart, and we did not remain in touch. To my surprise, he contacted me one day and needed a place to stay. He was divorced and his wife was keeping the home. Shockingly, he was now jobless and homeless. It even seemed that his grown children had now turned against him, and he was completely alone. There was a part of me that felt like he was another Job who God was testing because of his righteousness. But I really didn't have the whole story.

The last time I saw him was after his wife had passed away. We spent a day together driving through the mountains talking about life. One of the things he said to me has echoed through my mind across the decades.

As he told his side of the story about why he was let go from his teaching position, he shared a conversation he had with one of the Church leaders that interviewed him on the way out. In the interview, my friend was confronted with a behavior of his that was incompatible with a person in his position. It can be described in various ways, but it boils down to a lack of love. He was criticized by students, parents, and colleagues as being someone who preached a little too hard. Having heard him teach and preach, I knew that everything he taught was correct and true and he had many sources, especially the scriptures to back him up. He was a master at teaching correct principles.

As he explained this to the person interviewing him, he was told by the Church leader in a loving voice, "Stephen, people before principles."

"People before principles?" he mocked with his British accent, as we gazed upon a beautiful mountain valley.

"People before principles?" he wondered again, with a tone of disbelief tinged with disgust.

People before principles? I wondered to myself. If a principle is true, can it be excused for a person and their choices? If a principle is true in one circumstance, is it not also true always? Is it ever incorrect to teach a true principle? I didn't have the answers that day, but for some reason those three words impacted me deeply and I pondered them many times over the years.

It wasn't many years after that day that my friend passed away and I became a bishop. I was a believer in principles before people. But thankfully my years of service opened my heart, and I began to see the way God sees. I began to see that God looks on the heart and waits for the right time to teach the principles. A perfect example of this is when Christ was called to condemn the woman taken in adultery. Had he put principles before people, he would have commanded that such should be stoned. Instead, he was content to wait until a later time for the woman to receive the principle of chastity.

As I now consider my friend's plight in this life, I realize that his insistence at putting principles before people probably cost him his marriage. Because everything was so black and white for him, his children sided with their mother, and he lost them too. Because of his inability to consider the *people* he was teaching and was beholden more to the principles he was teaching, he lost his livelihood as well. Truth can have a powerful effect when taught boldly. As we are reminded by Mormon, "preaching of the word had . . . a more powerful effect upon the minds of the people than the sword, or anything else."[245] But timing is important, too.

---

[245] Mosiah 31:5.

A wise teacher will consider the student's preparation to receive. "Give not that which is holy unto the dogs, neither cast ye your pearls before swine, lest they trample them under their feet, and turn again and rend you."[246]

More important than preaching or teaching hard doctrine to those we are trying to persuade is the relationship we have with the hearer. The old adage, *'They don't care what you know until they know that you care,'* is wisdom and truth. If we are to plant the word as a seed into the heart of another, we must first prepare the soil of our relationship and ensure that it is soft and fertile. As correct as my teacher friend may have been in his teaching and doctrine, he lost his chance to influence his students and loved ones by ruining his relationships with them. Perhaps it would have made more sense for him to overlook some of the teaching opportunities he had and instead showed love and forgiveness and strengthened his bond with them through encouragement.

Influence Comes from Love

It is difficult to overemphasize the importance of demonstrating our love to those over whom we wish to have some influence. This idea was shared by Norman Nemrow with a congregation as he sought to persuade of the power of love in our families. "In order to have influence in the lives of our children, they need to know that you love them," he said.[247] (Nemrow, 2016) Is it not true that many times, our interactions with our children are based on our fear of what others will think of us if our children don't behave a certain way? People (especially our children) can sense when our behavior toward them is motivated not by love, but by the fear of looking bad. Over the years we have heard this type of sentiment expressed in a multitude of ways: "I'm making you do this because I don't want people to think I didn't raise you right." Or "If you don't learn some manners, people are going to

---

[246] Matthew 7:6.
[247] Norman Nemrow, Keynote Address, an address given at the Highland East Stake Conference General Session, October 16, 2016.

think you were raised on a farm." As if farmers are somehow notorious for bad manners.

When we really care deeply about the welfare of the souls of our family members, how we look from the outside becomes less important. After all, our success as a parent will be largely determined by the love our children feel from us rather than how we are rated by neighbors on an imaginary scale. Henry Eyring alludes to this idea as he contrasted the two concerns. "I have felt His hand and His closeness in my service with our children when I prayed to know how to help them find the peace that only the gospel brings. At such moments, I cared less about being seen as a successful parent, but I cared deeply about the success and well-being of my children."[248] (Eyring, Becoming True Disciples, 2017) This is an interesting confession if he is speaking about a certain occasion. As most of us suppose, the children of an apostle would never be unsure about how to find the peace of the gospel. Yet despite all his teaching, it sounds as if some of his children were still not getting it. Perhaps they were looking for peace in some other way and Eyring knew that the peace they were searching for could only be found through the gospel.

It appears his normal methods of counseling and teaching were not getting through, and he was brought to his knees in prayer to know how to help them get in tune with the gospel. Would an Apostle of Jesus Christ really need to resort to prayer to help his own children learn the gospel? Is the gospel that hard to catch? Maybe so. It is also interesting to note that while he cared most deeply about the well-being of his children, he also cared about begin seen as a successful parent, only less so. We wonder if his children were taking a position to make him fear that he would not be viewed as a successful parent.

His comment illustrates how even the brightest and humblest among us must battle against the fear of how we will be seen by others. These fears can cause even the best people to take a harmful course. It is an evil, driving force in the great and abominable church. "For the praise of the world do they destroy

---

[248] Henry Eyring, "Becoming True Disciples," *Ensign*, October 2017.

the saints of God and bring them down into captivity."[249] This destruction is obviously a spiritual one, for how can you be taken into captivity if you have already been destroyed? To destroy saints means to take away their "saint-ness." When a saint seeks after the praise of the world, it won't be long until they are no longer saints.

We should all know that it is more important to care for the well-being of our children than it is to have parenting fans, but sometimes in an effort to make ourselves look better to others we may say or do things that are not entirely in our children's best interest. Therefore, we must always be on guard against seeking the praise of the world.

It is somewhat of a fantasy to believe that parents have such a huge influence in the lives of every one of their children. While it is true that we can influence them through fear when they are younger, when they grow that influence wanes. Nor can we be easily convinced that "raising them right" with the proper instruction, care, and education is a guarantor of any desired outcome. Let's take for example the Duke of Sussex in 2020.

Henry Charles Albert David Mountbatten-Windsor (aka, Prince Harry) was born in 1984 to Prince Charles, the heir apparent to the British throne as the eldest son to Queen Elizabeth II. As a member of the British royal family, without question he received the most proper upbringing and education available in modern Western Civilization. At age 34, Prince Harry announced his engagement to an American actress which prompted "much comment about the possible social significance of Meghan Markle becoming a mixed-race royal."[250] (Wikipedia, 2020) Likely, marrying an actress, let alone an American one, was not one hundred percent in line with his parents' expectations. But to further the breach, Harry and Meghan announced they would be "stepping back from their role as senior members of the royal family" a few years later.[251] Without question, this was

---

[249] 1 Nephi 13:9.
[250] Prince Harry Duke of Sussex, Wikipedia, sourced September 5, 2020.
[251] Ibid.

not in alignment with his family's expectations.

Prince Harry's case is not unique. History is replete with similar stories of princes and kings abdicating thrones and inheritances. And in many cases, they all did it for the same reason: love. There was a person in their life who had more influence on them than their family and it is not a stretch to believe that they allowed themselves to be influenced because of the love they felt from and for this person. The point is that even with the best upbringing, nothing is a more powerful influencer in our lives than the love we feel.

Relationships Are All We Have

If we destroy our relationships over principles, no matter how lofty, in the end we have nothing. Relationships are all we have. Does it do any good to stand alone because our loved ones will not embrace our principles? No. In that situation we have lost all influence over them. We should hold ourselves to the highest possible spiritual standard without holding anyone else to that standard. Their obedience to correct principles has to come from within them. It cannot be forced on them from the outside. All we can do is encourage and teach and show forth an increase of love. Love sustains the relationship. The relationship sustains the influence. Thomas Monson has taught, "Never let a problem to be solved become more important than a person to be loved."[252] (Monson, Finding Joy in the Journey, 2008)

This idea is expounded upon beautifully by Rick Warren. He reiterates the importance of love and relationships. "Often we act as if relationships are something to be squeezed into our schedule. We talk about *finding* time for our children or *making* time for people in our lives. That gives the impression that relationships are just a part of our lives along with many other tasks. But God says relationships are what life is all about. Four of the Ten Commandments deal with our relationship to God

---

[252] Thomas Monson, *Finding Joy in the Journey*, an address given at the General Conference of the Church of Jesus Christ of Latter-day Saints, October 2008.

while the other six deal with our relationships with people. But all ten are about relationships!"[253] (Warren, 2002)

We are placed on this earth in families because families bring out the best and worst in us. Being forced to interact, to accommodate, to compromise, and to sacrifice for others is what is required to wear down the rebellious, selfish, natural man. Unfortunately, all of the accommodating and compromising can lead us to take a lonesome path. It is far easier to live alone than with a family as far as logistics, preferences, routines, and schedules go. But few people want to live alone for too long. Especially when they are preparing to step off into the abyss of death. Warren continues, "I have been at the bedside of many people in their final moments, when they stand on the edge of eternity, and I have never heard anyone say, 'Bring me my diplomas! I want to look at them one more time. Show me my awards, my medals, that gold watch I was given.' When life on earth is ending, people don't surround themselves with objects. What we want around us is people—people we love and have relationships with. In our final moments we all realize that relationships are what life is all about. Wisdom is learning that truth sooner rather than later."[254]

Compassion and Respect

By now we should have a good idea of what that love looks like that must be shown to family members in order to hope for the influence we wish to have in the lives of our loved ones. But what kind of influence can we expect to have? For a parent, we hope that the example we set for our children inspires them to live in a way that they can enjoy the benefits of a good life. For example, a mother who has spent many years learning about nutrition and exercise would hope that her children would follow in her footsteps and enjoy the vigor and energy in later years that comes from fitness and eating good foods. But sometimes it's hard for

---

[253] Rick Warren, *The Purpose Driven Life*, Zondervan, 2002, pp 124-125.
[254] Ibid., p 125

a parent to influence children in life matters. When people feel that they are being judged for being out of shape or have no interest in healthy foods or they feel that they are being forced to change from without, it's likely that they will dig in against even the most helpful advice.

Without the perspective of years, it is sometimes difficult for the younger generation to respect what their parents have gone through. Someday they may learn for themselves. In the meantime, the parent can show respect for other good attributes of their children, even if they are not the trait that they are most interested in.

Perhaps one of the most endearing traits we can learn that will strengthen our relationships is compassion. Having compassion for each other's challenges and trials in life goes a long way toward showing you understand another and what they are going through. We all have difficulties in our life. We all have hardships and trials. Having someone really try to understand what we are going through means a lot. Compassion can be defined as having concerns for the misfortunes of others. This means forgoing the "I told you so" response and the second-guessing suggestions of a better course of action that would have resulted in the avoidance of difficulty. Sometimes, even when we see the choices that led to a trial, a better response than highlighting them would be to put ourselves in the place of the other. Try to imagine what it would be like to be in a similar circumstance. Understand that in the heat of the moment, we do not always make optimal choices. Realize that, there, but for the grace of God, go I. Remember to feel the struggle your loved one is facing and help them to realize that you understand and will be there for them to help them get through.

"Nowhere is that bedrock foundation of love needed more than in the home," taught Thomas Monson. "If we would keep the commandment to love one another, we must treat each other with compassion and respect, showing our love in day-to-day interactions. Love offers a kind word, a patient response, a selfless act, an understanding ear, a forgiving heart. In all our associations, these and other such acts help make evident the love in our hearts."[255] (Monson, As I Have Loved You, 2017)

The other essential ingredient that Monson recommends to prove the love that is in our hearts is respect. While having respect for those we love seems too obvious to discuss, it is not uncommon to find it missing in the family setting. Perhaps this is because living so near to someone else, you get to see their weakness and flaws up close. Maybe familiarity really does breed contempt. But these responses must be overcome as we learn to show respect one to another.

We have discussed respect elsewhere in this work in the context of children respecting their parents and parents earning respect from their children rather than demanding it. Having respect for others means a lot of things. It can mean understanding when one comes home after a strenuous day of classes and work, they may not be able to mow the lawn. It may mean understanding that your spouse works as hard as you do when you are not together. It means respecting the other person's time, not making them late, or understanding when they are late. It means speaking calmly even when circumstances seem to demand a more forceful tone. It means respecting the reasonable wishes of a family member when they've asked you to adjust. Respect is essential and love cannot manifest without it. Compassion and respect are indispensable in forging relationships and lay the foundation for the love that is going to heal hearts and influence minds.

Toward the end of his life, Thomas Monson summed up his life lessons and his testimony was the importance of love in the family. "Love is the very essence of the gospel," he said. "The noblest attribute of the human soul. Love is the remedy for ailing families, ill communities, and sick nations. Love is a smile, a wave, a kind comment, and a compliment. Love is sacrifice, service, and selflessness."[256] What greater testimony to the power of love in

---

[255] Thomas Monson, "As I Have Loved You," *Ensign*, First Presidency Message, February 2017.
[256] Ibid.

the home can there be beyond that of a man who selflessly gave his entire life to the service of others?

Strive to Preserve

We have made a strong case for the importance of relationships in this life and highlighted what it takes to make them stronger. Rest assured that there are persistent forces in this world that work against human relationships and oppose our efforts to build and strengthen them. Evil will work to erode our relationships with others with the end being loneliness and fear. Often those we love most take a course of action that trespasses on our values or wishes. How we respond to their actions can determine whether we can sustain or will erode the relationship. It is a fine line we must navigate as we seek to hold onto our own values, be an example of the joy our values bring, and continue to support and sustain those who have paused or taken a detour in their course. As we walk this fine line, we cannot allow ourselves to cut off others from our love.

Dallin Oaks regularly teaches about the importance and difficulty of maintaining this balance. He has also observed the tactics others take in attempting to do so. At a BYU-Idaho campus devotional, Oaks warned against the path of failing to show love toward those who do not share our values at the moment. "At the most serious level," he said, "some [people] even withhold love and relationships from members of their own families and friends. To balance our commitments to love and law we must continually show love even as we continually honor and keep the commandments. We must strive to preserve precious relationships and at the same time not compromise our responsibilities to be obedient to and supportive of gospel law."[257] (Prescott, 2018)

His teaching is that we must strive to preserve our precious relationships. By using the verb "strive," it is evident that he

---

[257] Dallin Oaks, quoted in an article by Marianne Holman Prescott reporting on his address, November 1, 2018.

thinks our efforts to preserve relationships will be challenging. Because of the forces that work to disintegrate human relationships, we will find that we must always be seeking and granting forgiveness, patching over differences, ignoring idiosyncratic traits, focusing on the best in others and building them up. Often these efforts go against our natural tendencies to take offense, suspect mal intent, nurture resentment, and criticize. This is why it is so difficult. But overcoming these tendencies is what make success so rewarding.

Conclusion

In this chapter we have shown how relationships are the key to happiness in this world. We have taken the position that nothing in this life is worth ruining relationships with our loved ones, and it often requires a high degree of mutual toleration to preserve them. For families, the most important relationship is the marriage between the husband and wife. To strengthen and preserve this relationship, three key ingredients are essential: charity, intimacy, and security. We should seek to extend the life of these relationships as long as possible and there may be nothing better than time spent in the service of another to endear them and strengthen the relationship.

We have highlighted the fine line we must sometimes walk to preserve relationships with those we love when they depart from our expectations for them, and we have shown how putting principles before people can lead to tragic losses in our relationships with those we should be loving. If we desire to have influence in the lives of our loved ones, then we must show them that we care. Ultimately, people are only influenced by those from whom they feel love.

At the end of this life, our relationships will likely be the only things we care about. To help ensure that we have someone there for us when we pass, it helps to show compassion and respect for them throughout their life. Developing and nurturing relationships that will be lasting and endure forever is no easy task. Nevertheless, we must strive to strengthen them and at the end, we will be rewarded by having the companionship of those we love to get us through this difficult life.

References

Adams, S. (2019). *Loserthink: How Undtrained Brains Are Ruining America.* Harefield: Portfolio.

Alonso, J. L. (2017). Love One Another As He Has Loved Us. *General Conference of the Church of Jesus Christ of Latter-day Saints* (pp. 119-121). Salt Lake City: Intellectual Reserve, Inc.

Andersen, N. L. (2018). Wounded. *General Conference of the Church of Jesus Christ of Latter-day Saints* (pp. 83-86). Salt Lake City: Intellectual Reserve, Inc.

Arbinger Institute. (2015). *The Anatomy of Peace: Resolving the Heart of Conflict.* Oakland: Berrett-Koehler.

Ballard, M. R. (2003). Let Our Voices Be Heard. *General Conference of the Church of Jesus-Christ of Latter-day Saints* (pp. 16-19). Salt Lake City: Intellectual Reserve, Inc.

Ballard, M. R. (2016). Family Councils. *General Conference of the Church of Jesus-Christ of Latter-day Saints* (pp. 63-67). Salt Lake CIty: Intellectual Reserve, Inc.

Ballard, M. R. (2019). Giving Our Spirits Control Over Our Bodies. *General Conference of the Church of Jeus Christ of Latter-day Saints* (pp. 106-109). Salt Lake City: Intellectual Reserve, Inc.

Bednar, D. A. (2015). Chosen to Bear Testimony of My Name. *General Conference of the Church of Jesus Christ of Latter-day Saints* (pp. 128-131). Salt Lake City: Intellectual Reserve, Inc.

Bednar, D. A. (2016). If Ye Had Known Me. *General Conference of the Church of Jesus Christ of Latter-day Saints* (pp. 102-105). Salt Lake City: Intellectual Reserve, Inc.

Benson, E. T. (1985). Born of God. *General Conference of the Church of Jesus Christ of Latter-day Saints.* Salt Lake City: Intellectual Reserve, Inc.

Bingham, J. B. (2016). I Will Bring the Light of the Gospel into My Home.

General Conference of the Church of Jesus Christ of Latter-day Saints (pp. 6-8). Salt Lake City: Intellectual Reserve, Inc.

Boom, H. T. (2019). Knowing, Loving, Growing. *General Conference of the Church of Jesus Christ of Latter-day Saints* (pp. 104-106). Salt Lake City: Intellectual Reserve, Inc.

Braithwaite, S. P. (2018, October 14). *What Every Leader Needs to Know About Faith Crisis - An Interview With Scott Braithwaite*. Retrieved from leadingsaints.org: https://leadingsaints.org/what-every-leader-needs-to-know-about-faith-crisis-an-interview-with-scott-braithwaite/

Brown, B. D. (2013, December 10). *Brene Brown on Empathy*. Retrieved from YouTube: https://youtu.be/1Evwgu369Jw

Bryan. (2020, June 7). *Bryan on Scouting*. Retrieved from Scouting Magazine: https://blog.scoutingmagazine.org/tag/cub-scout-motto

Burton, L. K. (2016). I Was a Stranger. *General Conference of the Church of Jesus Christ of Latter-day Saints* (pp. 13-15). Salt Lake City: Intellectual Reserve, Inc.

Chambers, W. (1952). *Witness*. Retrieved from Goodreads: https://www.goodreads.com/work/quotes/748601-witness

Christofferson, D. T. (2015). Why the Church. *General Conference of the Church of Jesus Christ of Latter-day Saints* (pp. 108-110). Salt Lake City: Intellectual Reserve, Inc.

Christofferson, D. T. (2016, Marcy). *Finding Your Life*. Retrieved from Ensign: https://www.churchofjesuschrist.org/study/ensign/2016/03/finding-your-life?lang=eng

Christofferson, T. (2017). *That We May Be One: A Gay Mormon's Perspective on Faith and Family*. Salt Lake City: Deseret Book.

Church of Jesus Christ of Latter-day Saints. (2018). *The Aaronic Priesthood Leader Training*. Retrieved from churchofjesuschrist.org:

https://www.lds.org/callings/aaronic-priesthood/auxiliary-training?lang=eng

Clark, J. R. (1936). Conference Talk. *General Conference of the Church of Jesus Christ of Latter-day Saints* (pp. 114-115). Salt Lake City: Intellectual Reserve, Inc.

Cordon, B. (2018). Becoming a Shepherd. *General Conferene of the Church of Jesus Christ of Latter-day Saints* (pp. 74-76). Salt Lake City: Intellectual Reserve, Inc.

Cosby, B. (2012, May 8). *Fathers*. Retrieved from YouTube: https://www.youtube.com/watch?v=19YYCThl6lI

Covey, S. R. (1982). *The Divine Center*. Harrisonburg: R.R. Donnelly & Sons.

Craig, M. (2018). Divine Discontent. *General Conference of the Church of Jesus Christ of Latter-day Saints* (pp. 52-55). Salt Lake City: Intellectual Reserve, Inc.

Craig, M. D. (2018, December 11). *This Is My Day of Opportunity*. Retrieved from BYU Speeches: https://speeches.byu.edu/talks/michelle-d-craig_my-day-of-opportunity/

Danielson, I. (2017). *What We Cannot Afford to Live WIthout*. Retrieved from churchofjesuschrist.org: https://webcache.googleusercontent.com/search?q=cache:Pg-tqmaj-esJ:https://www.churchofjesuschrist.org/blog/what-we-cannot-afford-to-live-without%3Flang%3Deng+&cd=1&hl=en&ct=clnk&gl=us

Duperouzel, L. C. (2020, June 19). *Finding Compassion for the Crabs*. Retrieved from Dr. L Christian Duperouzel: https://drlchristianduperouzel.wordpress.com/2020/06/19/finding-compassion-for-the-crabs/

Dyer, F. L. (1910). *Edison: His Life and Inventions*. New York: Harper & Brothers.

Esplin, C. A. (2016). He Asks Us to Be His Hands. *General Conference of the*

Church of Jesus Christ of Latter-day Saints (pp. 6-9). Salt Lake City: Intellectual Reserve, Inc.

Eyring, H. B. (1991). Teaching Is a Moral Act. *BYU Annual University Conference.* Provo: Brigham Young University.

Eyring, H. B. (2013). To My Grandchildren. *General Conference of the Church of Jesus Christ of Latter-day Saints* (pp. 69-72). Salt Lake City: Intellectual Reserve, Inc.

Eyring, H. B. (2016, January). Happiness for Those We Love. *Ensign.*

Eyring, H. B. (2017, October). Becoming True Disciples. *Ensign.*

Eyring, H. B. (2017). My Peace I Leave With You. *General Conferene of the Church of Jesus Christ of Latter-day Saints* (pp. 15-18). Salt Lake City: Intellectual Reserve, Inc.

Eyring, H. B. (2019). A Home Where the Spirit of the Lord Dwells. *General Conference of the Church of Jesus Christ of Latter-day Saints* (pp. 22-25). Salt Lake City: Intellectual Reserved, Inc.

Eyring, H. B. (2020). He Goes Before us. *General Conference of the Church of Jesus Christ of Latter-day Saints.* (pp. 66-68). Salt Lake City: Intellectual Reserve, Inc.

Faust, J. E. (2000). Womandhood: The Highest Place of Honor. *General Conference of the Church of Jesus Christ of Latter-day Saints* (pp. 95-97). Salt Lake City: Intellectual Reserve, Inc.

Foster, B. (2015). It's Never Too Early and It's Never Too Late. *General Conference of the Church of Jesus Christ of Latter-day Saints* (pp. 50-52). Salt Lake City: Intellectual Reserve, Inc.

Gay, R. C. (2018). Taking Upon Ourselves the Name of Jesus Christ. *General Conference of the Church of Jesus Christ of Latter-day Saints* (pp. 97-99). Salt Lake City: Intellectual Reserve, Inc.

Heaston, S. (2015, June 23). *Keeping Your Fingers on the PULSE of Service.* Retrieved from speeches.byu.edu: https://speeches.byu.edu/talks/sondra-heaston_keeping-your-fingers-on-the-pulse-of-service/

Hidden Treasures Institute. (1994). *Hold Onto Hope: Suggestions for LDS Co-Dependents.* Springville, UT: Cedar Fort.

Hinckley, G. B. (1984, March). And the Greatest of These Is Love. *Ensign*, p. 3.

Hinckley, G. B. (1997, March). A Conversation with Single Adults. *Ensign*.

Hinckley, G. B. (1999). Thanks to the Lord for His Blessings. *General Conference of the Church of Jesus Christ of Latter-day Saints.* Salt Lake City: Intellectual Reserve, Inc.

Hodge, B. (2014, September 19). *The Five R's of Repentance.* Retrieved from bryanhodge.net: https://bryanhodge.net/2014/09/19/the-five-rs-of-repentance

Holland, J. R. (1980). *BYU Devotional.* Provo, UT: Brigham Young University.

Holland, J. R. (2010). Because of Your Faith. *General Conference of the Church of Jesus Christ of Latter-day Saints* (pp. 6-9). Salt Lake City: Intellectual Reserve, Inc.

Holmes, D. D. (2020). Deep in Our Heart. *General Conference of the Church of Jesus-Christ of Latter-day Saints* (pp. 23-25). Salt Lake City: Intellectual Reserve, Inc.

Hugo, V. (1862). *Les Miserable.* Paris, France: A. Lacroix, Verboeckhoven & Cie.

Hunter, H. W. (1984). The Pharisee and the Publican. *General Conferene of the Church of Jesus Christ of Latter-day Saints.* Salt Lake City: Intellectual Reserve, Inc.

Huntsman, E. D. (2018, August 7). *Hard Sayings and Safe Spaces: Making Room for Struggle as Well as Faith.* Retrieved from speeches.byu.edu: https://speeches.byu.edu/talks/eric-d-huntsman/hard-sayings-and-safe-spaces-making-room-for-both-struggle-and-faith/

Jackson, K. P., & Hunt, R. D. (2005). *Religious Educator Volume 6 Number 2*. Retrieved from rsc.byu.edu: https://rsc.byu.edu/vol-6-no-2-2005/reprove-betimes-sharpness-vocabulary-joseph-smith

Jones, G. (2021, May 2). *Perspectives on the Prophet Joseph Smith - Gracia Jones Episode 5*. Retrieved from churchofjesuschrist.org: https://www.churchofjesuschrist.org/inspiration/latter-day-saints-channel/listen/series/perspectives-on-the-prophet-joseph-smith-audio/gracia-jones-episode-5?lang=eng

Jones, H. (2021, May 30). *What Is Love?* Retrieved from Wikipedia: https://en.wikipedia.org/wiki/Human%27s_Lib

Keen, J. (2020, June 7). *6 R's of Repentance - Part 1*. Retrieved from Sermon Audio: https://www.sermonaudio.com/sermoninfo.asp?SID=107172212126

Lee, H. B. (2021, May 2). *Teachings of the Presidents of the Church: Harold B. Lee*. Retrieved from churchofjesuschrist.org: https://www.churchofjesuschrist.org/manual/teachings-harold-b-lee/chapter-14?lang=eng

Lewis, C. (1996). *Joyful Christian.* New York City: Simon & Schuster.

Lyon, J. M. (1996). *Best-Loved Poems of the LDS People.* Salt Lake City: Deseret Book Company.

McConkie, B. R. (1973, February 27). *Agency or Inspiration - Which?* Retrieved from BYU Speeches: https://speeches.byu.edu/talks/bruce-r-mcconkie/agency-inspiration/

McCue, J. (2020, January 19). *A Parent's Guide to Why Teens Make Bad Decisions*. Retrieved from The Conversation: https://theconversation.com/a-parents-guide-to-why-teens-make-bad-decisions-8826

Monson, T. S. (2008). Finding Joy in the Journey. *General Conference of the Church of Jesus Christ of Latter-day Saints* (pp. 84-87). Salt Lake City: Intellectual Reserve, Inc.

Monson, T. S. (2010). Charity Never Faileth. *General Conference of the Church of Jesus Christ of Latter-day Saints* (pp. 122-125). Salt Lake City: Intellectual Reserve, Inc.

Monson, T. S. (2015). Be An Example of Light. *General Conference of the Church of Jesus Christ of Latter-day Saints* (pp. 86-89). Salt Lake City: Intellectual Reserve, Inc.

Monson, T. S. (2017, February). As I Have Loved You. *Ensign*, p. 6.

Monson, T. S. (2017, February). As I Have Loved You. *Ensign*.

Montoya, H. (2015). Tested and Tempted - but Helped. *General Conference of the Church of Jesus Christ of Latter-day Saints* (pp. 53-55). Salt Lake City: Intellectual Reserve, Inc.

Nattress, B. K. (2016). No Greater Joy Than to Know That they Know. *General Conference of the Church of Jesus Christ of Latter-day Saints* (pp. 119-121). Salt Lake City: Intellectual Reserve, Inc.

Nelson, R. M. (2019). We Can Do Better and Be Better. *General Conference of the Church of Jesus-Christ of Latter-day Saints* (pp. 67-69). Salt Lake City: Intellectual Reserve, Inc.

Nemrow, N. (2016). Keynote Address. *Conference of the Highland East Stake of the Church of Jesus Christ of Latter-day Saints*, (p. from author's personal notes). Highland, UT.

New York Trust Co. vs. Eisner, 345 (United States 1921).

Oaks, D. H. (1994). Tithing. *General Conference of the Church of Jesus Christ of Latter-day Saints* (pp. 33-34). Salt Lake City: Intellectual Reserve, Inc.

Oaks, D. H. (2009). Love and Law. *General Conference of the Church of Jesus Christ of Latter-day Saints* (pp. 26-29). Salt Lake City: Intelletual Reserve, Inc.

Oaks, D. H. (2018, October 30). We Must Both Live God's Law and Love Those Who Don't. *Church News*.

Oaks, D. H. (2019). Trust in the Lord. *General Conference of the Church of Jesus Christ of Latter-day Saints* (pp. 26-29). Salt Lake City: Intellectual Reserve, Inc.

Oaks, D. H. (2020). The Melchizedek Priesthood and the Keys. *General Conference of the Church of Jesus Christ of Latter-day Saints* (pp. 69-72). Salt Lake City: Intellectual Reserve, Inc.

Oscarson, B. L. (2017). The Needs Before Us. *General Conference of the Church of Jesus Christ of Latter-day Saints* (pp. 25-27). Salt Lake City: Intellectual Reserve, Inc.

Packer, B. K. (2010). The Power of the Priesthood. *General Conference of the Church of Jesus Christ of Latter-day Saints* (pp. 6-9). Salt Lake City: Intellectual Reserve, Inc.

Palmer, M. (2017). Then Jesus Beholding Him Loved Him. *General Conference of the Church of Jesus Christ of Latter-day Saints* (pp. 114-116). Salt Lake City: Intellectual Reserve, Inc.

Patterson, J. (2006). Enmity. *Alpine North Stake Conference* (pp. 1-7). Alpine: Patterson.

Prescott, M. H. (2018, November 1). *Church News*. Retrieved from ChurchofJesusChrist.org: https://www.churchofjesuschrist.org/church/news/we-must-both-live-gods-law-and-love-those-who-dont-president-oaks-shares?lang=eng

Quote Investigator. (2020, January 20). *I Have GOtten a Lot of Results! I Know Several Thousand Things That Won't Work*. Retrieved from Quote Investigator: https://quoteinvestigator.com/2012/07/31/edison-lot-results/

Renlund, D. G. (2015). Through God's Eyes. *General Conference of the Church of Jesus Christ of Latter-day Saints* (pp. 93-95). Salt Lake City: Intellectual Reserve, Inc.

Renlund, D. G. (2016). Repentance: A Joyful Choice. *General Conference of the Church of Jesus Christ of Latter-day Saints* (pp. 121-124). Salt Lake City:

Intellectual Reserve, Inc.

Renlund, D. G. (2018). Choose You This Day. *General Conference of the Church of Jesus Christ of Latter-day Saints* (pp. 104-107). Salt Lake City: Intellectual Reserve, Inc.

Richards, S. (1950). *Conference Report, April 1950*. Salt Lake City: Intellectual Reserve, Inc.

Robbins, L. G. (2016). The Righteous Judge. *General Conference of the Church of Jesus Christ of Latter-day Saints* (pp. 96-98). Salt Lake City: Intellectual Reserve, Inc.

Rogers, S. (1996). *Hearts Knit Together: Talks from the 1995 Women's Conference*. Salt Lake City: Deseret Book.

Romney, M. (2009, March). The Celestial Nature of Self-Reliance. *Ensign*, pp. 61-65.

Saints, C. o.-d. (2021, May 2). *Topcis: Charity*. Retrieved from churchofjesuschrist.org: https://www.churchofjesuschrist.org/topics/charity?lang=eng

Smith, G. A. (2011). *Teachings of the Presidents of the Church: George Albert Smith*. Retrieved from churchofjesuschrist.org: https://www.churchofjesuschrist.org/study/general-conference/2016/10/the-righteous-judge?lang=eng

Smith, J. (2007). *Teachings of Presidents of the Church: Joseph Smith*. Salt Lake City: Church of Jesus Christ of Latter-day Saints.

Smith, J. (2021, May 2). *Joseph Smith - History*. Retrieved from churchofjesuschrist.org: https://www.churchofjesuschrist.org/scriptures/pgp/js-h1.19?lang=eng&clang=eng#p18

Smith, J. (2021, April 25). *Teachings of Presidents of the Church: Joseph Smith*. Retrieved from ChurchofJesusChrist.org: https://www.churchofjesuschrist.org/study/manual/teachings-joseph-smith?lang=eng

Smith, L. M. (2000). *The History of Joseph Smith by His Mother*. Salt Lake City: Covenant Communications.

Snow, S. E. (2016). Be Thou Humble. *General Conference of the Church of Jesus Christ of Latter-day Saints* (pp. 36-38). Salt Lake City: Intellectual Reserve, Inc.

Southland. (2014, March 20). *The Winds*. Retrieved from youtube.com: https://youtu.be/2-esjDFasPs

Stephens, C. (2015). If Ye Love Me, Keep My Commandments. *General Conference of the Church of Jesus Christ of Latter Day Saints* (pp. 118-120). Salt Lake City: Intellectual Reserve, Inc.

Townsend, C. a. (2002). *Boundaries in Marriage*. Grand Rapids: Zondervan.

Tyndale, W. (1528). *Obedience of a Christian Man and How Christian Rulers Ought to Govern*. London: Public Domain.

Tyndale, W. (2000). *The Obediance of a Christian Man*. New York: Penguin Books.

Uceda, J. A. (2016). The Lord Jesus Christ Teaches Us to Pray. *General Conference of the Church of Jesus Christ of Latter-day Saints* (pp. 30-32). Salt Lake City: Intellectual Reserve, Inc.

Uchtdor, D. (2016). In Praise of Those Who Save. *General Conference of the Church of Jesus Christ of Latter-day Saints* (pp. 77-80). Salt Lake City: Intellectual Reserve, Inc.

Uchtdorf, D. (2009). The Love of God. *General Conference of the Church of Jesus Christ of Latter-day Saints* (pp. 21-24). Salt Lake City: Intellectual Reserved, Inc.

Uchtdorf, D. (2013). Come, Join With Us. *General Conference of the Church of Jesus Christ of Latter-day Saints* (pp. 21-24). Salt Lake City: Intellectual Reserve, Inc.

Uchtdorf, D. (2015). A Summer with Great-Aunt Rose. *General Conference of the Church of Jesus Christ of Latter-day Saints* (pp. 15-19). Salt Lake City: Intellectual Reserve, Inc.

Uchtdorf, D. (2016). Fourth Floor, Last Door. *General Conference of the Church of Jesus Christ of Latter-day Saints* (pp. 15-18). Salt Lake City: Intellectual Reserve, Inc.

Uchtdorf, D. F. (2014). Lord, Is It I? *General Conference of the Church of Jesus Christ of Latter-day Saints* (pp. 56-59). Salt Lake City: Intellectual Reserve, Inc.

Uchtdorf, D. F. (2016). He Will Place You On His Shoulders and Carry You home. *General Conference of the Church of Jesus Christ of Latter-day Saints* (pp. 101-104). Salt Lake City: Intellectual Reserve, Inc.

Uchtdorf, D. F. (2016). In Praise of Those Who Save. *General Conference of the Church of Jesus Christ of Latter-day Saints* (pp. 77-80). Salt Lake City: Intellectual Reserve, Inc.

Uchtdorf, D. F. (2017). The Greatest Among You. *General Conference of the Church of Jesus Christ of Latter-day Saints* (pp. 78-82). Salt Lake City: Intellectual Reserve, Inc.

Warren, R. (2002). *The Purpose Driven Life*. Grand Rapids, MI: Zondervan.

Wikipedia. (2018, December 1). *Nature Versus Nurture*. Retrieved from Wikipedia.org: https://en.wikipedia.org/wiki/Nature_versus_nurture

Wikipedia. (2020, September 5). *Prince Harry, Duke of Sussex*. Retrieved from Wikipedia: https://en.wikipedia.org/wiki/Prince_Harry,_Duke_of_Sussex

Wikipedia. (2021, May 17). *Classical Conditioning*. Retrieved from Wikipedia: https://en.wikipedia.org/wiki/Classical_conditioning

Williams, C. J. (1996). *The Teachings of Harold B. Lee*. Salt Lake City: Deseret Book.

Wixom, R. M. (2015). Discovering the Divinity Within. *General Conference of the Church of Jesus Christ of Latter-day Saints* (pp. 6-9). Salt Lake City: Intellectual Reserve, Inc.

Young, B. (1954). *Discourses of Brigham Young*. Salt Lake CIty: Deseret Book

Co.

ABOUT THE AUTHOR

Jim Jensen is the father of five, including a daughter adopted from China. He lives in the outdoor-lovers' paradise of Utah in the United States, devoted to his family and right living.